MW00327731

DID YOU KNOW THAT . . .

. . . one of the most admired figures in American history was an art forger? Find out who!

. . . the Wright brothers were not the first to fly? Find out who did!

. . . once there was no summer? Find out when!

. . . a great city went missing for nearly five hundred years? Find out where!

. . . a housefly can defy gravity? Find out how!

. . . Saudi Arabia is not in the Middle East. Find out where!

. . . popular elections do not elect United States presidents? Find out why!

Knowledge is power . . . and it's entertaining, too! Learn the most fascinating facts about *history, science, inventions, geography, origins, art, music, and more* in this very "uncommon" compendium of knowledge.

DID YOU KNOW THAT. . .?

DID YOU KNOW THAT. . .?

"Revised and Expanded" Edition:
Surprising-But-True Facts About History, Science,
Inventions, Geography, Origins, Art, Music, and More

MARKO PERKO

All rights reserved, including without limitation the right to reproduce this book or any portion thereof in any form or by any means, whether electronic or mechanical, now known or hereinafter invented, without the express written permission of the publisher.

First Edition published in 1994 by Berkley Books

Copyright © 1994, 2014, 2017 by Marko Perko

ISBN: 978-1-5040-4073-0

Distributed in 2017 by Open Road Distribution
180 Maiden Lane
New York, NY 10038
www.openroadmedia.com

To my darling wife, Heather Mackay;
my wonderful son, Marko III;
and my beautiful daughter, Skye Mackay

CONTENTS

INTRODUCTION

Did you know that . . . Columbus did not discover America? The Wright brothers were not the first to fly? There is a famous manuscript that no one can read? Thomas Edison did not invent the electric light bulb? There was no gunfight at the O.K. Corral? The croissant is not French? A great city went missing for nearly five centuries? The bark of the willow tree can cure a headache? Greenland is white? America's illustrious Paul Revere never completed his midnight ride? Saint Patrick was not Irish? A dunce is a genius? Lightning can indeed strike more than once in the same place? Dinosaurs invented flowers? Betsy Ross never sewed the first American flag? The most expensive work of art in the world mysteriously vanished?

Did You Know That. . .? was written to set the record straight on these questions and hundreds more. It is a reference work of ambitious design; one that I hope will be of value to people of all ages. As an incurable lover of knowledge, I have spent the better part of my life pursuing my passion, gathering information from virtually every medium. This pursuit has caused me to read through tens of thousands of pages of published material, to listen to the radio with a different ear, to view television through a third eye, and to surf the Internet with a skeptic's suspicion, all in an effort to discern and distill the facts into an accessible form that I trust everyone will understand and find of interest.

It is my desire, first and foremost, that this book will be both informative and entertaining. I hope that it will edify, codify, demystify, and debunk; that it will astound and amaze; that it will fracture fabulous factoids; that it will be an arbiter of disagreements; and that it will stand cherished misconceptions right on their heads. I've sought to read between the lines to expose errors, unmask present-day orthodoxy, identify misinformation, clarify the confusing, and present new information. I have reached back into the depths of man's database of knowledge to retrieve the facts, and nothing but the facts.

I believe that the need to know and to be informed is ever present. The information age is upon us. We all exist in a global village where information is exchanged and consumed at a startling rate. Therefore, our ability to distinguish between what is fact and what is fiction has never been more important. Our present educational system, as well as the mongers of misinformation and disinformation, have placed many of us in a state of "information bankruptcy." *Did You Know That. . .?* was also written to encourage everyone to be inquisitive, and it is to this end that I hope I have succeeded.

In the writing of this book, I found it necessary to assume the identity of an information detective. Of the hundreds of subjects painstakingly researched, several were disregarded in the final analysis because the facts available just didn't add up, or there simply wasn't enough information to effectively verify the subject matter. From the beginning of this book, I felt it essential not to take any one source as gospel, thus virtually every entry is the result of numerous sources, in the belief that the truth will prevail.

It is my fervent hope that you will enjoy reading this "revised and expanded" edition of *Did You Know That. . .?* as much as I enjoyed writing it. It is also my hope that you will come away from this book eager to ask the next person you meet, "Did you know that. . .?"

DID YOU KNOW THAT. . .?

Knowledge is power
(Nam et ipsa scientia potestas est)
—SIR FRANCIS BACON, 1597 (Meditationes Sacrae)

CHAPTER ONE

HISTORY AND PEOPLE

George Washington started a war and then surrendered.

The illustrious Father of His Country, George Washington (1732–99), was inexperienced as a soldier but eager to prove his mettle in 1754. Along with a Virginia regiment of soldiers and several Iroquois Indian braves as guides, twenty-two-year-old Lieutenant Colonel George Washington was dispatched by Virginia Governor Robert Dinwiddie to the Pennsylvania wilderness to evict the French from Fort Duquesne, which they inhabited, and to inform them that they were encroaching on Virginia's territory. Washington surprised thirty Frenchmen at their encampment in the Great Meadows, Pennsylvania region. The battle lasted about fifteen minutes and resulted in ten French casualties, one of whom was their commander, Coulon de Jumonville, and the imprisonment of much of the remaining French contingent.

Shortly thereafter, Washington and his men hastily erected minimal fortifications in the area, appropriately naming the redoubt Fort Necessity. In spite of his success, things would soon go against Washington and his militia regulars, for ironically, Washington was to learn from his prisoners that they were only a group of plenipotentiaries and not the French soldiers as he had thought.

On July 3, 1754, while still basking in the glory of a dubious victory and not having established a more secure place to bed down his men for the night, the French soldiers attacked during a rainstorm. Thirty Americans were lost, including one of Washington's slaves, and an additional seventy were injured. With only one option open to him other than imminent death, Washington, in the early hours of July 4, 1754, surrendered to the French. Then, in a moment of unexplained benevolence, he was released to return to Williamsburg, Virginia.

Although Washington had unknowingly started the French and Indian War (1754–63), he was nevertheless applauded as a hero for confronting the bitter enemies of the English crown. The war itself was the prelude to and chief reason for the larger Seven Years' War (1756–63), and the Europeans referred to it as such.

It must also be noted that the war was not fought between the French and Indians, but rather between the French and English. The Treaty of Paris, signed on February 8, 1763, ending the global conflicts between the French and English, established England as the undisputed power in colonial America.

The father of history was Greek.

The recording of events of the past was not new, for men had been doing it for centuries, but prior to the Greek historian Herodotus (c. 485–430 B.C.), no individual had ever attempted to write down a logical account of events, comprising a beginning, a middle, and an end.

It was the Greek victory over the Persians in 490–480 B.C. that precipitated the eventual "invention" of history. The Greek triumph proved to be the most wonderful and inspiring occasion in Greek life up to that point. The Greeks were insistent upon trying to understand their good fortune over the Persians. Moreover, they were armed with the belief, taught them by Thales and others, that since nature itself is governed by underlying principles that make it understandable, then the actions of men must have discernible underlying principles that would help in understanding why men did what they did, and thus, possibly predict their future actions.

Herodotus, a Greek with an insatiable appetite for discovery, traveled much of Persia, Egypt, the Fertile Crescent, and most of Greece itself. He assiduously chronicled his every move, noting what he saw and what he heard. He would spend much of his life in pursuit of understanding what happened and why. Moreover, he would be remembered for his narrative *The History* of the Greco-Persian Wars, though he called it his "Researches": the oldest existing major Greek prose and the first history of the western world.

Because of Herodotus's *The History*, an organic work, he is justifiably called the "Father of History."

The Declaration of Independence was not on July 4, 1776.

One of America's most historic and cherished documents is dated July 4, 1776, and any real American knows that the Second Continental Congress first adopted the resolution and unanimously signed it on July 4, 1776. Not true. July 4 merely represents the day the last draft was voted on and not all delegates approved it. In addition, there were no signers on that day.

The legitimate story is that on June 7, 1776, Richard Henry of the Virginia delegation introduced a motion for an unequivocal declaration of independence from England. Five men were appointed to form a committee to produce the document. One of them was the brilliant anti-Federalist, Thomas Jefferson, then just thirty-three years old. He did the actual writing, and with few changes, the Declaration of Independence is primarily a product of his genius.

On July 2, the Second Continental Congress adopted a resolution of independence. That was the day, not July 4, when the action was taken and the declaration itself was concise—total independence was achieved. On July 3, several newspapers published the declaration, and on the next day, July 4, a Thursday, Congress voted on the declaration. Then, on July 8 the document was read aloud from the balcony of Independence Hall in Philadelphia, and then again on July 9 in New York to George Washington and his troops.

The committee's original document is a much more complete statement illuminating the reasons for the Declaration of Independence. The final draft was not approved unanimously by July 4, considering the State of New York did not even vote on the declaration until July 9. The document was officially called "The Unanimous Declaration of the Thirteen United States of America." Nowhere in the title does the word *independence* appear.

The signing of one of America's most famous documents was an even more laborious process. It is deceptive to think there were fifty-six "original" signers of the Declaration of Independence. By August 2, the majority had indeed signed the document, but at least six signatures were affixed to the document sometime later.

One signer, Thomas McKean, signing as Tho. M:Kean, did not sign it until 1781! Some signers were not present in Congress when the Declaration was agreed upon, and some who voted for it in Congress never signed it: Robert R. Livingston, a member of the celebrated committee of five, aided in drafting it and voted for it, but never signed it.

Lincoln's Emancipation Proclamation did not free the slaves.

It is common belief that President Abraham Lincoln's celebrated Emancipation Proclamation, issued January 1, 1863, freed the slaves. The truth is, the proclamation had no legal power and it did not free a single slave. As it was, it only applied to slaves in areas under Confederate control. It excluded the slave-holding states, of which there were four—Kentucky, Maryland, Delaware, and Missouri—all of which elected to remain in the Union. Even certain areas under Union command in Confederate territories were not subject to the emancipation.

The Emancipation Proclamation held no currency in the Southern states and as such the Confederacy simply rejected it without reservation. Even the antiwar Democrats of the time opposed any effort to free slaves and called for a retraction of the emancipation.

The proclamation did curry favor with abolitionists and at the same time it allowed the Union forces to conscript secessionists' slaves. More than 500,000 blacks sought freedom in the North by the war's end, with some 200,000 contributing to the war effort as soldiers, sailors, and laborers. These forces contributed greatly to the ultimate victory of the Union.

So, although Lincoln abhorred slavery, his Emancipation Proclamation freed not one slave, but it did lead to the Thirteenth Amendment, which on December 18, 1865, abolished slavery throughout the United States.

Plymouth was not the first English settlement in New England.

Although the settlement of Plymouth, in southeast Massachusetts, was established in 1620, and thought to be the first, that distinction goes to a group of colonists who settled in Virginia, in 1607—or does it?

Supporters of George Popham believe his settlement was the very first English settlement in New England. On August 18, 1607, George Popham and 120 brave souls founded a settlement on the western side of the mouth of the Kennebec River in Maine. In fact, Maine historians claim that the first Thanksgiving was celebrated by the Popham colonists in appreciation of their safe voyage and subsequent landing. Nevertheless, their stay was short, for the harsh winter and the loss of two major supporters resulted in the settlers vacating their settlement the next year.

However, on May 14, 1607, the same month that the Popham colonists set sail from England for America, 105 colonists disembarked from three ships to establish a settlement in Virginia that was to be called Jamestown, the first permanent English settlement.

Lincoln did not write his famous address on the back of an envelope on the train to Gettysburg.

Lincoln did not write the address while on a train en route to Gettysburg, Pennsylvania. To think that such an auspicious hour would have been dealt with so flippantly is absurd. The speech was given at the dedication of a cemetery for the thousands who died at the Battle of Gettysburg, the greatest battle ever fought on American soil.

Although the Gettysburg dedication was given on November 19, 1863, Lincoln began the first draft on November 8, nearly two weeks before. It took five drafts before the speech was complete, although it is entirely feasible that Lincoln may have made a revision on the train. In addition, he wrote the speech on regular White House stationery.

As for the address itself, it was less than enthusiastically received, for Lincoln had to follow the last of the illustrious orators, Edward Everett. Many people did not even know that Lincoln was speaking. The address was little more than two minutes in length and was delivered slowly and with deliberation. There was little if any applause: the famous Gettysburg Address was less man an unqualified success at the time of its delivery, but in time it became a true classic. Lincoln had said what had to be said with power and grace.

The story that the address was written on the back of an envelope was told in a letter by Lincoln's son, Robert. Robert assumed that the address was fashioned in such a manner, though he had no definite knowledge of its derivation.

A cow did not start the infamous Chicago Fire.

The Chicago summer of 1871 was hot and dry—very dry. Between July and October of that year, the city experienced only one-fourth of its normal rainfall, leaving the countless wooden buildings prey to the slightest hint of fire. On October 8 the worst happened, a fire started on the southwest side of the city, leaving in its wake, some two days later, mass destruction. Hundreds of people were killed and thousands were left homeless, with property damage around $200 million.

Mrs. Catherine O'Leary's cow has been blamed for the confla-
gration known as the Great Chicago Fire, but the fact remains: Mrs.
O'Leary was fast asleep when the fire broke out, having milked her
cow sometime earlier in the day. There is no proof that a cow was the
cause, and sometime later, a reporter named Michael Ahern confessed
to having concocted the story in an effort to embellish his description
of the fire.

The Rough Riders should be called the Rough Walkers.

Rough Riders is the celebrated sobriquet given to the First Regiment
of U.S. Cavalry Volunteers in the Spanish-American War of 1898. It is
commonly believed that Teddy Roosevelt (1858–1919) was their commander and led this regiment up hill and down dale in various flourishes of bravado against the enemy.

As Assistant Secretary of the Navy, Roosevelt did acquire Congressional approval to recruit a volunteer regiment of cavalry. He per-
sonally selected several hundred men, mostly Harvard blue bloods,
horsemen, cowboys, and famous athletes. In effect, Roosevelt did
organize the Rough Riders, but command of them fell to Colonel
Leonard Wood, who had legitimate military credentials and was also
a physician.

Lieutenant Colonel Teddy Roosevelt did not lead the charge up
San Juan Hill, but he did lead the charge up nearby Kettle Hill on his
horse, Texas. His success helped the Americans win the battle of San
Juan Hill, and therein lies the confusion. Roosevelt's ride became
mistakenly associated with the San Juan Hill assault. He was second
in command to Wood, whose Rough Riders soon called themselves
"Wood's Weary Walkers," because they fought much of the war entirely on foot.

What happened to the horses? They had to be left in Florida because the ships that were transporting the cavalry soldiers to Cuba
had no room for the horses the soldiers were supposed to have
ridden.

There was never a battle fought at Waterloo.

The famous battle at Waterloo, in Belgium, on June 18, 1815, between Napoleon Bonaparte (Napoleon I, 1769–1821) and General Wellington (Arthur Wellesley, Duke of Wellington, 1769–1852) never occurred at Waterloo. The actual battle, the last of the Napoleonic Wars, was fought approximately four miles south at a site somewhere between the two villages of Plancenoit and Mont-Saint-Jean. The addition of the Prussian troops, some 45,000 strong—the principal fighting force under General Gebhard von Blücher's command—proved the turning point in the battle. Their support helped General Wellington, with his Allied forces of 68,000, hand the brilliant Napoleon, with about 72,000 troops, his final defeat and brought about the conclusion of the Great War.

It seems that the victorious Wellington was quartered at Waterloo before and after the battle, hence the association. Waterloo is, in fact, a suburb about nine miles south of Brussels and north of the actual battlefield.

The U.S. fired the first shot at Pearl Harbor.

President Roosevelt so emphatically asserted, "This day shall live in infamy," in response to the Japanese attack on Pearl Harbor, December 7, 1941, but the fact remains that the U.S. actually fired the first shot.

Just before sunrise on that fateful day in December 1941, the U.S. World War I destroyer *Ward* was plying the waters off Pearl Harbor when it was notified by the minesweeper *Condor* that an unknown submarine had been sighted making its way toward Pearl Harbor. A small, two-man midget submarine was then was located by the crew of the *Ward* and the captain, Lieutenant. W. W. Outerbridge, exhorted his men to stand ready and then to fire upon the enemy submarine. The submarine was hit in the conning tower and subsequently sank at 6:45 in the morning. The *Ward* followed up the attack by sending four depth charges down to eliminate any possibility of the submarine surviving the assault. So the U.S. fired the first shot at Pearl Harbor and the Japanese shed the first blood of World War II in the Pacific.

In a strange twist of fate, precisely three years later to the day, on December 7, 1944, the *Ward* was attacked by kamikaze pilots, and it sank off the Philippine coast.

There was no gunfight at the O.K. Corral.

The famous gunfight, or more accurately murder, did not occur on October 26, 1881, at the O.K. Corral in Tombstone, Arizona.

To begin with, there were two opposing factions.

The first consisted of the three famous Earp brothers, Wyatt, Virgil, and Morgan, and their partner in crime, the consumptive John H. "Doc" Holliday, a now-and-again frontier dentist. Some historians argue that Wyatt Earp was nothing more than an outlaw with a badge, a larger-than-life folk hero, undeserving of his reputation as a peacekeeper.

The other faction consisted of the scandalous outlaws, Ike and Billy Clanton, and their neighbors, Tom and Frank McLaury.

The two sides were always at each other's throats, just like many young miscreants of today.

Although conflicting testimony regarding the fight still clouds the true facts of what happened, what is known is that the actual gunfight occurred in a vacant lot between Camillus Fly's Rooming House and Photographic Studio and lumber dealer W. A. Harwood's private home, and not in the O.K. Corral, which was nearly one hundred feet east of the vacant lot.

About thirty shots were fired in nearly as many seconds. Witnesses to the fight said that the Earps and Holliday fired without just cause, and Billy Clanton and both McLaurys were killed, while Ike Clanton escaped. Virgil and Morgan Earp and Doc Holliday were wounded; Wyatt was unharmed. Despite damaging testimony against the Earp bunch, the Earps and Doc Holliday were exonerated of all charges.

Why, then, is it called the Gunfight at the O.K. Corral? It was author Stuart Lake who, in his 1931 biography *Wyatt Earp: Frontier Marshal*, erroneously placed the gunfight at the O.K. Corral.

In an effort to remain true to the myth and at the same time increase its revenues, years ago the town of Tombstone, reputedly the toughest town in the West, enlarged the size of the O.K. Corral to encompass the place where the actual gunfight took place.

The United States Congress sold the Liberty Bell.

That grand old icon of American independence was once traded as scrap metal and valued at only $400.

The illustrious bell supposedly signaled the first public reading of the Declaration of Independence on July 8, 1776, although there exists no concrete evidence to support the claim. The bell was installed at the Pennsylvania State House in Philadelphia in 1753 and bore the biblical inscription, "Proclaim Liberty throughout all the land unto all the inhabitants thereof," which, by the way, had nothing whatsoever to do with the American Revolution. It seems that the myth surrounding the bell is most likely the work of a nineteenth-century author by the name of George Lippard.

It is also interesting to note that the Liberty Bell that is seen in the Liberty Bell Pavilion is actually a second bell; the first bell, cast in England in 1752 at a cost of $300, cracked when first struck by its clapper after its arrival in America. The second bell was quickly recast from the same metal in 1753.

Although hidden for security reasons in Allentown, Pennsylvania, during the winter of 1777–78, while the Revolutionary War raged on, it reappeared at the State House to continue its charge of announcing state meetings and summoning congregations. By 1800, the bell and the State House were no longer in use, since the U.S. Congress had moved to new quarters in Washington, D.C., and the state legislature of Pennsylvania had also relocated to Lancaster.

In 1824, the now deteriorating State House—Independence Hall— was partially restored to its former beauty in time to receive a visit from Lafayette, the French general who led his soldiers of fortune in defense of the Colonies against the British. The old bell sounded for the great general's arrival, and then again upon his death in 1834. By 1828, the restoration of the State House was complete and the final touch was to have yet another Liberty Bell made.

The bell-maker, John Wilbank, of Germantown, Pennsylvania, was the city fathers' choice to cast a new bell for the recently constructed new steeple of the State House. It was to be twice the size of the old bell, and Wilbank agreed to reduce his fee by $400 in exchange for the old, one-ton artifact. Subsequently, he decided the old bell wasn't worth it. After all, the cost of drayage was more than the scrap value of the bell. The city sought legal action against Wilbank to remove the bell, but acquiesced when he decided to pay legal costs and to make a gift of the bell to the city. This second bell also cracked in 1835, so the legend goes, when it was rung at the funeral of Chief Justice John Marshall. John Wilbank went on to cast a new bell for the steeple, while the old, "great bell" still hung below it.

We should all be thankful that John Wilbank decided not to destroy one of America's greatest symbols of freedom, the Liberty Bell. It was not named so until 1839, when it signaled a clarion call to action for abolitionists. Prior to that, it was simply called the Old State House Bell.

Lincoln never slept in the Lincoln Bedroom.

Abe Lincoln, the Great Emancipator, and possibly America's most revered and honored president, slept for years in the White House. However, what is most curious is that he never slept in the bedroom named after him.

The celebrated Lincoln Bedroom was used by Lincoln as well as several other presidents from 1830 until 1902, as an office and Cabinet Room. The room was also a repository for the myriad papers that Lincoln issued during the Civil War. Lincoln even signed the illustrious Emancipation Proclamation on January 1, 1863, in the room, but once again, he never spent a night's slumber there.

President Truman was the one who decided to place bedroom furniture from the Lincoln period in this room. Besides the American Victorian furniture from the period between 1850 and 1870, exhibited on the desk is a holographic copy of the Gettysburg Address that Lincoln delivered before a less-than-enthusiastic crowd on November 19, 1863. One prominent piece of furniture is the famous eight-foot-long redwood bed, purchased by Mrs. Lincoln, which was in a second-floor guest room, and had been used by such presidents as Woodrow Wilson and Teddy Roosevelt, but never by Lincoln.

Untold history-making events occurred in the Lincoln Bedroom through many a turbulent year, but as for Abraham Lincoln ever having made the room his sleeping quarters, it just did not happen.

John Paul Jones never said, "I have not yet begun to fight."

On September 23, 1779, the stylish and often courageous John Paul Jones, aboard his warship *Bonhomme Richard*, named in honor of Benjamin Franklin's *Poor Richard*, engaged the British warship *Serapis*. When called upon to surrender, Jones refused such a request as an obvious affront to his bravado. Whether he said this often quoted phrase is not altogether clear, given the fact that his own personal account of the battle never made mention of this famous saying, and it's certainly not something one would easily forget.

By the way, John Paul Jones, the Father of the American Navy, didn't surrender, the British did.

Paul Revere never finished his famous ride.

Paul Revere (1735–1818) was an accomplished silversmith, engraver, political cartoonist, a veteran of the French and Indian war, father of sixteen children, iron founder, inventor, avocational dentist, artist-engraver, and a nefarious art forger. However, Paul Revere's greatest concern was for the success of the American Revolution, and it is to this extent we have all become familiar with his renowned midnight ride. It's folklore at its finest.

"Listen, my children, and you shall hear, of the midnight ride of Paul Revere . . ." was Paul's moment of greatness—or was it? The distinguished poet, Henry Wadsworth Longfellow (1807–82), in his description of Paul Revere's ride, changed a few facts about that glorious gallop. Such are the benefits of poetic license.

In truth, Paul Revere made many important rides for the American cause, but none were as significant as the two rides he made in April 1775. He rode first to Concord on April 16 to tell the patriots to move their munitions to a safer place. It was this first ride that Longfellow refers to in his poem. The lanterns were to be hung in the steeple of the North Church: "One, if by land, and two, if by sea." Paul Revere, in his own account of that midnight ride, said the lanterns were to notify others in case he could not make it across the Charles River or over the Boston Neck, the isthmus that connected the town to the mainland. Oddly enough, since the British approached both by land and by sea, the lanterns were of little consequence anyway.

On the second ride to Concord on the night of April 18–19, 1775, Paul Revere took to his mighty mount and raced, hell-bent-for-leather, throughout the villages and farms of Middlesex, but contrary to Longfellow's brilliant flourish of words, Paul Revere never completed his ride.

It turns out that he did go in a boat with "muffled oar" to the Charlestown bank. Once upon horseback, he realized that in all the confusion he had forgotten his spurs. Nevertheless, the unfortunate oversight did not deter him from his objective. Despite warning the countryside along the way, his primary charge was to inform John Hancock and Samuel Adams of the British plan and to carry the signal to the rebels of Concord.

He did warn both Hancock and Adams, who were the targets of General Gage, and then left for Concord with William Dawes and Samuel Prescott. In time, the three were observed by British scouts. Prescott jumped a fence and somehow made it to Lincoln and Concord to warn of impending trouble. Dawes created a diversion that caught the British officers off guard. Ultimately, he backtracked to Lexington, but a little while later, his horse threw him and he was finished for the night.

As for Revere, he tried to escape by hightailing it for a grove of trees, but six British soldiers snatched his bridle and caused him to stop by putting pistols to his chest. Revere was able to convince the officers that since he had already alerted the countryside, 500 Minutemen would be waiting in Concord to decimate them in short order. A Fifth Regiment major named Edward Mitchell was infuriated by Revere's story and immediately put a cocked pistol to his head and demanded the truth or Major Mitchell would blow Revere's head off. Revere held steadfast to his story. The officers were somewhat confounded. They conferred among themselves for several minutes and then commanded Revere to mount up, but without reins to guide his horse.

The officers then proceeded to march Revere and four other suspected messengers toward Lexington. Suddenly, with less than a mile to go from Lexington, a shot was heard. An officer asked Revere what that meant and Revere informed them that it was to warn the countryside of their impending approach. At that moment, the British realized their captives, excluding Revere, were a liability, and they were subsequently set loose on foot. Then a second shot was heard, and the officers concluded that Revere was a liability as well. He, too, was set afoot, and he raced toward Lexington.

Paul Revere ultimately found his way to Lexington and made good by rescuing a trunk of important documents that Hancock had inadvertently left behind. Sad to say, he never made it to Concord and he never fought in the battle of Lexington. He was, however, paid five shillings for his efforts that night.

Jefferson never spoke of the best government being one that governs least.

Numerous writers and speakers often quote Thomas Jefferson's famous statement, "That government is best that governs least." The problem with this quote is that Jefferson never said it.

Henry David Thoreau, in the opening of his celebrated essay, *Civil Disobedience*, which was published in 1849, made use of the Jefferson quote that never existed, and even Thoreau set it off by quotation marks, implying that it was a well-worn phrase. Moreover, in his essay he also stated, and he quotes, "That government is best which governs not at all." This is also not a Jefferson quote.

Humphrey Bogart never told Sam to play it again.

Yes, it's true. Bogart never uttered the line, "Play it again, Sam," in the Warner Brothers celebrated World War II movie, *Casablanca* (1942). The correct line is, "Play it, Sam. Play 'As Time Goes By.'" Moreover, Ingrid Bergman (Ilsa), not Bogart (Rick), said the line when she asked the pianist-singer Arthur "Dooley" Wilson (Sam) to play the song. Incidentally, Sam didn't actually play it—he didn't know how to play the piano—that was dubbed in. He just sings it. In fact, Dooley was once asked to perform at a nightclub, and he had to admit that he couldn't play the piano, he was only a singer. Also, the song was not written just for the movie, it was first introduced in the stage revue, *Everybody Welcome*.

When casting for *Casablanca*, former President Ronald Reagan was the first choice to play Rick, but it was ultimately decided that someone tougher was needed. George Raft turned the part down, but Bogart accepted it; he was the seventh choice.

W.C. Fields was wrongly accused of having said, "Anybody who hates children and dogs can't be all bad."

The actual phrase was, "Anybody who hates dogs and babies can't be all bad," and W. C. Fields (1880–1946) didn't say it. Leo Rosten, the humorist, political scientist, and pedant said it while introducing Fields at a Friar's Club banquet to honor his fortieth year in entertainment. Rosten apparently thought he was echoing a belief that Fields had expressed. Anyway, Rosten invented the line W. C. Fields is most famous for.

James Otis may have never spoken about taxation without representation.

Many Americans are familiar with James Otis's phrase: "Taxation without representation is tyranny." The simple fact is that Otis probably never uttered the words that were thought to be the rallying cry of the American Revolution.

It seems that in February 1761, Otis (1725–83), a lawyer, was contesting search warrants imposed by the British administration in the Colonies before a Boston court. No modern record of Otis's supposed utterance about taxation exits. In reality, the mention of the spurious quote did not occur until 1820, when John Adams was paraphrasing the Otis argument in notes that he was taking.

George Washington never wrote his own war correspondence.

It is not commonly known, but General George Washington most probably never wrote his own military correspondence or speeches during the American Revolution. Washington had only a few years of what was essentially informal schooling, and no one ever considered him an educated man. It was Alexander Hamilton (1755–1804), a lieutenant colonel and Washington's private secretary, who wrote nearly all of Washington's war correspondence, especially that which was top-secret in nature. He was indispensable to Washington, who considered him a member of his family.

In America's quest for freedom from mother England, Hamilton distinguished himself as a courageous supporter of the war and as one of the principal forces behind the ratification of the U.S. Constitution. He was undeniably the gray eminence of the revolution and the new country's first Secretary of the Treasury.

Galileo was not the man we think he was.

Galileo (1564–1642) was an inventor, astronomer, mathematician, and heretic. It is commonly believed that Galileo invented the telescope; however, it was most likely invented in 1608 in Holland by Hans Lippershey, a Dutch optician. Galileo simply recognized the telescope's potential and adapted it as a device for examining the heavens. The mistake for many crediting him with the discovery of the telescope lies in a paper that he published in 1610, *Nuncius Siderius*, in which he speaks of discovering the telescope and understanding the universe like no man before. He did not say he invented the telescope, but he was the first to utilize it for astronomical purposes, while at the same time improving upon its mechanics.

Another misconception attributed to Galileo was his run-in with the Inquisition in 1633. He was never subjected to the dreaded authority of the auto-da-fé, which inflicted physical torture, execution, or imprisonment on its victims. However, considered a heretic by the clergy, Galileo was forced to recant his beliefs regarding the Copernican theory (the belief that the Earth and other planets revolve around the Sun) in order to save himself from further harassment by the Church. The Church believed the theory antithetical to the Bible and unorthodox at the very least. After Galileo's recantation, he was placed under house arrest and left to live the last eight years of his life in Arcetri.

On October 31, 1992, Pope John Paul II, before the Pontifical Academy of Sciences, formally recognized that Galileo was correct in believing the Copernican theory for which he was condemned in 1633. The Pope apologized for the Church's myopic view at the time, but defended it, saying that little knowledge was available to its theologians in the seventeenth century. After a 13-year investigation and some 360 years of "no comment," the Roman Catholic Church had finally righted a very grievous wrong, and the most infamous confrontation between the Church and science ended.

In addition, it is believed that Galileo never proffered any theories about the pendulum after presumably observing a swinging lamp in the cathedral in Pisa. He also never dropped any weights from the

Tower of Pisa to prove objects of different weights achieve the same velocity in a free fall. Galileo himself never spoke of these purported experiments nor did any of his disciples make mention of such investigations. Others have since mistakenly made those attributions.

Finally, his full name was Galileo Galilei, son of Vincenzio Galilei, who himself was a musician and a Florentine aristocrat of limited influence and wealth.

Magellan was not the "first" to circumnavigate the Earth.

Imagine circumnavigating the Earth today, much less in the early 1500s. What a feat! Ferdinand Magellan (in Portuguese, Fernão de Magalhãnes, c. 1480–1521), the Portuguese explorer, had planned to be the first, but he met with an untimely death on the Isle of Mactan, in the Philippines. Instead, his faithful second, Enrique de Malacca, the Malay slave he had acquired in Malacca, has the honor of being the first person to do so, not the surviving crew members of the *Victoria*, and most certainly not Sir Francis Drake.

When Magellan, his crew, and Enrique reached the Malayan Peninsula, Enrique found himself among locals who spoke his language. As he was conversing with them, Magellan realized that by sailing westward they were back in the land where they had first met in 1512. At that point, he knew Enrique was the very first circumnavigator of the Earth, and he also knew that the Earth was round, for Enrique had gone round it.

After Magellan's death, his expedition continued westward, led by Juan Sebastiàn del Cano, completing the circumnavigation on September 6, 1522, some three years after Magellan had set sail on September 20, 1519, in search of a shorter route to the Spice Islands (Moluccas).

Although Magellan never lived to complete what some consider to be the greatest navigational feat in history, his friend Enrique did; he was the first. However, to Magellan's credit, he was the first to traverse the vast Pacific Ocean from east to west, and the completed voyage by his crew was proof positive to the civilized world that the Earth was indeed round.

Stonehenge was not erected by the Druids.

Much to the amazement of most individuals, and history buffs in particular, the Druids (from the Celtic, meaning "knowing the oak tree" or "deep knowledge") did not erect the curious arrangement of stone monoliths that are located in southern England. Who erected Stonehenge is not known for sure, although it is speculated that the structure, built in three phases during the Bronze Age (3500 B.C. to as late as 1500–1000 B.C.), may have had some astronomical or religious importance. So why the association with the Druids?

It seems that the seventeenth-century author and antiquarian John Aubrey (1626–97), one of the discoverers of Stonehenge, promoted the idea that the Druids, a religious order of Celts in Britain during the Iron Age (the period succeeding the Bronze Age), were the constructors of Stonehenge. However, it is an impossibility that the Druids could have built Stonehenge, since they appeared at least one thousand years after it was erected. Nevertheless, this inaccuracy persists to this very day. There is even a modern sect called the Ancient Order of the Druids that annually celebrates the summer solstice at Stonehenge.

An interesting sidelight to what is known about the Druids is that Julius Caesar is one of the primary sources concerning their origins and practices. Even the earliest Greek accounts show the Druids appearing around 200 B.C., more than one thousand years after Stonehenge was completed.

Whoever erected this curious monument is unknown, but it certainly wasn't the Druids, despite what Mr. Aubrey said.

Hitler did not create the swastika symbol.

The swastika has been inextricably associated with Hitler and his Nazis of World War II, although it was officially recognized in 1920 and began to be used on party banners at that time. It was probably Hitler's most effective propaganda tool. However, frankly, the mad Austrian was not the first person to utilize the swastika as a symbol of a group or cause.

The swastika is, in fact, an ancient sign dating back to prehistoric times; it first appeared in approximately 3000 B.C. in the Indus and Harappa cultures. The word comes from Sanskrit, the oldest of the Indo-European family of written languages. The early Aryans of India drew the sign of the swastika to represent the Sun's motion across the sky and it symbolized the Sun's goodness and rejuvenating power. The swastika is also found in ancient Greek pottery in about the first millennium B.C. Some have preferred the belief that Hitler stole the symbol from the American Indians, which is patently false, though they did employ the symbol to depict peace or the four directions.

The true meaning of the swastika is lost with time; however, in Sanskrit it roughly translates to "conducive to well-being." Thus, the symbol was probably associated with goodness more often than not. In the Buddhist culture, it was used to signify rebirth and prosperity. Moreover, the Roman holy cross has a swastika at its center. In Scandinavia, it was once known as Tor's hammer, and thought to possess power and energy.

A point of added interest: the non-Nazi use of the swastika always has the arms pointing left, while the infamous symbol of the Third Reich has the arms pointing right.

Franklin D. Roosevelt was not the first to speak of "fear."

"The only thing we have to fear is fear itself. . . ." It is postulated that these immortal words were uttered by FDR in his inaugural address on March 4, 1933, but he was not the first to speak of fear. There are Biblical references to this quote, but more specifically, the sixteenth-century French essayist Michel E. Montaigne (1553–92) said, "The thing of which I have the most fear is fear." In the seventeenth century, the English philosopher and statesman Sir Francis Bacon (1561–1626) is credited with having said, "Nothing is terrible except for fear." Even America's Henry David Thoreau (1817–62) said, "Nothing is so much to be feared as fear."

No Salem witch was ever burned at the stake.

Although it makes for good copy, of the 165 people charged in 1692 with witchcraft at the Salem Witch Trials in Salem, Massachusetts, only 20 were executed and none were burned at the stake. This was not the normal method of execution in the Colonies. To be specific, 19 were hanged at Gallows Hill and 1 was crushed to death—maybe burning would have been less painful.

The ages of those imprisoned ranged from seven to one hundred, with two dogs having been put to death. It should also be noted that witches were not exclusive to Salem and that other towns in New England during the Puritan era were inflicted with the demons of witchcraft. As such, more than two hundred times before the Salem trials, witchcraft raised its hideous head and twenty-five individuals were put to death.

Paul Revere was an art forger.

The much revered Paul Revere (1735–1818), consummate revolutionary, silversmith, father of sixteen children, and sometime maker of teeth, was also an accomplished and notorious forger of art. Quite frankly, he stole other artists' work ad libitum.

Paul Revere's most outrageous forgery was his biggest seller, the *Boston Massacre of 1770*. It wasn't so much a massacre since only a few died; it was more a precursor to the Revolutionary War, and a great propaganda tool to unite the Colonists against inequitable British practices. Nevertheless, engraver Henry Pelham's original print of that momentous day entitled *An Original Print . . . Taken on the Spot*, was intercepted on its way to the printers by none other than Revere himself. Revere immediately copied Pelham's engraving, signed it as if it were his own creation, and started selling it two weeks before Pelham knew what had happened.

When Pelham, the half-brother of the famed portraitist John Singleton Copley, heard of this egregious deed, he wrote Revere stating that Revere had flagrantly copied his original work. The grievance proved academic, because before Pelham could get his print to market, Paul Revere had a hit on his hands.

Revere's avocation as an art forger continued throughout his life, despite having been accused of infringing upon the copyrights of others. He continued to pursue this illegal trade with vigor and reckless abandon. Moreover, to find an original engraving by Paul Revere would take some doing.

A dunce is a genius, sometimes.

Oddly enough, the word *dunce*, meaning a dull or ignorant individual, originates from one of the geniuses of the Middle Ages.

John Duns Scotus (c. 1265–1308) was a Scottish theologian and philosopher who was considered the equal of Thomas Aquinas—the other great theologian and thinker of the Middle Ages—though he was in opposition to Aquinas's teachings. Duns Scotus wrote illuminating treatises on subjects as varied as logic, grammar, metaphysics, and theology. Often called the "subtle doctor," known for his genteel yet incisive views, Duns Scotus received his education at both Cambridge and Oxford and was even granted a master's degree from the University of Paris.

It was while he was engaged in study at the University of Paris in 1303 that he became entwined in one of the most heated donnybrooks of the day. France's King Philip IV had decided to help finance the war effort against England by taxing the Church. Duns Scotus took the side of Pope Boniface VIII, who threatened to excommunicate King Philip IV. For his efforts in supporting the pope, Duns Scotus was banished from France and lived out his last days as a university professor in Cologne, Germany, where he died in 1308. He is buried in the choir section of the Franciscan church and was revered as a saint by his disciples.

It wasn't until about two hundred years later that the term *dunce* was coined by Renaissance humanists and Reformation leaders who were decidedly against his teachings and support of the papacy. It was believed that any disciple of Duns Scotus was therefore a "Duns," or

"Dunce"—obstinate, dull, or incapable of academia. Unfortunately, this misnomer persists to this day.

Abraham Lincoln's son Robert was a jinx.

Robert Todd Lincoln (1843–1926), the eldest son of President Abraham Lincoln, earned the unfortunate distinction of being present or nearby at three out of the four presidential assassinations (John F. Kennedy being the fourth.)

Young Robert received the benefit of the finest schooling, something his father never had, and 1859 saw him enter Harvard, carrying with him a letter of introduction from none other than his father's political adversary, Stephen A. Douglas. Although Robert was studying at Harvard during much of his father's White House years, he did arrive in Washington after witnessing Lee's surrender at Appomattox, for a visit on April 14, 1865. That fateful day proved to be his illustrious father's undoing, for later that night, Lincoln was shot by John Wilkes Booth, an actor, while attending the play *Our American Cousin* at Ford's Theater. Robert came to his father's side, remaining with him throughout the night and into the next morning, when President Lincoln died of a gunshot wound.

After his father's assassination, Robert moved to Chicago. Despite his reclusive nature, he was successful as an attorney, becoming a founding member of the city's bar association. He disliked the political spotlight and thought politics to be a loss of privacy, not something to aspire to. Moreover, to follow in his illustrious father's footsteps would have been an obvious impossibility. However, in 1881, President James A. Garfield asked Robert to join his cabinet as Secretary of War. Robert accepted the appointment, but with great reservation. Nevertheless, he was regularly considered a possible Republican presidential candidate.

In July of the same year, Robert arrived at a train depot in Washington to bid his president a safe journey, only to witness the assassination of the nation's twentieth president by a lawyer and political aspirant, C. J. Guiteau, on July 2. Garfield held on to life for a short time, but he expired on September 19.

In 1889, President Benjamin Harrison appointed Robert to the post of U.S. Minister to London. By 1897, Robert had become a very wealthy industrialist and held the position of president of the Pullman Company from 1897 until 1911, when he became its chairman.

In September 1901, Robert traveled with his family to Buffalo, New York, to visit the Pan-American Exposition. Upon approaching the city, he was given the grave news that the president had just been shot on September 6 by an anarchist, L. F. Czolgosz. Robert rushed to William McKinley's side before he died eight days later.

Macabre as it seems, happenstance brought Robert Todd Lincoln in immediate proximity to three of the four U.S. presidents as each one ultimately succumbed to assassins' bullets. A final twist to this weird confluence of events is that he is buried only one hundred yards from the fourth victim, John F. Kennedy.

Betsy Ross never sewed the first American flag.

Fooled again! Betsy Ross, a seamstress and upholsterer, did not sew the first American flag. Even the house (Flag House) she supposedly lived in was refused as a gift by both the U.S. Congress and the City of Philadelphia because its authenticity could not be verified. She was also not the first to call the flag "Old Glory." The whole story was a complete fabrication.

It seems that on March 4, 1870, the Pennsylvania Historical Society was entertained by William Canby, Betsy Ross's grandson. He related how in 1776, prior to the signing of the Declaration of Independence, George Washington, Robert Morris, and George Ross (a relation by marriage), members of the congressional flag committee, came to Betsy's shop in Philadelphia and asked if she would sew a flag of their design. Betsy took their design and added a proportional arrangement of five-pointed stars, and thus was born America's first flag.

Balderdash.

Nevertheless, by 1885, Betsy Ross was a household heroine and remains so, despite the fact that no record exists of a 1776 flag committee or that Betsy Ross had anything to do with the first American flag.

It appears to have been a family anecdote concocted by her grandson and perpetuated by her descendants to make them appear more important in the annals of history. If anyone must be given credit for having designed the first flag, it must go to Francis Hopkinson. After all, he is recognized by Congress. However, it appears that the final design of the flag was a collaborative effort. As for Betsy, she was the official maker of flags for the Pennsylvania Navy in 1777.

The truth is that it was not until June 14, 1777, that the Second Continental Congress agreed upon the design of the Stars and Stripes (a derivative of the British flag) and passed legislation to make it the official flag of the United States. The first flags had stars with six or eight points, the stripes had no specific meaning, nor did the colors, and no one knows who actually sewed them. What we do know is that Betsy Ross most certainly did not sew them or design them.

Captain William Bligh was involved in not one, but three mutinies.

For more than two hundred years, the infamous Captain William Bligh (1754–1817), who had once sailed under the famous Captain Cook, has been remembered as the man who caused the mutiny on the *HMS Bounty*. Portrayed in film and chronicled in numerous books, Bligh was the quintessential madman. What few know, however, is that he was actually involved in not one but three mutinies and that his madness did not prevent him from achieving a high rank in the British navy.

In 1789, Master's Mate Fletcher Christian, rebelling against Bligh's coercive disciplinary tactics, took command of the *Bounty* near the Friendly Islands in the southwest Pacific. However, one account suggests that the mutiny was more a product of overcrowding and too few deck hands, which was common on ships of that time. Christian's mental state was also in question.

It appears that Christian was called out by Bligh for his poor performance as a master's mate. In a moment of embarrassment and outrage, Christian ordered Bligh and eighteen of his minions set adrift in a small boat. Christian recognized the instigation of a mutiny to be perilous at best, so he tied a heavy weight around his neck just in case his ploy was not accepted by the crew. Success was his, and Bligh, along with a crew of six, spent six weeks at sea traveling some 3,618 miles in their small vessel. Somehow, they miraculously reached land in the East Indies.

Bligh's troubles didn't end, for in 1797, he was commander of the *HMS Director* and was drawn into a series of events that resulted in a mutiny involving the entire fleet at The Nore, England. The mutineers demanded more pay and better grog as well as the dismissal of brutal captains. Curiously, Bligh was not one of the captains singled out for dismissal, but nevertheless, he was summarily relieved of his command.

Finally, in 1808, acting as governor of New South Wales, Australia, Bligh became intolerant of insobriety and ended the sale of alcohol. His actions triggered the Rum Rebellion and he was eventually removed from office and subsequently imprisoned.

Ultimately and ironically, Bligh proved victorious, despite his notorious reputation. He returned to England and rose to the rank of vice admiral in 1814, but he held no naval commands. He died in London on December 7, 1817.

There was a man who was the President of the United States for just "one" day.

Although some view it as a technicality, others insist that David Rice Atchison (1807–86), a lawyer, major general, and senator from Missouri, was also the President of the United States for just one day. Atchison was also a very powerful figure in Washington during his tenure as president pro tempore of the Senate, a position he was elected to sixteen times.

This presidential fluke came about when Zachary Taylor's inauguration date fell on Sunday, March 4, 1849, although he did not take the oath of office until the following day, Monday, March 5. The term of the previous president, Polk, expired at noon on March 4, and the vice president, George M. Dallas, resigned his position as president of the Senate on Friday, March 2. In order to fill the office of the presidency until Taylor took his oath on March 5, Atchison was elected president pro tempore of the Senate on March 2, and as the next in line, he became the President of the United States on March 4, 1849, if only for a day.

Thomas Edison was not the father of the "age of electric light."

Today, little is remembered of the "genius of invention," the man who made life easier for all Earth's inhabitants. Many experts freely admit that he is probably the greatest inventor of his or any time.

Nikola Tesla (1856–1943) was born of Serbian parents in what is now Croatia (at one time part of Yugoslavia). His father was an Orthodox Christian clergyman and his mother was a clever inventor of home and farm implements. Tesla showed himself early on to be a dreamer, a loner, an eccentric, and most of all, a visionary. He received an extensive education in engineering while a student at the University in Graz, Austria; then in 1884, he immigrated to the United States. In no time at all, he found himself in the employ of none other than Thomas Edison, who would later prove to be his adversary in the historic "battle of the systems."

A year later, Tesla left Edison's laboratory because of a disagreement over his system of alternating current versus Edison's long-outdated system of direct current. This disagreement would soon manifest itself as one of the legendary confrontations in modern science, with Tesla ending up the victor, and Edison relegated to the ranks of the used-to-be's.

From 1888 to 1896, Tesla acquired the necessary patents on his system of alternating current and electric motors. The rights to his patents were ultimately purchased by the American industrialist, George Westinghouse. Tesla's system proved to be the only logical method of electrical current transmission and it enabled the large-scale harnessing of Niagara Falls, thus establishing the foundation for what was to become the modern electrical power industry.

In 1893, Tesla's alternating current system illuminated the World's Columbian Exposition in Chicago. That same year, he predicted wireless communication, a whole two years before Marconi's claim of inventing the medium. In 1898, Tesla also foresaw the possibility of radio-guided missiles and aircraft, as well as radio-guidance systems for ships and torpedoes. By the turn of the century, his name was as world-renowned as Edison's.

In 1917, Tesla predicted the eventual invention of radar. His inventions were countless, his honors were numerous, but he never stopped to take notice. Financial gain was not a motivating force in his life; he was after something much more elusive. He was a driven man, who, in his later years, shut himself off from much of the world, associating with only a few others, among them, Mark Twain.

Tesla died lonely and essentially unknown to the world that he illuminated, though no less than three Nobel Prize recipients eulogized him by saying that he was a "world-class intellect" who made possible many of the technological developments of modern times. Even today, scientists peruse his notebooks, looking for additional inventions and discoveries.

Tesla never realized all of his dreams, but he did die knowing that he won the "battle of the systems," and today, virtually all the electricity used in the world is the result of Tesla's alternating current system and his electric motors. Because of this, he is the undisputed father of the "age of electric light."

America was not discovered by Columbus.

The legacy of Christopher Columbus (1451–1506) is unequaled in the annals of western history. As much as most Americans fervently believe that the Italian navigator Christopher Columbus (Cristoforo Colombo, in Italian) discovered their country, nothing could be farther from the truth. The image of Columbus and his three ships, the *Pinta*, the *Niña*, and the *Santa Maria*, sailing out of the port of Palos, Spain, on August 3, 1492, only to discover "the land of the free and the home of the brave" reads like an epic novel—fiction, of course. Columbus himself set out to discover a sea route to Asia, not America, and was insistent, even as he took his last breath, that he had done so.

No one should discount Columbus's bravery, tenacity, or efforts, but the true record of his exploits indicates a somewhat different picture of just what happened.

Columbus spent several years trying to convince the royals of Portugal, France, and England to support his voyage in search of riches to be found in the Indies. After being rejected by all, he returned to Spain's Queen Isabella I and King Ferdinand, both of whom had once before scoffed at his proposal. Ultimately they acquiesced, and agreed to finance the voyage, although Isabella did not have to hock her jewels in the process. The terms of the agreement between Columbus and the Spanish court would give him 10 percent of the profits, governorship of all the lands that he discovered, and the aristocratic title of Admiral of the Ocean Sea.

So, before dawn, on October 12, 1492, after thirty-three boring days at sea, a crew member aboard the ship *Pinta* sighted land. Columbus christened the island in the Caribbean San Salvador, Spanish for "Holy Savior," thinking it was close to where Japan ought to be. On October 28, he sighted Cuba, believing it to be the mainland of China. He also came upon an immense island he named Hispaniola, now the countries of Haiti and the Dominican Republic. All are a considerable distance from Florida.

It was during this foray into the Caribbean Islands that he met and called the islanders there Indians (*Indios*), once again thinking he had reached his predetermined destination somewhere in Asia, possibly an island of the East Indies. It was more than a few decades before people realized that Columbus had not found the East Indies, but the misnomer, East Indian, endures to this very day.

On January 16, 1493, Columbus turned the bow of the *Niña*, the *Santa Maria* having been wrecked near Cap-Haïtien at Christmas, northeast and set sail for home, reaching Palos on March 15. He made four voyages of exploration westward between 1492 and 1504, never once reaching the shores of the United States of America. Remember, he went to his grave believing he had discovered the Indies of the East. Columbus's body was laid to rest in Valladolid on May 20, 1506, though its present whereabouts is in doubt. He died in relative obscurity and broken by litigious matters.

It cannot be denied that Columbus's impact, both positive and negative, on European western expansion is without equal. He most assuredly deserves the title Admiral of the Ocean Sea, for all it entails. Who, then, did discover America?

There's as much controversy over who really discovered America as there is over the exploits of Columbus himself. Many claims have been made over the years to suggest that any one of a number of individuals could have discovered America, but the most logical claim, bolstered by archaeological proof, points to the Norse sea captain Leif Eriksson (c. 980–1025). He not only reached the shores of North America but founded a settlement he called Vinland (present-day Newfoundland), sometime around A.D. 1000, some five centuries before Columbus discovered the West Indies. However, Eriksson was not the first to sight North America, for Norse sagas suggest it was another Norseman, Bjarne Herjulfsson, who in 985 or 986, caught a glimpse of Labrador and Baffin Island. Nevertheless, Eriksson gets the credit for being the discoverer of America, for unlike Herjulfsson, he landed on the continent and established a colony.

There are others who also lay claim to the title of discoverer of America. The Irish voyagers of the ninth or tenth century purport to have sailed across the Atlantic to discover America, despite no tangible proof. Another theory intimates that one of the oriental civilizations, possibly the Japanese or Chinese, may have landed on the Pacific coast of America before Eriksson. Recent evidence has come to light to suggest that the Scottish nobleman Prince Henry Saint Clair of Orkney, with an Italian crew, may have landed in North America virtually a century before Columbus's failed attempt to reach the Orient.

As for who was the first to set foot on what is now considered the United States, that distinction goes to the Spanish explorer and conquistador Juan Ponce de León (1460–1521), of the "fountain of youth" fame. Thinking it was an island, he landed on Florida's coast on April 11, 1513, and named it *La Florida*, for it was the Easter season (*Pascua Florida*).

Although Columbus did not discover America or Asia, he did leave an indelible mark on the history of exploration and discovery.

Lincoln never spoke about the abundance of the common people.

Arguably the most notorious of the multitude of spurious quotes attributed to Abraham Lincoln has the Great Emancipator saying, "God must have loved the common people; he made so many of them." There is no proof that Lincoln ever uttered anything of the kind. The culprit was James Morgan, in his book, *Our Presidents* (1928), who evidently had Lincoln uttering this phrase.

Morgan writes that Lincoln dreamed one night that he was in a large crowd and heard someone in the crowd, startled to see the president, exclaim in astonishment: "He is a very common-looking man." Apparently Morgan himself was misquoted, for in his work Lincoln presumably answers: "Friend, the Lord prefers common-looking people. That is the reason he makes so many of them." The truth is, Lincoln simply never said it!

Saint Patrick was not Irish.

Much to the dismay of the Irish, tradition, and the like, Saint Patrick, the apostle and patron saint of the Emerald Isle, was not Irish; he simply converted the locals to Christianity.

Actually, Saint Patrick was born in Roman-occupied Britain to an imperial officer and his British wife in the fifth century A.D. The exact place of his birth is unknown, although some scholars postulate that he was born at Dumbarton on the Clyde in Scotland, while others believe his birthplace to be near Hadrian's Wall or at the mouth of the River Severn. Be that as it may, he most certainly was not Irish.

Patrick, whose original name was Magonus Sucatus, made two trips to Ireland. The first was at the tender age of sixteen as the captive of Irish sea rovers who sold him into bondage as a shepherd. Approximately six years after being abducted, Patrick escaped his captors and returned to Britain. He then traveled to Gaul in about 395, where he began religious studies, under Saint Martin at Tours, that would prepare him for his life's work: to impart religion to the heathens of Ireland. Upon his investiture (c. 417) he was given a formal name, Patricius, the nobleman, in order to erase his slave background and less than appropriate education. He was ordained a bishop in 432.

Patrick practiced his faith and made every attempt to civilize the heathens of the Emerald Isle, but he never forgot his first visit. He was constantly aware that violence could change his life, and he expected that he would be robbed or enslaved once again.

Although Saint Patrick was not Irish, he does much to warm the souls of the Irish, whose ancestors abducted him many centuries ago. Saint Patrick's Day is celebrated every March 17—the feast day of Saint Patrick—in Ireland and the United States as well, with the largest parade commemorating the day to be found in New York City.

Lincoln never talked about the impossibilities of deceiving all of the people all of the time.

Possibly the most famous quote attributed to Abraham Lincoln was his statement: "You can fool all the people some of the time and some of the people all of the time, but you cannot fool all of the people all of the time." Lincoln was presumed to have spoken these words when addressing the people of Clinton, Illinois, on September 8, 1858, during his senatorial campaign (Lincoln versus Douglas). However, the editor of the Bloomington *Pantagraph* made no reference to the statement in his account of the speech. Furthermore, it cannot be substantiated by any of Lincoln's printed speeches.

George Washington was not the "first" President of the United States.

Yes, it's true. Gallant, a man of uncommon bravery and resolve, the quintessential revolutionary, George Washington, Father of His Country, was not the first President of the United States. That honor falls to a lesser-known man, one John Hanson (1721–83).

Born into a Maryland family, whose ancestors were said to be distantly connected to Sweden's Queen Christina, young John had a distinguished political career before his election in 1779 as a delegate to the Second Continental Congress in Philadelphia, where he took his seat in June 1780. Always the consummate patriot, he was an early proponent of independence, having opposed British tax acts in the 1760s and organized troops to fight the British during the Revolutionary War.

John Hanson was instrumental in gaining support for the Articles of Confederation—the first American constitution—to which he was a signatory on March 1, 1781. His tireless efforts on behalf of the new nation were rewarded on November 5 of the same year when he was elected by Congress as "President of the United States in Congress Assembled." It is to this extent that John Hanson can truly be called the first President of the United States. His tenure saw the initiation of peace terms and treaties being signed, as well as the creation of government agencies.

Although many take issue with this distinction, since the office of the President of the United States was not officially established until the Constitution of the United States was ratified, it must be pointed out that General George Washington himself applauded Hanson on his election to "the most important position in the United States."

From 1781 until 1789, when the Constitution of the United States was ratified and George Washington was duly elected as President of the United States, seven other men served as President of the Congress, thus making the man who did not cut down the cherry tree the ninth president.

Joseph Stalin was not really Joseph Stalin.

Joseph Stalin (1879–1953)—dictator of all Soviets—originally went by the Georgian name Ioseb Vissarionovich Dzhugashvili. Oddly enough, his passport, while he lived in Vienna in 1913, read Stavros

Papadopoulos. He even made an attempt to speak with a slight Greek accent in the hope that his assumed name would be more believable. All these machinations were an endeavor to mask his true identity during the time he spent in Vienna prior to World War I.

As Stalin began his long climb to the top of the socialist hierarchy, he took the name Stalin ("The Man of Steel") as his pseudonym in *The Social Democrat*, published in Russia. This political instrument afforded him the ability to oftentimes wage polemical war against the Vienna *Pravda*, edited by Leon Trotsky (1879–1940).

In time, Stalin was befriended by none other than Vladimir Lenin (1870–1924) himself, if only for a brief moment while in Cracow. This liaison was to prove to be an experience from which Stalin would learn the art of political exile and the fundamentals of, of all things, biking.

To further complicate matters, Stalin was also known to his comrades as Koba, the name of a mythical folk hero from his beloved Georgia, meaning "The Indomitable."

The communist/socialist program of deception obviously had its beginnings with the man we know as Joseph Stalin—or is it Ioseb Vissarionovich Dzhugashvili—or is it Stavros Papadopoulos—or is it K. Stalin—or is it simply Koba?

There are "no" American Indians.

Common convention dictates that the original inhabitants of the Americas were the American Indians, but the truth is, there were and are no American Indians.

On August 3, 1492, Christopher Columbus (1451–1506) left Spain and sailed across the Atlantic Ocean in search of a short sea route to the Indies, which then consisted of India, China, Japan, and the East Indies. At that time, the existence of North and South America was unknown to the Europeans. When Columbus finally landed in the West Indies, he thought he was in the East Indies, so as a result, the first inhabitants he made contact with he named Indians (*Indios*). By the time people realized his error, it was too late, so the misnomer persists to this very day.

To further confuse matters, in 1735, Swedish taxonomist Carolus Linnaeus, the "father of taxonomy," came up with a specific biological classification for these "Indians," by calling them the "American," or "red" race. In one fell swoop he unknowingly grouped together over 2,000 different cultures known throughout North, Central, and South America. These people, native to the Americas, were neither Indians nor were they colored red. In fact, the Indians had no word for themselves that had any similarity to the word *Indian*.

The word *Indian* denotes a native or inhabitant of the subcontinent of India, regardless of color, religion, or race. There is absolutely no relationship between the racial types found in India and those of the Americas. The original inhabitants of the Americas were not indigenous, for their ancestry dates back tens of thousands of years to the nomadic hunters of Asia. They are, nevertheless, natives, having arrived long before Columbus or anyone else from the European Continent.

Christopher Columbus was never aware of his infamous error in naming the inhabitants of the West Indies *Indians*, for he died still believing he had discovered the Indies of Asia.

Richard I and Berengaria are unique among British monarchs.

King Richard the Lion-Heart (1157–99), also called the Lion-Hearted (French: Richard Coeur de Lion), the King of England from 1189 to 1190 and again in 1194, was a man of bravado, with the heart of a lion, but he was hampered by ill health most of his life. The campaigns of the Third Crusade consumed much of his time, and as a result, he spent less time in England than any king before or since. He was obsessed with victory, and to that extent, he is the subject of countless heroic legends and his daring deeds live on in both prose and verse.

Enter the queen-to-be. While Count of Poitou, Richard was smitten by a young maiden, Berengaria, daughter of Sancho VI (the Wise) of Navarre. She wooed him with her extraordinary beauty, wisdom, and genteel deportment, thus winning his favor.

Shortly after Richard I's ascension to the throne, he ordered his mother to send Berengaria to him so that he could take her as his wife and queen. So began the perilous journey of a future queen to join her king.

Berengaria and Richard's mother set out to meet Richard in Messina, Italy. On their way, they passed through the ominous Great Saint Bernard Pass, and in February 1191, they entered Naples, where ships of Richard's navy awaited their arrival.

The two ladies, joined by a significant escort, continued on to Messina where they were initially turned away by retainers of Tancred of Sicily. They then proceeded on to Brindisi. During their stay in Brindisi, Richard was engaged in an imbroglio with King Philip II of France regarding the king's insistence upon Richard marrying his sister, Alice. With the dispute finally settled, and both agreeing to the shared defense of their kingdoms, Berengaria and Richard's mother, Queen Eleanor, finally entered Messina, where the queen entrusted Berengaria with her daughter, Joanna, the Queen of Sicily. Richard then set sail from Messina on April 10, having sent his wife and sister ahead of his naval fleet.

Berengaria and Richard's sister ultimately ended up, after a series of tumultuous events, in Limassol, Cyprus. Finally, on May 12, after Richard's defeat of the Cypriots, he and Berengaria were married in Limassol by his chaplain, Nicolas, and later by the Bishop of Le Mans. The same day Berengaria was crowned Queen of England by the Archbishop of Bordeaux and the bishops of Evreux and Bayonne.

On June 1, Berengaria and her retinue set sail for Acre and arrived shortly thereafter. Richard made his way to Berengaria about one week later. After Richard's conquest of the city, he divided the spoils of war with Philip II. Richard's share included a palace where he lodged his queen, his sister, and the daughter of Isaac, the emperor of Cyprus.

On August 21, Richard left yet again for the campaigns, leaving behind his queen and her entourage in the keeping of Stephen of Longchamps and Bertram of Verdun (it is believed that Richard was possibly a homosexual and that he never consummated his marriage to Berengaria, despite one illegitimate son by another woman. It has even been suggested that Berengaria's brother may have been one of Richard's early swains). They were to wait in Acre, Palestine, until Richard's return in September 1192. In spite of this plan, Berengaria, and her company departed for Rome, where they planned to reside for about six months with Celestine Ill's blessings. They then moved to Poitou, during which time Richard set sail for home to see his queen. On his journey home from the Crusade, he was shipwrecked and forced to travel over land. He was captured by Leopold V, Duke of Austria, in December 1192, and subsequently given over to Emperor Henry VI of Germany, where he was held prisoner for more than a year (December 1192–February 1194).

As a reprisal for having humiliated the Duke in the Holy Land, Richard was ultimately coerced into a substantial ransom and to do homage for England. It was during his absence from England that his brother John had engineered a duplicitous arrangement with King Philip II of France to assume the crown. Apparently, the king was still outraged by Richard's earlier refusal to marry his sister. Nevertheless, Richard returned to his motherland one last time and was re-crowned at Westminster Abbey in 1194.

Surprisingly, surviving a dreadful illness, Richard continued to live a questionable personal life. However, he was most likely reunited with his queen on Christmas 1195 in Poitiers. Soon Richard was once again occupied with war as he undertook the siege of Châlus, near Limoges, against King Philip II. There he succumbed to the vicissitudes of war by taking an errant arrow in the shoulder and died of gangrene on April 6, 1199.

Richard was buried at Fontevraud Abbey and his heart, as was the tradition, was buried at Rouen next to his father. After Richard's portentous death, Berengaria lived out her days in Le Mans, France, which she received as a dower. Richard's brother, John, subsequently swindled her out of a great deal of land, tin mines, and monies.

Berengaria was then forced to live the life of a supplicant with her sister, countess of Champagne. Many influential entities, including Pope Innocent III, entreated John to return to Berengaria what was rightfully hers. John eventually acquiesced, but his untimely death ended any attempt to repay Berengaria. With the reign of Henry III, she did receive partial payment and secured the Templars as her agents, thus preventing further financial distress. Berengaria lived at Le Mans as countess and in 1226, she shared in the estate of a distant relation, William, bishop of Chalons.

She established the Cistercian abbey called Pietas Dei at Espau (Abbey of L'Espau) in Maine in 1230 and died shortly thereafter. Queen Berengaria was buried in the church she founded. A macabre sidebar to the fate of this little-known English queen was that by the seventeenth century, the abbey she founded fell into a state of disrepair and her physical remains, along with her tattered effigy, were discovered beneath a stack of wheat. Moreover, Berengaria bears the bizarre distinction of being the only Queen of England never to have been in England.

King Arthur was not a king.

King Arthur was the boy who drew the sword Excalibur from the stone; the founder of the Knights of the Round Table; the king of Britain's kings; the savior of the Christian world; the paladin of the people; and the great Celtic freedom fighter immortalized in prose and song—or was he?

To begin with, it is not truly verifiable whether King Arthur ever existed as anything more than a mythological character. We have come to know King Arthur as the man who was born to King Uther Pendragon and the Duchess of Cornwall, and who became king of the Britons sometime during the sixth century A.D., and held court with the men of his Round Table (the author Sir Thomas Malory places Arthur's Round Table at Winchester, not Camelot, as the French poets describe). Literature suggests that the trysts between his knight, Sir Lancelot, and his queen, Guinevere, and the pursuit of the Holy Grail contributed to his ultimate death and the ruin of his kingdom.

Arthur's popularity dates back to Wales before the eleventh century and his fame on the continent is attributed to the chronicle *Historia Regum Brittaniae* (1135–39), by Geoffrey of Monmouth. It is in this work that Arthur is depicted as a gallant leader who defeats the Roman army but was killed while engaged in the Battle of Camalan

(537) at home. Many insist that Geoffrey dealt with Arthur's exploits in a wholesale manner, invoking the right of poetic license.

The Arthurian legend continued to gain converts with French poet Chrétien de Troyes (late twelfth century) portraying Arthur caught up in numerous romantic escapades. He also originated the theme of the Holy Grail (the chalice from which Christ took His drink at the Last Supper and into which His blood was placed at the Crucifixion) and its Arthurian connection. The Lancelot and Guinevere liaison was first associated with the Holy Grail theme in the thirteenth century.

The *Vulgate* is a Latin Bible used by the Roman Catholic Church. The name derives from "vulgar," the "common people," and it was largely translated by Saint Jerome. Various editions also speak of Arthur's military adventures in an ersatz-historical account.

The legend, set forth in the *Vulgate* and later writings, was presented to English-speaking readers in Sir Thomas Malory's *Le Morte d'Arthur.* Arthurian legend was further infused into present-day culture with the publication of Alfred Tennyson's *Idylls of the King* (1859–85) and T. H. White's *The Once and Future King* (1958). Lerner and Loewe gave the world additional reason to fall under the spell of the Arthurian legend with the mounting of their Broadway musical, *Camelot*, in 1960.

Some historians argue, however, that if indeed King Arthur existed, he may have not been a king at all. Arthurian expert Leslie Alcock postulates that Arthurian legends give evidence that Arthur's alternate title was *dux bellorum*, "leader of battles." The manuscripts pertaining to the legends of King Arthur imply that while he was fighting with the kings of the Britons, he himself was the leader of battles, not a king.

The identities of the supposed kings of the Britons are unknown, but what is known is that Arthur was not one of them. Arthur was more likely a warlord or mercenary. Nevertheless, the legend lives on.

The Royal Canadian Mounted Police do not ride horses.

The Royal Canadian Mounted Police (RCMP) is Canada's national police agency. They have jurisdiction over all of Canada and perform duties ranging from provincial (except in Quebec and Ontario) and municipal policing, to investigating subversion and espionage (Canadian Security Service).

Historically, the RCMP was established as the North-West Mounted Police (NWMP) on May 23, 1873. With 150 original recruits, its charge was to police "on horseback" the immense North-West Territories. With the anticipated influx of miners to the Klondike gold rush of the late 1890s, members of the mounted police positioned themselves in the Yukon. In 1904, the NWMP became the Royal North-West Mounted Police, and by 1920, the force had undertaken the responsibilities of policing all of Canada and acquired the name, the Royal Canadian Mounted Police.

Where are the Mounties today, attired in scarlet jackets and jodhpurs, and perched atop their mighty steeds? You won't find them. They haven't existed as such for decades. In over a century since the founding of the RCMP, they have been known to everyone as Mounties, but the Mounties are a legend created by the filmmakers of Hollywood, who have popularized their exploits and perpetuated beliefs that only the uninformed hold to be true.

Hollywood movies have shown the Mounties chasing cars and trains full of outlaws, forging rivers, singing proudly, and always getting their man—all on horseback. However, Canadians refer to them as the RCMP, not the Mounties. More importantly, the Mounties call themselves "the force." As for their daring deeds performed on horseback, the Mounties—excuse me, the RCMP—do not ride horses. They haven't ridden horses for decades. Even the universally accepted motto, "He always gets his man," is pure fabrication. However, the RCMP does have a saying, "Uphold the Right."

If you travel in Canada today and look for the Mountie as depicted on tourist posters—attired in a scarlet jacket, jodhpurs, hat, and sitting atop his mount—you won't find him. The Mountie today dresses in a standard police uniform and rides in a police car. The dress of yesteryear is used for state functions only.

Even if they don't ride horses anymore; even if they aren't called Mounties; and even if they don't always get their man, the Royal Canadian Mounted Police will continue to be the model of civility and the pride of Canada.

Only one woman was ever awarded the Congressional Medal of Honor.

It was the bloodiest and cruelest war ever fought by Americans. Brother was pitted against brother in a battle to the end. It was fought to preserve the Union and free the disenfranchised; it was fought to safeguard a genteel way of life and slavery. It was the Civil War (1861–65).

Many individuals stood out among the millions who were combatants during the war, but Dr. Mary Edwards Walker (1832–1919) was unique. She was a nineteenth-century woman who wore pants, practiced medicine, and championed the right of women to vote—and she was irrefutably before her time.

At the outset of the war, she made her way from upstate New York to Washington in the hope of receiving a military commission. She was refused on the grounds of her sex, but stayed on in Washington to treat wounded Union soldiers. Ultimately, she was permitted to take her services to the battlefields.

For the next two years, she gave her all, without pay, on the front lines. Attired in officer's trousers and a straw hat accented by an ostrich feather, she was eventually put on the payroll as an assistant surgeon in 1864, but still she received no commission.

Later in 1864, she was captured by Confederates and imprisoned for four months. Upon her being freed in a prisoner exchange, she comforted soldiers on the Atlanta battlefield, worked in an orphanage, and administered help in a female prison.

Dr. Mary Walker never gave up hope of becoming a commissioned officer in the Union Army. She wrote letter after letter to then President Andrew Johnson (Lincoln's vice-president) stating that her loyalties to the Union and her duties performed on the fields of battle qualified her for a military commission.

In an effort to quell Walker's incessant plea, the president directed Secretary of War Edwin Stanton to think of some appropriate way to recognize her service and devotion to her country. The answer was to present her with the Medal of Honor.

One must understand that the Medal of Honor was conceived during the Civil War to inspire the Union's apprehensive citizen-soldiers to fight. On December 21, 1861, President Lincoln called for the Navy to produce two hundred such medals at a cost of $1.83 apiece. Months later, the Army began issuing the medal as well.

At the time of the Civil War, the medal was the United States' basic military medal. In many cases, the medal was given to individuals whose deeds were less than heroic by today's standards. In total, twenty-four hundred men and one woman, Dr. Mary Walker, received the Medal of Honor for their participation in the Civil War.

Dr. Mary Walker wore her medal with pride until her death. She even earned money as a sideshow attraction, sporting her medal affixed to the lapel of her manly jacket, with bow tie and top hat.

By 1916, Congress decided to stiffen the Medal of Honor standards to require combat with the enemy. By 1917, Walker's medal was revoked, as were hundreds of others who had not received their medals for engaging the enemy upon the field of battle.

Dr. Walker refused to yield to the Congressional demand to surrender her medal. She even went to Congress to beseech its members to reconsider, and while on the Capitol steps, she fell and suffered injuries that precipitated her death in 1919 at the age of eighty-six.

Almost six decades later, after a descendant of Dr. Mary Walker's asked the Army to restore her medal, they did so in 1977, making her the only woman ever to have been awarded America's highest honor—The Congressional Medal of Honor.

A saint conceived of communism.

The creation of communism was not the genius of Marx, Lenin, or any other individual of modern times. It was the work of the English lawyer, scholar, author, and subsequent martyr, Sir Thomas More (1478–1535). More, a friend of Erasmus, was destined to collide with his grace, King Henry VIII, but before his imbroglio with the man of many wives, More first set down the precepts of a new world order.

In 1516, More published his seminal work entitled *Utopia*, the "golden little book." More's *Utopia* created a world liberated from the depravity of Europe, a pagan and communist city-state, where its citizens were all equal and all facets of life were ruled by reason. He conceived of the first communist state, a utopia (a word he coined from the Greek *ou-topos*, meaning "no place"). His contribution to communism did not go unnoticed, for his name is recorded in Red Square as one of the champions of the Russian Revolution.

More's last years were spent in service to his king. Henry VIII made him the second most powerful man in England when he raised him to Lord Chancellor in 1529. The enjoyment of such a station in life was short-lived, for when Henry VIII divorced Catherine of Aragon and took Anne Boleyn as his wife, More was overwhelmed with grief and distaste for such impieties. Henry VIII rejected the Pope's disapproval and when the Pope excommunicated him, he proclaimed himself the absolute leader of the English Church.

More could take no more and he opposed the declaration by Henry VIII, king of England, that he was also the leader of the Church. More was convinced that the unity of Christendom should be under the auspices of papal authority. Henry VIII respected More, but pursued with a vengeance More's disapproval of his actions. Charged with treason, More was sentenced to death by the cruelest of means: he was to be drawn, hanged, and quartered. However, Henry VIII proved benevolent, and commuted More's sentence to a simple beheading. More departed this earthly life on July 6, 1535.

Sir Thomas More, a saint (canonized by Pope Pius XI in 1935), was the father of communism, yet he was married to the Church and God.

George Washington never signed the Declaration of Independence.

Yes, the Father of His Country and defender of liberty, the illustrious George Washington (1732–99), never signed one of America's most cherished documents. It's hard to fathom that Washington was not among those who affixed their names to the piece of paper that declared the Colonies to be free of British rule. After all, he was the young country's general of generals, so why didn't Washington sign the declaration?

The Second Continental Congress adopted a resolution of independence on July 2, 1776, and not July 4, as most believe. The fifty-six delegates to the Second Continental Congress then began the laborious process of signing Thomas Jefferson's masterwork, and most had done so by August 2, 1776.

On July 8, the declaration was publicly announced in Philadelphia and on the next day the same was done in New York City before the Continental Army and its leader, George Washington, who, it has been said, was actually in his office, and did not hear the announcement and reading.

Washington could not have signed the declaration because he was not a member of Congress; he was a general. He did, however, sign one of the other most significant documents in the history of mankind, the Constitution of the United States. He was also only one of two signers of that document to become president, the other being James Madison.

The Pilgrims "did not" land at Plymouth Rock.

In December 1620, the Mayflower party of English Separatist Puritans sailed into a wide and circular harbor on the western shore of Massachusetts—Cape Cod Bay—and disembarked. They had already first anchored in Provincetown Harbor, Massachusetts, the month before in order to consider a proper location for their colony and to sign the *Mayflower Compact*.

Soon the colonists, small in number and without many possessions, founded their settlement, known as New Plymouth (they spelled it *Plimouth*), in Plymouth, Massachusetts, about forty miles south of Boston. Their endless search for religious freedom had given them the will and desire to survive their arduous journey, and they became known as Pilgrims, establishing the Congregational Church in their new homeland. They remained autonomous until they became part of Massachusetts Bay Colony in 1691. Plymouth Colony was the second permanent English settlement in America, the first being Jamestown (1607), in Virginia.

As for the renowned *Plymouth Rock*, there wasn't one, not at least when the Pilgrims first landed. Local legend has it that when the Pilgrims disembarked from the *Mayflower*, they stepped ashore onto a granite boulder, Plymouth Rock. What's interesting is that no historical account makes mention of Plymouth Rock with the date 1620 carved into it.

It seems that the whole idea was the work of Elder Thomas Faunce, who, in 1741, at the advanced age of ninety-five, identified the rock as the place where the Pilgrims landed after their journey from England. It also seems that Faunce was repeating a story told to him as a boy by his father, a colonist who himself landed in America several years after the first Plymouth settlers. There may have been a rock in the vicinity and they may have landed on a rock at some later date, but the Pilgrims didn't see or use a rock when they first landed. Nevertheless, the rock became an icon of American freedom when it was split in two while being dragged to Liberty Pole Square during some confusion prior to the American Revolution. It has withstood its share of abuse between 1774 and 1921, and has since been restored. Plymouth Rock now rests, housed under a granite canopy, at the site where the Pilgrims supposedly landed in 1620.

Uncle Sam was a real person.

Yes, that ever present icon of the United States Government and a symbol of the national spirit, "Uncle Sam," was in fact a real man. Cartoonists are responsible for the image of the Uncle Sam we are all familiar with. First pictured seated, sans beard, in a striped gown and nightcap (1834), the image has since evolved to embody the essence of the American Flag, credited to cartoonist Thomas Nast in the 1870s, whose model was none other than Abraham Lincoln. It depicts a tall, slender figure with white hair and chin whiskers, adorned in red stripped trousers, a swallow-tail coat embellished with stars, and a top hat with both stars and stripes. This image was first seen in a military recruiting poster painted by J.M. Flagg, who himself once posed as the model, and was issued during World War I. It showed a friendly but stern Uncle Sam pointing to "you," urging you to enlist in the U.S. Army. So who was this Uncle Sam? Was he really fact or simply fiction?

Uncle Sam was in truth Samuel Wilson (1766–1854). As a young lad, he assisted as a drummer boy during the American Revolution, and later as a fighting regular at the tender age of fourteen. After victory over the British was a fait accompli, Sam moved to Troy, New York in 1789. There he started a meat-packing company, and success was soon to follow.

Samuel Wilson was always known as an equitable man, whose integrity was beyond reproach. It was because of his honorable business practices that his company was awarded a military contract to supply beef and pork to the U.S. Army during the War of 1812. To show that specific crates of meat were bound for the military, Sam would order them stamped with the initials "U.S.," meaning United States (the acronym was not yet in everyday use).

From time to time government inspectors would make an unannounced tour of his facilities, to insure that everything was up to government standards, and October 1, 1812, was certainly no exception. The inspectors were curious as to what the numerous crates of meat branded with the initials "U.S." represented. It is believed that a workman, uncertain himself as to the answer, replied that the initials were those of his employer, Samuel "Uncle Sam" Wilson. The inaccuracy took hold and before too long just about everything that had to do with government-issued supplies was deemed the property of Uncle Sam. The moniker Uncle Sam was soon commonplace, and in 1816, the name found its way on to the title of a book, *The Adventures of Uncle Sam*.

Although the origin of the term Uncle Sam may not survive the scrutiny of some critics, a historian found an 1830 newspaper which gave credence to the story. Moreover, it was also convincing enough to compel the 87th Congress in 1961 to issue a resolution honoring Samuel Wilson as the prototype of America's national symbol: "Uncle Sam."

George Washington "never" chopped down the cherry tree.

Americans have always had a love affair for larger-than-life heroes to whom they could look with pride, and George Washington (1732–99), the Father of His Country, is certainly no exception. He is the most real, yet mythical man to have ever graced the pages of American history books.

Little is known of Washington's childhood, so much of it was left up to others to fill in the gaps. Let's take the famous cherry tree story. It appears that "Parson" Weems (Mason Locke Weems, 1759–1825), a clergyman, author, and Washington's biographer, was ever the blithe man. He sought to instill high morals and ethics in the youth of America, and it was to this end that he created the most celebrated American anecdote of a six-year-old George chopping down the cherry tree and then admitting his guilt to his father: "I cannot tell a lie. . . ."

This story, as well as others, was purely the product of Parson Weems's imagination. Even Washington tossing the coin across the Potomac—actually the Rappahannock—was a complete fabrication as well.

Though Weems took great poetic license, even admitting it to his printer, Mathew Carey, that his biographies of Washington and others were often seen as excursions into hero worship, it was something the nascent country truly needed.

George Armstrong Custer was not a general at his "last stand."

Perhaps no single military battle in American history draws more attention and is surrounded by more controversy than George Armstrong Custer's (1839–76) "last stand" against the Sioux Indians on June 25, 1876. It seems extremely bizarre and yet fascinating, that a soldier, who not only graduated at the bottom of his class at West Point, but lost a major military battle, would be remembered as one of America's greatest warriors.

However, what's more interesting is that unlike the depiction of Custer: fighting the thousands of Indians at Little Big Horn, dressed in his Civil War uniform, with his long, yellow locks following in the breeze, and sporting the stars of a general's rank upon his epaulets, while at the same time flaunting his saber in defiance, astride his mighty steed, the actual truth is much less romantic.

Custer did not wear his Civil War uniform; he wore basic buckskins and a simple flannel shirt, and his well-known locks had been cut off prior to the battle. As for his general's rank, he was not a general, but rather a lieutenant colonel of the 7th U.S. Calvary, having surrendered his field rank of major general given to him during the Civil War (he was the Union Army's youngest). As for his saber, it was left behind at the encampment.

George Armstrong Custer died on June 25, 1876, in the Battle of the Little Big Horn—none of his men survived; all were subsequently butchered by the Indians, save Custer himself. He was taken down with just one bullet to his left temple, causing some historians to hypothesize that he died by his own hand.

Despite the less than romantic circumstances of his "last stand," Custer will always be remembered as a bona fide American war hero, a winner in the minds of millions, a legend for all time, a general of generals, and a man of undeniable bravado.

Darwin was not the only man to conceive of the "theory of evolution."

No greater coincidence exits in the world of science than the fact that two men, both independent of each other, developed virtually identical theories of evolution. Popular consensus dictates that the father of the theory of evolution is Charles Robert Darwin (1809–82). After all, this noted British naturalist did publish the classic work, *On the Origin of Species*. From that point on, he has been credited with originating the theory. Although he did do just that, so did someone else.

Let's step back a few years to 1855. Another British naturalist, Alfred Russel Wallace (1823–1913), less well-known than the eminent Darwin, and whose life started out less auspiciously, published a paper in the scientific journal, *Annals and Magazine of Natural History*, entitled, "On the Law Which Has Regulated the Introduction of New Species." Wallace postulated that new life was not regularly being created, but rather, new forms were slowly evolving out of old ones. Wallace was an incurable collector of botanical specimens and insects (numbering 125,660). While living in the Spice Islands, Wallace produced another paper that literally came out of nowhere. It rocked the scientific community to its very core, and no one was as surprised as Darwin himself.

Darwin was vaguely aware of Wallace's existence, but that's about all. He was in a state of panic to say the least; he had assumed that the theory was his child. Contemporaries such as Lyell and Hooker urged Darwin to publish or perish. After all, others were flirting with the theory of evolution, and if Darwin were to make his twenty years of work on the subject pay off, he'd better do something quick.

By May 1856, Darwin was knee deep into his colossal book that would set him apart from the rest and establish him as the sole creator of the theory that Wallace had already conceived of himself, thousands of miles away. Soon Darwin received an unsolicited letter from none other than Wallace himself, asking Darwin to discuss their independent theories. Darwin answered by saying that they thought alike and then summarily dismissed Wallace. Darwin forged on, tired, troubled, and in poor health.

What brought Wallace to conceive of his theory? It seems that his collecting excursions throughout South America and the Pacific caused him to marvel at the variation of nature. He noted that the geographical distribution of species and genera demanded that some type of evolutionary force must be at work. In 1858, while convalescing from the ills of tropical fever in the Molucca Islands (Spice Islands), Wallace hit upon the idea that natural selection was the governing force behind evolution. He recorded his ideas and dispatched them to Darwin for his opinion.

June 18 was to prove to be a gray day in Darwin's life, for he received yet another unsolicited missive, this time containing Wallace's manuscript. Darwin perused Wallace's work and horrified, he concluded that Wallace's ideas were so much like his own that he could have written them himself.

Totally nonplussed, Darwin once again summoned his friend, the eminent geologist Sir Charles Lyell. Lyell notified Hooker and the three met in secret. After much deliberation, Darwin decided that he could not conceal Wallace's manuscript. He hurriedly found one of his earlier efforts on the subject dated 1844 (and a letter from 1857) and had his and Wallace's manuscripts read before the Linnaean Society on July 1, 1858. The two manuscripts, plus Darwin's letter, were published in the Linnaean Society in 1858. Wallace's work was entitled "On the Tendency of Varieties to Depart Indefinitely From the Original Type." The hope was that the Society would select Darwin's work as being truly original inasmuch as he had been working on it for some twenty years. The Society's response to the papers was polite and curiously without comment. In fact, in the yearly report from the Society there was no reference to any major discoveries having been made that year.

Darwin, downtrodden but not without hope, continued his work on what he called an "abstract" of his theories. On November 24, 1859, Darwin published his unprecedented work, *On the Origin of Species by Means of Natural Selection*. It was an immediate success and five more editions were to follow during Darwin's lifetime. Its greatest impact was that natural selection, as the driving force of evolution, worked automatically, thus all but ruling out any divine intervention.

Wallace received a copy of Darwin's book and was genuinely impressed and humbled, likening it to the importance of Newton's *Principia Mathematica*. In 1862, the two giants of science met for the very first time. They developed a close relationship through correspondence, with Wallace always deferring to Darwin, his senior by some fourteen years. They remained devoted friends right up until Darwin's passing.

To his credit, Darwin always made it known that he shared the credit for the theory with Wallace. When Wallace found himself in financial straits, it was Darwin who had successfully petitioned the government for a pension on Wallace's behalf.

Both men viewed their greatness in different ways. To Darwin, the theory was his reason for living, but for Wallace, it was simply a moment of marvelous revelation, not something that should detract him from his first love, collecting insects. In fact, Wallace freely admitted that he never could have written as complete a book as Darwin's *On the Origin of Species*. He even expressed the belief that he was relieved not to have been the one to give the theory to the world.

Wallace continued to have financial troubles, yet he was able to publish substantial works. He became chief of the Entomological Society and president of the British Association. A recipient of many awards, including the Order of Merit in 1910, Wallace continued to be active up into his eighties. He died of a chill one day in 1913.

Darwin lived a life plagued by ill health and personal tragedy, but he never gave up. During the early part of his life, he spent five years aboard the H.M.S. *Beagle* as a naturalist. It was then that he became persuaded that there was a gradual evolution of the species. He observed firsthand the changes that occur in nature, and because of these observations, he was to later conceive of his theory. His final years were spent as the protector of the theory of evolution and the consummate scientific iconoclast. Forever prolific and enigmatic, Darwin died in Downe, Kent, England, on April 19, 1882. He was interred in Westminster Abbey, near Sir Isaac Newton, on April 26 of the same year.

Sadly, it seems almost scripted that these two great men of science would independently conceive of the same seminal theory of evolution, meet for a brief moment, and then go their separate ways . . . one into the history books and the other into the dustbin of history.

CHAPTER TWO

LANGUAGE AND LITERATURE

There is a famous manuscript that no one can read.

Hard as it may seem to believe, there exists a famous manuscript that no one can read. It is an archaic scientific text that comprises 102 vellum leaves, detached from vellum covers. The manuscript is embellished with several hundred multicolored drawings, mostly botanical and biological in nature, and is handwritten in a stylish black ink script, in an unknown alphabet, in cipher.

In 1912, New York rare-book dealer Wilfrid Michael Voynich purchased the manuscript, believed to be medieval in origin, from the Mondragone Jesuit College in Frascati, Italy. The manuscript has had many owners throughout the centuries, not the least of which was the Holy Roman Emperor Rudolf II (1522–1612), a man possessed by the world of alchemy.

Voynich, familiar with symbolism and armed with what he thought to be powerful circumstantial evidence, had posited the theory that the manuscript's author might have been the thirteenth-century Franciscan monk, alchemist, and scientific experimenter, Roger Bacon (c. 1220–92). With this in mind, he subsequently had copies made and offered them to anyone who thought they could decipher it. Although the groups of letters and words appeared at first to be rather rudimentary, a second look revealed otherwise. Even the pictures accompanying the text yielded no information. Philologists and cryptologists struggled with the manuscript without success. Even a division of United States Military Intelligence became intrigued by the Voynich manuscript, but its experts failed, too. The manuscript refused to give up its secrets.

Of the many excited scholars who attempted to break the code, none had any success until 1921, when Professor William Romaine Newbold, a cryptologist and a specialist in medieval history and philosophy at the University of Pennsylvania, said he had deciphered the arcane alphabet. For two years prior, Newbold had meticulously examined the vellum leaves. By a very complicated method he had arrived at an answer, which he presented to the American Philosophical Society in Philadelphia in April of that year.

Newbold came to the same conclusion that Voynich had: it was written by Roger Bacon. Newbold stated that Bacon encoded the manuscript to avoid being branded as a heretic, for it contained scientific knowledge unheard of at the time. The manuscript even suggested that Bacon had invented and successfully utilized microscopes and telescopes nearly four centuries before their documented inventions.

The crowd of academicians that gathered at the meeting was astonished, some thinking Newbold was really reaching, but Newbold's reputation and presentation were very convincing: the preliminary findings demonstrated that the Voynich manuscript had been deciphered. However, Newbold continued analyzing the manuscript up until his death in 1926.

It seems that shortly after Newbold's death, most of his claims about the manuscript were proven false and relegated to the dustbin of historical sophistry. It was pure bunk and the manuscript had yet again claimed another victim. That didn't stop the dreamers, those who fantasized about cracking the uncrackable code. Many more tried their hand, and many more failed.

Upon the death of Wilfrid Voynich in 1930, his famous manuscript became the charge of his wife, Ethel Lillian. She was an independent woman in her own right, as well she could afford to be, for in 1897, she authored a book entitled *The Gadfly*, which before her death had sold over 2.5 million copies, making her as big a seller as Shakespeare, Dickens, and Burns. Since she had no interest in the hullabaloo surrounding the manuscript, she placed it in her safe-deposit box in a New York bank and promptly forgot about it.

Ethel Lillian died in 1960 at the age of ninety-six, leaving the manuscript in the hands of executors. The manuscript was auctioned off to the highest bidder, Hans P. Kraus, a noted New York collector of rare books. Two years later, he offered it for sale at the then ungodly sum of $160,000.

Kraus advertised the book by saying that when deciphered, it might reveal a new understanding of the history of man. Needless to say, no one thought the work worthy of such a lofty figure, and in 1969, he presented the Beinecke Rare Book and Manuscript Library at Yale University with the Voynich manuscript (MS 408). The Voynich manuscript now reposes within the walls of academia, still refusing to give up its many secrets.

The Bible never spoke of cleanliness being next to godliness.

John Wesley (1703–91), the eighteenth-century British cleric who founded the Methodist Church, is the man credited with the phrase, "Cleanliness is, indeed, next to godliness," not the Bible. In his *Sermon 93, On Dress*, he admonished his congregation to revere cleanliness. Slovenliness has no part in religion. The Bible makes no mention of the necessity of being clean in order to be next to God.

Wesley himself was quoting the Hebrew sage Phinehas ben-Yair, who lived in the latter part of the second century and who spoke of the "doctrines of religion." Phinehas drew the distinction between cleanliness and godliness, not the Bible.

The first novel written in English was about cats.

In 1553, the first English novel, entitled *Beware the Cat*, was written by William Baldwin, a distinguished man of letters. The book, a landmark example of English Renaissance literature, was not published until 1570, seven years after its author had succumbed to the ominous plague. The illustrious Huntington Library has since reprinted this first effort.

The book itself is representative of Baldwin's activities as a zealous supporter of the Protestant Reformation and a vehement foe of the Roman Catholic Church. It is a religious satire exposing the presumed cruelty and voracity of cats that represent the purported indulgences of the clergy. Maybe it was the first metaphor, as well.

Think of it: to be the first novelist; what power! Baldwin had the ultimate carte blanche, poetic license. His book is narrated by Master Streamer, arrogant and not to be trusted. He is a louse and a ne'er-do-well. So what's changed?

Baldwin's work most likely pandered to an audience of the well-to-do, for after all, it was the first novel written in English, and only the wealthy could read.

A side note to the first novel written in English, the first "modern" novel to be written in English is said to be *Pamela: or, Virtue Rewarded*. Written in two parts by Samuel Richardson between 1740 and 1742, the book's central character is a naive teenage country girl, Pamela Andrews, who has a propensity for self-analysis. What would Freud think?

A bellwether has nothing to do with the weather.

The mistake is common: *bellwether* (Middle English) is not an incorrect spelling of *bellweather* (inasmuch as bellweather is not even a word). Moreover, *bellwether* has nothing whatsoever to do with the weather.

A castrated ram (wether) that is the leader of a flock of sheep is fixed with a bell; hence, he is the bellwether of the flock. Moreover, a bellwether can also be an entity that influences trends or foretells of future events.

The oldest publication in English was not even printed in England.

William Caxton (1422–91) was a wealthy and scholarly English businessman living in Bruges, ("City of Bridges") Belgium. At that time, Bruges was one of the central trading centers of Europe. In 1475, Caxton, fascinated with the recent developments of printing in Germany and having learned the art of printing on the Continent, thought that there might be money to be made, so he established his own publishing house in Bruges. That same year, he published *Recuyell of the Historyes of Troy* (translated by Caxton himself from the French), the oldest publication in the English language. The oddity of that historic moment was that the book was printed in Flanders, not in England.

Caxton is credited with publishing about one hundred books, totaling eighteen hundred leaves. He published works by such literary luminaries as Chaucer, Malory, and Gower. As a man of letters, Caxton also contributed greatly to English literature as a translator and editor.

The expression O.K. is truly American.

Considering all the new words that are produced in America each year, nothing remotely approaches the impact of O.K. O.K. can be used for various parts of a sentence ranging from a verb (Please O.K. the letter) an adjective (The O.K. Corral is in Tombstone), to a noun (We must have your O.K. before we can proceed), and an adverb (Tom ran O.K.). It can even express variations of meaning from informal permission (Shall Dorothy come too? O.K.) to the mundane (O.K., let's get out of here). O.K. is simply the most useful word in the English language, and it is a word that is often heard in most other languages.

Many believe the source of O.K. can be traced to the misspelling of *all correct* (oll kurrect) by Andrew Jackson. Allen W. Read, reporter for the *Saturday Review of Literature*, wrote on July 19, 1941, that O.K. was first seen in print in the New York *New Era* (in 1839 the *Boston Morning Post* may have printed the O.K. expression as an abbreviation for all correct) on March 23, 1840(?) as an element of the name, The Democratic O.K. Club. The organization, comprised of Martin Van Buren partisans, utilized the expression as an acronym for (Old) Kinderhook, New York, Van Buren's birthplace. Read also makes reference to a group of young turks in Boston who would intentionally speak in abbreviations based on obvious illiteracies.

O.K. ultimately became the chant that represented the constituency of Van Buren—he lost to William H. Harrison ("Tippecanoe and Tyler Too."). It is understood that other explanations, more likely suppositions, exist as to the origin of O.K., but none have the logic, history, or documentation that the Van Buren connection has.

O.K., so where did the sign O.K. come from? The sign of the thumb and forefinger joined together originated with the famous first-century Roman rhetorician Quintilian, who made use of the sign, signaling approval, in his discourse on oratory.

Horace Greeley did not originally say to go west.

One of the more well-worn phrases, "Go west, young man . . . ," is attributed to Horace Greeley (1811–72), the founder of the powerful *New-York Tribune*. It seems that Greeley used the expression in his paper, and many individuals also stated that he gave them advice to go west; hence, he was credited with having originated the exhortation.

However, Greeley was insistent upon giving John Babsone Lane Soulé, the editor of the Terre Haute *Express*, credit for creating the slogan that has characterized Greeley. In fact, Greeley, both publicly and in print, disclaimed having ever said any such thing. But despite Greeley's endless efforts to make known the source of the phrase, it has forever been associated with him.

Mark Twain was not really "Mark Twain."

Modern convention has it that the illustrious and talented author Mark Twain was a pseudonym originated by Samuel Langhorne Clemens (1835–1910). Mr. Clemens, or Mark Twain to his true believers, was an honest man who never really claimed credit for his pseudonym. He cites in Chapter 50 of his *Life on the Mississippi* (1883) that Captain Isaiah Sellers, an old riverboat pilot (Mark Twain also piloted riverboats from 1853 to 1862) and an occasional journalist, penned a prosaic column for a New Orleans newspaper under the name Mark Twain. Clemens, having made fun of one of Sellers's journalistic efforts, may have adopted the man's name after his death as a penance for supposedly hurting his feelings.

There exists some refutation to the Clemens's story by the author Milton Meltzer. In 1960, Meltzer wrote in his *Mark Twain Himself* that Sellers never employed the sobriquet Mark Twain, and that Clemens had been mistaken. Meltzer further stated that the name originated with the duties of a "leadsman" on a Mississippi riverboat, whose job it was to take soundings with a line affixed to a lead weight. Once the line was in the water, he would then call out "by the mark, twain (twine)," meaning that the line showed a marking of two fathoms deep, or a "twain" of water. Two fathoms translates to twelve feet of water, sufficient for any riverboat to safely negotiate the waters of the Mississippi River.

As for the celebrated white suit that was synonymous with Twain himself, he never lectured in such attire. In fact, he only took to the white suit well into his seventh decade of life. For most of his professional career, he wore basic black.

It's okay to spell Christmas with an "X."

It is a mistaken belief that to spell Christmas as Xmas is sacrilegious and vulgar. However, dating back to the ancient Greeks, the word for Christ began with the Greek letter *chi*, or *X* for Christos. According to the *Anglo-Saxon Chronicle*, in the early twelfth century, the Old English word for Christmas began with an *X*.

The term *Xmas* was first cited in 1551. The scholarly abbreviation for *Christianity* is *Xianity*. Therefore, one is perfectly correct to spell the celebration of Christ's birth with an *X*, hence, Xmas.

A Kodak is not a bear.

No, a Kodak is not a bear, but a Kodiak is. So what is a Kodak? It is the most famous name in photography. It all started with a small, inexpensive camera, called the Kodak No.1, which George Eastman (1854–1932) introduced in 1888. The Kodak No. 1 brought photography to the masses in a big way, with its inventor claiming, "You press the button, we do the rest."

Since Eastman had a camera and a slogan, he needed a name before he could market his product. He claimed that *Kodak* was his own creation, believing that a trade name must be short, powerful, pronounceable in virtually any language, and easy to spell. Since he favored the letter *K*, thinking it was a letter with presence, he used it as his starting point. Also, trademark laws are very specific regarding names, and he felt that his trade name should have no meaning. After mulling over numerous combinations of letters that created words beginning and ending with his favorite letter, he hit upon *Kodak*.

George Eastman patented the name and the camera on the same day, September 4, 1888.

There was a book written without ever using the letter "E."

Try to write just a paragraph in English without ever using the letter *E*. Seems impossible. After all, it's one of the five principal vowels. Well, Ernest Vincent Wright (1872–1939) achieved the seemingly impossible with his novel *Gadsby*. It is 267 pages in length, containing some 50,000 words, with nary the letter *E*.

What Wright did was to write a novel-length lipogram. A lipogram is a written work composed of words selected so as to refrain from the use of one or more specific alphabetic characters. Tryphiodorus, a letter-dropper of antiquity, is believed to have composed a version of the *Odyssey* in which he completely excluded the letter Σ (sigma), while the earliest composer of lipogrammatic verse is thought to have been Lasus (b. 538 B.C.)

Cinderella didn't wear glass slippers.

Cinderella ("the little cinder girl") is the heroine of a universal fairy tale: with the help of a fairy godmother, she marries a prince. So what about the glass slippers? The fairy tale, which originated in ninth century China and has since been published in countless versions, never spoke of glass slippers. The facts are overwhelmingly against such a happening.

Despite the worldwide acceptance of the story of Cinderella in all languages, the slippers made of glass exist only in the French versions and those influenced by the French. Of the 345 different adaptations of the story studied by Marian Roalfe Cox, she demonstrates that the error occurred in the French versions.

In truth, many qualified authorities believe that the slippers in the earliest, and verbal, tradition were "*pantoufles en vair*," slippers of gray and white squirrel (ermine). The French writer and commentator Charles Perrault (1628–1703) is thought to have confused *vair*, meaning "ermine" or possibly "gray and white squirrel," with *verre*, meaning "glass." The error gave Cinderella this improbable, fragile footwear.

A sidebar to the story of Cinderella is that there are many grisly details in the unabridged story, which are not found in most children's books. Rossini's enchanting *La Cenerentola* (1817) was inspired by a corrupted version of the story.

It seems that only in the United States, Scotland, the Netherlands, Chile, Catalonia, England, and France does Cinderella wear the proverbial glass slippers. In other parts of the world she wears slippers made of gold or silver, sometimes pearl-embroidered or bedecked with jewels, and even white ermine, but not glass.

To live in Luxembourg one must be a polyglot.

The country of Luxembourg is an independent grand duchy situated in Western Europe, bordered by France, Germany, and Belgium. If one lives there, one must be a polyglot (one who has a command of several languages). It is essential to know German to read the newspapers, French to attend school, and Luxemburgish, a local Germanic dialect, to speak at home. All three languages are official.

The first sentence written in English was about a "she-wolf."

The Anglo-Saxon variety of the runic alphabet (also referred to as "Futhark" and of uncertain origin) was used in Britain from about the fifth century to about the twelfth century. A rune, from the Anglo-Saxon *rûn*, meaning "secret" and *runa*, meaning "magician," is a character in the runic alphabet, with only priests or sorcerers having knowledge of the runes.

In 1982, a gold medallion resembling an American half-dollar was discovered in an outlying field in Suffolk, England. It had apparently been inadvertently left behind or buried by one of the earliest interlopers sometime between A.D. 450 and 480.

The medallion's runic inscription says something to this effect: "This she-wolf is a reward to my kinsmen." It's not Lord Byron, but it is the earliest existing specimen of Anglo-Saxon writing in Britain—the first sentence ever written in English.

The word "set" has more uses than any other word in the English language.

The English language possesses arguably the richest vocabulary, coupled with the most mixed shadings of meaning, of any language today. We have an inexplicable practice of endowing a single word with myriad meanings. This condition of having multiple meanings is known as *polysemy*.

For example, the word *fine* has fourteen definitions when used as an adjective, six as a noun, and two as an adverb. The *Oxford English Dictionary* devotes two complete pages and five thousand words of explanation to the word *fine*. The word *round*, without its mutations (rounded and roundup), consumes nearly eight pages and about fifteen thousand words in the same dictionary. But the polysemic king of the hill is the simple, monosyllabic word *set*.

Set can be used 58 ways as a noun, 126 as a verb, and 10 as a participial adjective. Because of the word's diversity, the *OED* devotes an astonishing sixty thousand words to examine them all—that's about the length of many books.

Some English word endings are very rare indeed.

The English language is a font of surprises, contradictions, and curiosities. Here are a few of its most interesting examples.

Take what appears to be a typical word ending, *-gry*. The first two words that come to mind are *angry* and *hungry*. Now try to think of another word with the same ending. Can't think of one? That's because there are no other common words in English that end in *-gry*. But wait a minute, what about the word *gry*. It doesn't count, since it is an obsolete unit proposed by Locke in his system of linear measurement and equivalent to a hundredth of an inch.

With that in mind, look at *-dous*. It appears in just a few words: *horrendous, stupendous, hazardous, tremendous,* and *jeopardous*. Similarly, *-red* is essentially found only in *hatred* and *kindred*. Some word endings are very rare indeed.

Shakespeare did not spell his name Shakespeare.

He is called the Bard of Avon or the Swan of Avon, a man of the late sixteenth and early seventeenth centuries, who is most assuredly the greatest writer of all time. While the likes of Homer, Tolstoy, and Dickens are well-known, no writer has ever transcended national boundaries quite like William Shakespeare (1564–1616), or is it Shakspere? The relationship between this lord of the language and the mother tongue he helped so much to develop is undeniable, but what is strange is how he spelled his own name.

It was not uncommon during Shakespeare's time to find many words in the English language with more than one spelling, but William Shakespeare's very own surname may have one of the greatest variances of all. In fact, it numbers more than eighty, with such examples as Shagspeare, Skakestaffe, and Skakspere. Even the man himself couldn't make up his mind as to how he wanted to spell his own name: he did not spell his name the same way twice in any of the six authenticated signatures attributed to him. Furthermore, in his will he spelled it two different ways: in one place he signed Shakspere, and in another Shakspeare.

It is accepted that a man's signature is not always the best source of the correct spelling of his name because of the problem of legibility, and the same can be said for Shakespeare's signature. Nevertheless, Shakespeare is how his name is found on most documents involving him, though he most likely never used the spelling himself.

A dollar is a "daler."

The English language is an amalgamation of virtually every language under the sun, to a greater or lesser degree. Many words reach us in a most roundabout manner. Since America represents the land of opportunity, the almighty dollar is ever present. So where did the word for the American dollar come from?

The word actually originates from Joachimsthaler, the sixteenth-century silver mine in Joachimsthal, Germany, where a large silver coin was first struck in 1519 under the aegis of the Count of Schlick. The word's first known use in English was in 1553 and was spelled *daler*. This spelling lasted for the next two hundred years. By 1782, it found its way into general American usage, although it had appeared on Continental currency prior to that date. Thomas Jefferson, in his *Notes on a Money Unit for the United States*, recommended the acceptance of *dollar* as the name of the national currency. It was his contention that since the Spanish dollar circulated (and did for many years) in the English-American Colonies, it was a recognized monetary unit. By July 1785, Jefferson had his way, though the first U.S. dollars were not struck in silver until 1794.

America was named after a man who never saw the New World.

America, the New World, was named after Americus Vespucius, a Latinized spelling of Amerigo Vespucci (1454–1512). Vespucci was a Florentine businessman and sea pilot who acted as a chandler on Columbus's vessels, and whose sailing exploits were far more celebrated in his time than those of Columbus himself. The number of voyages he made is in doubt, but most historians agree that it was most likely four. Nevertheless, in 1499, he sailed along the shore of South America, but never once having set eyes upon North America.

It seems that in 1507, a coterie of academics at St. Dié in the Vosges Mountains of Lorraine produced a treatise on geography entitled *Cosmographiae Introductio* (Introduction to Cosmography), wherein they described current discoveries. Martin Waldseemüller, a cartographer, who drew the map for this treatise, wrote the name *America* across the portion that is now called Brazil, thinking Vespucci was its discoverer. When he realized his mistake, he removed the name, but it was too late: the book had become very popular, and so did the name. It stuck, and soon the name was applied to the entire hemisphere. Vespucci, in a letter published in 1504, called the area Mundus Novus ("New World").

The word "air" has numerous spellings.

Once again, a single-syllable, three-letter word holds the record, this time, as the word with the most diverse spellings in English. If you include proper nouns, the word *air* has an incredible thirty-eight: *aire, ayr, e'er, ere, aër, aier, heir, eyere,* and on and on.

Frankenstein was not a monster.

Mary Wollstonecraft Shelley (1797–1851) was an English romantic novelist whose renowned masterwork (entitled *Frankenstein, or, The Modern Prometheus*) was published in 1818. It was a tale of Gothic romance and science fiction. Many people believe that Frankenstein was a vile monster, who has been the subject of countless horror films and popular literature. However, he was in fact, not a monster at all.

The hero of Shelley's *Frankenstein* was a young Swiss scientist named Victor Frankenstein. Frankenstein, having discovered the secret of life, creates an eight-foot monster, devoid of soul, from corpses gathered from churchyard graves, butcher shops, and dissecting rooms, and gives him life by means of galvanism. The animated monster, unloved and rebuked by everyone, becomes evil and, infuriated at Frankenstein for playing God, commits heinous crimes, killing those closest to his creator. The denouement of this tale is the death of both Frankenstein and his monster.

Shelley's monster was nameless, though he is usually confused with the mad scientist who created him.

How did Mary W. Shelley come up with such a bizarre tale of terror? Lord Byron suggested to the Shelleys that the three of them should each write a ghost story. The story itself was the result of a dream Mary W. Shelley experienced. And who was the third person? Why, the famous English Romantic poet, Percy Bysshe Shelley, of course. After all, he and Mary were husband and wife.

There was no real McCoy.

Here's an oft quoted phrase—"the real McCoy"—whose origin is enveloped in controversy. Nevertheless, its derivation most likely stems from the heather-covered Highlands of Scotland, not from the boxing rings where Charles "Kid" McCoy, aka Norman Selby, plied his trade.

Despite many who believe the phrase originated with the unscrupulous American fighter and welterweight champion of 1896, Kid McCoy, who himself never denied the association; it is weak at best, and most likely a product of American folklore. Numerous stories abound concerning Kid McCoy's association with the phrase, but the most popular has the Kid entertaining a lady in a saloon when a drunk approached the couple and began bothering them. The Kid informed the intoxicated annoyance, in no uncertain terms, just who he was dealing with. Not seeming to convince the drunk in a peaceful manner, the Kid administered a one-two punch. When the drunk regained consciousness, he exclaimed, "It's [you're] the real McCoy, all right."

The story reads well, as do others put forth by both H. L. Mencken and Alistair Cooke regarding the origin of the phrase, but convincing evidence suggests that the phrase was in use some years before there was ever a Kid McCoy.

Evidently, sometime around 1870, a Scottish distiller of whiskey spirits, Messrs. G. Mackay of Edinburgh, Scotland, began advertising their fine whiskey products as "the real Mackay." It was the buyer's assurance that he was purchasing the very best whiskey available. This phrase, though modified somewhat, was used for decades to come, especially during Prohibition in the United States. It was then that only true quality liquor was referred to as "the real McCoy," or "the McCoy," an apparent corruption of "the real Mackay."

"The real Mackay" stood for the real thing, something that was bona fide, something that was the nonpareil, the genuine article. In 1883, Robert L. Stevenson, the famous Scottish novelist, was quoted as having used the phrase "the real Mackay" in his correspondence. It is also believed that it was in use at least a century earlier, and possibly as far back as the Jacobite rebellions of 1715 and 1745.

As for how "the real Mackay" metamorphosed into "the real McCoy," some word historians postulate that "real" is a corrupted form of Reay, in Sutherland, Scotland. The Mackays of Reay declared themselves the leaders of the Clan Mackay. It is surmised that "the Reay Mackays" in time became "the real Mackay." It must be stated that the phrase is associated with other abridgements and spellings, as well, such as Macoy, McKie, McKay, and McKaye.

Although it seems the actual origin of the phrase still proves controversial, the Reay Mackays are a very persuasive lot.

A lawyer wrote Treasure Island and Kidnapped.

Robert Louis Stevenson (1850–94) was born into a family of distinguished civil engineers in Edinburgh, Scotland. It was his father's wish that he follow in the footsteps of his family and become yet another civil engineer, noted for their expertise in harbor and lighthouse design (Sir Walter Scott wrote *The Pirate* in 1821, inspired by a tour of lighthouses taken with Robert's grandfather, in 1814).

Stevenson was encumbered by ill health most of his life, a victim of recurring respiratory ailments. At his father's behest, he entered the celebrated Edinburgh University at the age of sixteen, first to study engineering and then the law, but the pen and paper held a greater attraction. By this time, he had proclaimed himself an agnostic and began to feverishly write. Poor health continued to menace his future as an engineer, so in an effort to appease his father, he was admitted to the bar in July 1875, though he had no intentions of ever practicing.

His maturity as an author was slow and deliberate, but before he passed on at the tender age of forty-four, the lawyer who never practiced the law left behind a legacy of classic literature: *Treasure Island* (1883), first published in serial form in 1881, and inspired by a map he concocted with his stepson, Lloyd Osbourne, to amuse themselves while on vacation in the magnificent Scottish Highlands; *Kidnapped* (1886), set in Scotland after the failed Jacobite rebellion of 1745; and *The Strange Case of Dr. Jekyll and Mr. Hyde* (1886), exposing the struggle between good and evil in man.

Though these works are now recognized as masterpieces of juvenile literature, Stevenson's genius as a novelist, poet, and essayist went far beyond the boundaries of such a genre.

The sandwich is James Montagu's doing.

Who doesn't like a well-made sandwich, stuffed with all of one's favorite meats and cheeses? Where did such a name come from?

The concept of the sandwich is centuries old, for many a Roman would make a light meal of a sandwich, as did the peasants of Medieval Europe, sans meat, and probably very little of anything else. However, the name of this easily made and deliciously filling edible finds its origin among the bluebloods of Britain.

Legend has it that the sandwich was named after an English aristocrat, Cambridge-educated James Montagu, fourth Earl of Sandwich (1718–92). It seems that the earl was a confirmed gambler and rogue extraordinaire, who was known to spend endless hours, sometimes as many as twenty-four, at the gambling tables without leaving for any refreshment. To regain his strength and not interrupt his gambling, he would order several slices of cold meat, probably roast beef, served between two slices of bread, and so the sandwich was born in 1762.

Some years later, in 1778, Captain James Cook named the Sandwich Islands in the earl's honor. Today they are known as the Hawaiian Islands.

The oldest novel is Japanese.

The Tale of Genji (in Japanese, *Genji Monogatari*) is thought to be the oldest full-length novel in the world. Also considered one of the finest examples of literature anywhere, this lengthy romantic tale of the Heian period (794–1185), written by Lady Murasaki Shikibu (c. 978–1031) in the beginning of the eleventh century, is a chronicle of court life in Kyoto and focuses mainly on the exploits of Prince Genji, the son of an emperor, his concubine, and his various love interests.

Shikibu's masterpiece is Japan's greatest gift to the world of literature, and was first translated by Arthur Waley (1925–33). The tale was written in a very elaborate style, embellished by both poetry and intricate wordplay. As a reflection of Japanese culture, *The Tale of Genji* is revered as the finest example of Japanese fiction, and Murasaki Shikibu is Japan's most distinguished literary genius.

A "papal bull" is not an animal.

Sounds like some sort of sacred animal, but a papal bull in Roman Catholicism is an official letter or document issued by the pope. The expression derives from the Medieval Latin term *bulla*, meaning the seal historically attached to such documents. In English, *bulla* translates as bull.

Since the eleventh century, official edicts or decrees have been written on parchment, with only the most holy and consequential of papal bulls having affixed to them a round seal of lead embellished with cords of silk or hemp inlaid into the seal. The obverse of the seal shows the name of the current pope, while the reverse depicts the likenesses of both Saints Peter and Paul divided by a vertical cross and their names placed beneath their respective images. When the ruling pope dies, his seal is summarily destroyed.

By the fifteenth century, papal briefs became commonplace, and papal bulls were generally retained for only the most sacred of matters such as Church decrees, canonizations of saints, and Henry VIII's release to marry Catherine of Aragon. In 1878, Pope Leo XIII limited the use of papal bulls, to matters concerning primary benefices and edicts of the Holy See. Since then, the majority of bulls have been stamped with a wax seal.

All original papal bulls—the language of which is stylized Latin, written in the standard Latin hand—are archived in Rome, with copies sent to Catholic churches all over the world.

Mark Twain didn't ask anybody to do anything about the weather.

Arguably the most famous words ever uttered regarding the weather were, "Everybody talks about the weather, but nobody does anything about it." This quote is most often attributed to Mark Twain, and sometimes to Will Rogers. However, neither of them said it, although they probably would have liked to have originated such a bon mot. The quote is the product of Charles Dudley Warner (1829–1900), a lawyer, prolific writer, and editor, who in an editorial in the Hartford *Courant*, dated August 24, 1897, actually wrote the now famous words regarding the weather.

Warner also coauthored with Mark Twain the celebrated book *The Gilded Age* (1873). In addition, he coined what is possibly the most prophetic phrase with respect to politics. In *My Summer in a Garden* (1871) he wrote, ". . . politics makes strange bedfellows." So true, so true!

Two bits are a quarter.

The U.S. quarter is worth twenty-five cents, not pennies—the U.S. Mint has never minted a penny, but the British do—and 6,146 quarters were first minted in 1796, and were officially referred to as a quarter dollar. The present quarter, with a likeness of George Washington on the obverse, was first minted in 1932, and commemorated the two-hundredth anniversary of his birth.

The word *bit* has been in use in Britain for centuries as a term that alluded to money itself or any small silver coin. However, *two bits* got its start in the West Indies of the seventeenth and eighteenth centuries. There, a bit was a small silver coin whose value was a fraction (slice of the pie), one-eighth, of the Spanish dollar. This use of the word soon made its way to the southern United States. Known as the *real*, the Spanish dollar circulated in the U.S. until the mid-1850s. Since one bit equals one-eighth of a Spanish dollar, or twelve and a half cents. Hence, two bits are equivalent to twenty-five cents. When the Spanish dollar ultimately vanished from circulation in the United States, *bit* continued to be used in the phrase *two bits*.

Many English monarchs never spoke English.

The Norman conquest of Britain in 1066 did much to alter English vocabulary. The Normans were Vikings who had colonized northern France around 866. Upon their arrival in France, they deserted their language and took on French conduct and speech. The Normans rejected their language so completely that not one word of Norse has survived in Normandy, save a few names of places. This is extraordinary, when you consider that the Normans imbued English with ten thousand words.

It is astonishing that no king of England spoke English for the next three-hundred years; the official language was French. It wasn't until 1399 that Henry IV ascended to the throne and revived the mother tongue, English. Even England's King George I (1660–1727) had no understanding of the English language since he was German.

John F. Kennedy was not the first to ask what you can do for your country.

Although President Kennedy is credited with having been the first to utter the now immortal words that inaugurated his presidency on January 20, 1961, ". . . ask not what your country can do for you; ask what you can do for your country," neither he nor any of his speech writers can claim any modicum of originality. He simply paraphrased the sentiments of many who came before.

Famed Supreme Court Justice Oliver Wendell Holmes, Jr., said in a speech at Keene, New Hampshire, on May 30, 1884, ". . . it is now the moment . . . to recall what our country has done for each of us, and to ask ourselves what we can do for our country in return." Also, before the Republican National Convention, on June 7, 1916, President Warren G. Harding spoke the words, ". . . we must have a citizenship less concerned about what the government can do for it and more anxious about what it can do for the nation."

Still others spoke the same sentiments long before Kennedy's utterance, most notably, the profound writer and philosopher, the Prophet himself, Kahlil Gibran, during an excited oration before his countrymen. He asked, "Are you a politician asking what your country can do for you, or a zealous one asking what you can do for your country?"

Kennedy may have made the phrase famous, but it was most certainly not his own.

CHAPTER THREE

INVENTIONS AND DISCOVERIES

Thomas Edison "did not" invent the electric light bulb.

Lodged in the collective consciousness and chronicled in countless history books is the belief that Thomas A. Edison (1847–1931) invented the electric light bulb, or incandescent lamp. Just as Singer did not invent the sewing machine but simply improved upon it, Edison did much the same with the light bulb. He simply perfected a commercially salable light bulb and the equipment needed to create a practical lighting system.

As early as 1802, before the birth of Edison's parents, the English chemist Sir Humphrey Davy (1778–1829) produced an arc light, and in 1844, three years before the birth of Edison, Jean Foucault (of pendulum fame) experimented with an arc light powerful enough to light up the Place de la Concorde in Paris.

Moreover, in 1841, the Englishman Frederick de Moleyns was granted the first patent for an incandescent lamp. A fellow countryman, physicist Sir Joseph W. Swan, fashioned a crude light bulb in 1860, and in 1878 he introduced a functioning carbon-filament lamp at Newcastle, almost a year before Edison was able to introduce his original "Edison's Light" bulb. No less than two dozen inventors constructed light bulbs before Edison. Then again, it seems that Mr. Edison had a penchant for claiming the originality of others.

Interestingly enough, Edison was aware of his fondness for taking the credit due others. One time, when asked about his inventive genius in a discussion with the governor of North Carolina, Edison responded by admitting that his real genius was in his ability to absorb the ideas of others, much like a sponge, and then improve upon them.

The seismograph was not invented in California.

The seismograph makes a record of the ground movements caused by earthquakes, explosions, or various other phenomena that release energy into the Earth's interior. The seismograph is the primary instrument of seismology, the branch of science that is concerned with such movements. The seismograph was not the invention of a coterie of brilliant minds quartered within the walls of the California Institute of Technology, as most would assume, given the regularity with which California is rocked by earthquakes. Rather, its development dates back to a time shortly after the birth of Christ. The place was another equally shaky region of the world, China.

In A.D. 132, the first seismograph was developed by Chang Hêng, a pundit and inventor. The focal point of his seismograph was an enormous urn. At its upper circumference, strategically positioned, were eight finely carved ivory dragon heads, each holding a ball in its mouth. At the bottom circumference of the urn were eight finely carved frogs, with open mouths as well, each placed directly under a dragon head. When an earthquake happened, one or more of the balls would be dislodged from the dragons' mouths and fall into the frogs' mouths. Each falling ball caused a sound upon impact, indicating that an earthquake had occurred. The direction of the earthquake could be ascertained by observing which balls fell and which did not.

Others followed Hêng's lead by developing devices that could detect earthquakes. In seventeenth-century Italy, a device similar to Hêng's utilized water spillage from an upper receptacle to a lower one to detect earthquakes. Then, in 1855, Italian inventor Luigi Palmieri constructed the first electrical seismograph, whose accuracy was infinitely more reliable.

Though Hêng's device was primitive in nature, its concept formed the basis for the development of today's more precise seismometers and the science of seismology, which hopes to one day predict, with the utmost accuracy, "the big one."

The modern flush toilet was invented by a man whose name is synonymous with less than polite matters.

Many World War I U.S. soldiers were delighted to be the first to make use of a device that has made life easier for all of us. They loved the device so much that they took it home with them after the war and christened it the crapper. But wait a minute. But what is it? And why call it a crapper? The man responsible for this utilitarian invention is Thomas Crapper (1837–1910), the English sanitary engineer and inventor whose valve-and-siphon adaptation gave birth to the modern flush toilet.

It's not that Crapper invented the flush toilet, for the ancient Romans used a primitive version of it; running water transported the human waste away. However, what he did was to develop a mechanism by which the water could be automatically shut off after its job had been completed.

We should all give thanks to the man whose name is now an eponym.

Robert Fulton did not invent the steamboat.

One of the most significant by-products of the great Industrial Revolution (1700s to early 1800s) was steam power and ultimately the steamboat. The advent of the steamboat, and hence the steamship, revolutionized transportation on inland waterways and the open seas, and made possible the transport of goods and people in an economical, comfortable, and expedient manner.

Since the celebrated Robert Fulton (1765–1815) produced the first commercially successful steamboat, it is thought that he was its inventor. In fact, Fulton did not invent the steamboat, although he did take advantage of the accomplishments of others, most notably James Rumsey and John Fitch, whose boats had coursed the waters of the Potomac and Delaware rivers respectively, some two decades before Fulton's supposed invention. In addition, Fulton never called his steamboat the *Clermont:* he called it the *North River Steam Boat.*

The guillotine was not a French invention.

Although the origin of the guillotine is in doubt, we do know that it was in use for hundreds of years prior to the French making it famous—or infamous, as the case may be.

Legend has it that the Chinese, Persians, Romans, Germans, and numerous others claimed to have had machines for decapitating unwanted citizens. The noble Scots admit that the Halifax gibbet in England was the precursor to their Maiden, used to decapitate Regent James Douglas Morton in 1581. Even the lighthearted Italians made use of the device for centuries.

When the guillotine was first introduced in France, it was not called the guillotine. The French doctor Antonin Louise adapted the device for French purposes, and it was built by a German named Tobias Schmidt. Originally called a *Louison* by the French, it took its much-recognized name from Dr. Joseph I. Guillotin (1738–1814), a man who convinced the National Assembly that the guillotine was a much more humane method of execution than the methods then used. After testing on human cadavers and live sheep proved the device to be effective, the French adopted the more humane method of execution on March 25, 1792.

The first Frenchman to fall victim to the guillotine was a common bandit named Nicolas J. Pelletier. The guillotine's most infamous victims were King Louis XVI and Queen Marie Antoinette. Subsequently, 2,498 individuals were decapitated during the Reign of Terror (the French Revolution, 1789–99), often at the rate of 60 victims per hour.

Dr. Guillotin was so distraught over its obvious abuse, that upon his death in 1814, his children officially changed the family name.

The guillotine was in use until September 30, 1981, when France officially abolished the death penalty.

Clarence "Bob" Birdseye invented frozen foods.

At age twenty-six, Clarence "Bob" Birdseye (1886–1956) traveled to Labrador, between 1912 and 1915, to work for Sir Wilfred Grenfell on his famous hospital ship. When his tour was up, he opted to stay, and he assumed the life of a fur trapper and trader. While in Labrador, Birdseye noticed that one of the basic shortages in his diet was the lack of vegetables. After pondering the dilemma for sometime, he chanced upon the process of preserving cabbage. When thrown into seawater, he observed that the cabbage retained its inherent flavor without destroying the consistency of the vegetable itself. He continued experimenting with the technique, inspired by his observations of the Eskimos' methods of quickly freezing fish and caribou. The quick freezing prevented the large crystals responsible for cell destruction in meat from forming, and the result was edible meat and vegetables after defrosting.

In 1924, Birdseye established the Freezing Company and thus began the frozen-food industry. He would freeze up to five-hundred tons of fruit and vegetables per year. Birdseye proceeded to refine his technique of freezing. In 1929, he invented the double-band freezing device, and in 1935, he created his multiple-plate freezer, the basis of freezers in use today. Even the American Medical Association approved of his methods.

After many triumphs and defeats, Birdseye finally realized his dream and sold his company to General Foods for a tidy sum, while retaining a consulting position with that company. He is credited with numerous additional patents during his lifetime, one of which is the process of food dehydrating (1949).

Baseball was the inspiration for the fly swatter.

In the spring of 1905, Dr. Samuel Jay Crumbine (1862–1954), a well-respected physician, health propagandist, and member of the Kansas State Board of Health, was attending the opening game of the Topeka, Kansas, softball season. It was a day of relaxing outdoors, a day away from his job as a doctor driven by the need to eradicate the common housefly. Dr. Crumbine understood the potential of this ubiquitous insect to spread deadly diseases and persistently tried to inform the public of the necessity of exterminating these little pests.

It was at a critical point near the end of the baseball game when frenzied fans shouted to the batter, "Sacrifice fly! Sacrifice fly!" Still others yelled out, "For Pete's sake, swat it! Swat the ball!" Then the proverbial light bulb went off in Dr. Crumbine's head. He thought, *if you can swat the ball, why not swat the fly?*

In his very next issue of the *Fly Bulletin*, "Swat The Fly" appeared emblazoned across the first page, and the catchphrase spread across the country in no time. It was Frank H. Rose, a schoolteacher, who heard the phrase and was inspired to fashion a fly-swatting device out of a yardstick and a wire screen. Originally called a fly bat, Dr. Crumbine christened it a fly swatter.

So the next time fly season comes around, think of "swat the fly," just like Dr. Crumbine did so long ago.

Hitler was responsible for the Volkswagen.

Prior to World War II, Hitler was disturbed by the fact that few working-class members of his Third Reich could afford automobiles. Around 1933, he decided to have an inexpensive car designed and manufactured with Third Reich funds, so that his people could become more mobile. The car, the Volkswagen, was to be the "people's car."

Hitler summoned one of the auto world's most successful designers, Austrian engineer Dr. Ferdinand Porsche, to do the honors. That's right. The father of the renowned Porsche designed the Volkswagen.

The car was initially named by Hitler the KdF-Wagen, meaning the Kraft-durch-Freude-Wagen or "Strength-Through-Joy-Wagon." The first cars were assembled at the Fallersleben plant in 1938 and sold for an unbelievably low price of $250.

Hitler had collected the equivalent of $68 million from workers, and in return they would each receive a car for their financial contributions to the cause. However, the project was ended in 1941, when the plant was retooled for arms production. The workers never got their cars or their money back. The few cars that were made went to the Nazi hierarchy. In 1961, the German courts ruled that the workers who paid into Hitler's project were to be compensated, either with cars or money. Nearly 120,000 claimants received cars or their money back.

The Volkswagen quickly became a worldwide phenomenon, except in the United States, where its small size, peculiar styling, and historical affiliation with Hitler and his Nazis caused sales to be slow at the beginning. As one would expect, in 1959, a U.S. ad firm took on the onerous task of marketing the car that looked like a little bug and dreamed up the idea of calling it the "Beetle," and also referred to it as the "Bug." By the next year, the Beetle was the number-one selling import in the United States.

Today, the little Bug, developed at the behest of Hitler by the man who designed the famed Porsche sports cars, is still sold in the United States and is remembered as a triumph in the automotive world.

Paper came from the land of the pyramids.

Sometime around the third millennium B.C. (First Dynasty), the Egyptians produced paper from the fibers of the papyrus plant, common to the Nile Valley and Delta of ancient Egypt. This reed represented the first pliant material used by the Egyptians for chronicling the momentous events in ancient Egypt. The word *paper* derives from the name *papyrus*.

The continued development of paper brought about various changes, the most significant being rag paper, similar to what is used today. It was first produced in the Chinese imperial court of Emperor He Di in A.D. 105 by a clerk, Ts'ai Lun, who originated the formula, using mostly the fibers of the mulberry bush. Later, the Chinese discovered that fishnets, old rags, and hemp waste made an excellent pulp from which to make paper. One Chinese emperor's personal library was said to contain over fifty thousand books, while at the same time Europe was virtually illiterate.

With the invention of the printing press around 1450, the demand for paper escalated. Refinements continued, and in 1774, with the discovery of chlorine, the snow-white paper that twentieth-century man is familiar with was first produced. In 1798, the Frenchman Nicolas-Louis Robert invented the first machine to manufacture paper in continuous rolls, rather than in single sheets.

Sometime in the first part of the eighteenth century, a major breakthrough occurred purely by accident. The brilliant French scientist, René-Antoine Ferchault de Réaumur, was walking through the forest when he noticed an abandoned wasps' nest. He discovered that the wasps' home was made from a crude paper, but used no rags. He then noticed small twigs at his feet and concluded that it had to be made from wood processed in the wasps' stomachs, then excreted to be used in building the nest. In 1719, he submitted a paper to the French Royal Academy describing what he had observed. By 1841, the first paper made from ground wood pulp was seen in Nova Scotia, produced by Charles Fenerty. Today nearly 90 percent of all paper is made from wood, thanks to the lowly wasp and de Réaumur.

Braille was invented by a boy.

Imagine not being able to read the newspaper or the classics; imagine not being able to write a love letter or jot down a shopping list. Millions of people throughout the world are handicapped by being sightless, and their need to read and write is vital. A solution to this difficult predicament was found by the most unlikely of individuals.

Braille, the universally used method of writing and reading for the sightless, was invented by a fifteen-year-old French youth in 1824.

The system takes its name from its inventor, Louis Braille (1809–52), who had been blind since the age of three because of an unusual accident: his eyes were accidentally pierced while he was playing with his father's tools. Despite his handicap, Louis Braille became an accomplished cellist, organist, and scholar.

Like other blind individuals of his time, the prosaic methods of reading available to the blind were cumbersome at best. Inspired by French army Captain Charles Barbier, whose system was invented in 1819 for military communication at night and was called "nightwriting," young Braille reduced Barbier's twelve-dot configuration to a six-dot cell configuration, which renders a code of sixty-three characters, each composed of one to six embossed dots arranged in a six-position cell or matrix.

Louis Braille, a professor and former student at the Institute for Blind Children in Paris, published his results in 1829, and then again in a more comprehensive form in 1832. Through a long period of fermentation and modification by others, Braille, as a system of communication, achieved worldwide prominence and acceptance in 1916, when the U.S. Senators met with the English in London to accept the system. It is commonly referred to as Standard English Braille, Grade 2.

The basic Braille code has since been modified to represent mathematical and technical symbols as well as musical notation, shorthand, and other common languages. In the end, a young Louis Braille gave to the sightless the ability to see in their own way.

The French did not invent wine.

Vitis vinifera, the finest grape species for producing wine, was discovered by archaeologists to have been cultivated in the Near East as early as 4000 B.C. Earlier inhabitants of the Nile Valley region had domesticated the feral grape species *Vitis sylvestris*, which thrived from the Nile to Gibraltar on the far side of the Mediterranean. This species proved to be the predecessor of *Vitis vinifera*.

Initially, wine was used in temple rituals and it did not achieve prominence as a drink until sometime in the first millennium B.C.

Denizens of the Near East soon established wine as a principal product of commerce and the Minoan and Greek civilizations quickly followed. The Greeks were responsible for introducing wine to the Western world, specifically Italy and France. Greek wines ultimately lost their attraction after the first Roman (Italian) wines appeared.

The Romans did much to spread the pleasures of the grape throughout their immense empire, and by the fifth century wine made its mark in Europe and was refined in the vineyards of France, where the climate and rolling hills produced much of the world's superior wines.

Vitis vinifera gave birth to the world of wine, and through the process of evolution and hybrid creations, the grape today grows in more than five thousand varieties with more than two hundred used for wine making. Most recently, some of the finest are to be found in California.

The Chinese invented liquor.

Common sense would yield to the canon that the venerable Scotsmen invented liquor. After all, they did invent Scotch whiskey and modern golf; nevertheless, the taciturn Chinese get the credit for its invention, or rather, discovery.

They stumbled upon the realization in 800 B.C. that distilling beer produced an alcoholic drink with a substantially greater kick. Their potent potion was produced by gathering and consolidating vapors of boiled rice beer and then returning the liquid back to the original concoction. Through repetition, the procedure could turn 10 percent alcohol beer into 40 percent alcohol arrack.

Arrack was produced in the East Indies from sugarcane and rice. Soon, others caught on to this simple process and the Arabs, who gave us the word *alcohol*, created an inebriating liquor from their favorite wine. In time, the Romans of the first millennium A.D. were hard at work producing distilled spirits, but nothing much was accomplished until commerce with the Arabs began in the eighth century. By the early nineteenth century, the distilled spirits industry was in full swing throughout France and England.

Although the Scots did not invent liquor, their whiskeys are the most widely consumed liquors in the world.

Millions of lives are saved yearly because of a simple discovery.

Millions of lives are lost because rudimentary infections overcome individuals at will. Children succumb to a common cold. Men fight for their lives as they attempt to stave off impending death. Women fall prey to unknown invaders. All this happened daily until an accidental discovery by one man.

Sir Alexander Fleming, the noted Scottish bacteriologist, is the individual to whom mankind is forever indebted. By dint of fate or luck, his research into a simple laboratory accident resulted in the discovery of one of medicine's greatest achievements.

In 1928, in his laboratory at Saint Mary's Hospital in London, while diligently at work with a culture plate of bacteria, Fleming inadvertently dropped some green mold on the plate near the culture. This mold was *Penicillium notatum.*

A short time later, Sir Alexander noticed that close to the spot where the mold landed, all the bacteria were dead. He did not think much of his *Penicillium notatum;* he simply thought it too unstable for any real practical use. Sometime later, others, Howard Florey and Ernst Chain specifically, recognized the potential of this bacterial killer. In 1945, Fleming's peers recognized his accomplishments by awarding him, along with Florey and Chain, the Nobel Prize.

Today, all the world benefits from this ingenious and visionary scientist's discovery—penicillin—the world's first wonder drug.

Samuel Morse did not invent the telegraph.

The telegraph is an electrical apparatus for transmitting messages over a distance by using a code of some kind, and Samuel Morse (1791–1872) was not its inventor. The term *telegraph* derives from the Greek *tele,* "far," and *graphein,* "to write." It was coined by Claude Chappe, a physician and inventor, in France in 1792 to describe a visual signaling system, the semaphore, that he had invented. But it is believed that the Swiss inventor, Alessandro Volta, constructed the very first model, though primitive, of the telegraph in the early 1700s.

In 1829, a productive and spirited inventor, Joseph Henry, devised and built the first electric motor and functioning electromagnet, mechanisms that paved the way for the eventual invention of telegraphy. Just two years later, he built an electric telegraph, yet he took no credit, for he thought scientific discoveries to be the domain of all mankind. As is not that unusual, in 1844, Samuel Morse, of Morse Code fame, applied for the patent on telegraphy, never acknowledging the earlier efforts of Joseph Henry, and subsequently Morse received the adulation of his peers and all the financial rewards that come with such an invention.

Thanks to Mr. Bell we can now call home.

Arguably one of the most important inventions of mankind, save alternating current, is the telephone. The name derives from the Greek *tele*, "far," and *phonē*, "sound." Alexander Graham Bell is given the credit for its invention, but did he do it?

Prior to Bell's work with the telephone, several others earnestly studied the concept of transmitting sound over a distance based on a mechanical system rather than electrical means. The English scientist, Charles Wheatstone, worked with the transmission of sound through wooden rods as early as the 1830s. The American inventor Elisha Gray built a primitive system of communication consisting of two cans, the centers of which were connected by a taut string to carry vibrations. By speaking into one can, the vibrations would travel along the string and could be heard in the other can. It was dubbed the *lover's telegraph*. Then, in 1861, a German schoolteacher devised an electrical device that could transmit musical notes; whether it could transmit speech was never proven.

However, by the mid-1870s, numerous men recognized that speech could be transmitted via electrical means. The two pathfinders were Elisha Gray and Alexander G. Bell, with a guest appearance by none other than Thomas Alva Edison. Working autonomously, both Gray and Bell experimented with this new mode of transmitting speech between 1872 and 1875. Gray built the first receiver in 1874. Bell originated his own receiver, and the race, so to speak, was on.

Both men—Gray, the telegraph-line superintendent, and Bell, the schoolteacher for the deaf—continued their efforts to build the first practical telephone. Bell grew weary of his time spent on his dreams and abandoned his work for a while. Gray charged forward, and before long, he filed a notice of invention, notifying the patent office of his impending invention. Bell once again resumed his experiments, and in an unusual moment of synchronicity, he finished designs for his telephone, had them notarized on January 20, and made his way to the U.S. Patent Office. There he submitted his paperwork for a patent, just hours before Gray did the same.

Bell was granted the patent (No. 174,465) for the telephone on March 7, 1876, despite the fact that Gray's invention was superior. On March 10, Bell, then only twenty-nine, transmitted the first words ever heard on a telephone to his assistant: "Mr. Watson, come here, I want you." Bell went on to fame and fortune and Gray faded away.

The first commercial phone exchange was inaugurated in New Haven, Connecticut, in January 1878, while the prior year, the first private telephone was installed in the home of Charles Williams, who was the manufacturer of record for Bell's invention. By 1887, exchanges became almost commonplace throughout the country with over 150,000 subscribers. The first pay phone was installed in the Hartford Connecticut Bank in 1889. In that same year, the direct dial phone became a reality.

Thanks, Mr. Bell, now I can phone home.

The potter may have used the first wheel.

The verdict is still out as to what came first, the vertical wheel or the horizontal wheel—the potter's wheel—but what is known is that, unlike other inventions, the invention of the wheel happened only once.

Historians are still grappling with the issue, for we know that in ancient Sumeria a pictograph was discovered, dated approximately 3500 B.C. that shows a sledge fitted with wheels. Yet, at the same time, the use of the wheel as a turntable for potters had also come about in Mesopotamia around the same time.

Some engineers believe that since the horizontal use of the wheel was easier to apply, it must have come first. Use of the vertical wheel required precise balancing of weights and forces and the knowledge of how to surmount the negative aspects of friction.

Despite this argument, the wagon wheel revolutionized transportation of crops and man. It remained unchanged for at least a millennium after its discovery. Referred to as the tripartite wheel, it was a wooden disc made up of three carved planks held together by transverse struts with an opening in the center to allow for an axle. It is not known whether the wheel moved separately or turned with the axle. Nevertheless, the wagon wheel found its way to China, Syria, Great Britain, Northern Europe, and the Balkans.

Spoked wheels made their appearance about 2000 B.C. Used on chariots in Asia Minor, these wheels were much lighter in mass, thus permitting faster transportation. This modification to the original wheel was also discovered just once, and it, too, appeared among the Syrians, Egyptians, and other eastern Mediterranean civilizations.

By the Middle Ages, the wheel had proved its worth by better harnessing the three principal power sources: animal, water, and wind. Today, cars are manufactured that can reach previously incomprehensible speeds, supported on wheels not much more circular than the original.

The parachute came before the airplane.

It seems that falling through the air to a safe landing has always held a fascination for man, but why would anyone invent a parachute who wasn't able to fly? There is some evidence to suggest that Chinese acrobats, as early as 1306, used primitive models of parachutes to do just that—fly—in the most literal sense. Even the genius of the arts,

Leonardo da Vinci, toyed with the idea and rendered a sketch and instructions for the construction of a pyramid-like parachute. But what of the parachute of today?

The modern parachute did indeed come before the airplane. In fact, unrefined canvas devices were used to descend from hot-air balloons (invented by the Montgolfier brothers in 1783) from the late eighteenth century onward. It wasn't until Françoise Blanchard dropped a dog from a balloon in 1785, that the parachute demonstrated its viability and the possibility of safe landings.

The first man to utilize a parachute with repeated success was Frenchman André J. Garnerin, who made several successful jumps between 1797 and 1804, the highest being from the lofty altitude of eight thousand feet. Garnerin's last parachute design included the essential gore and vent construction built into today's parachutes and thus he is credited with inventing the first useful parachute, a century before man's first airplane flight.

The Wright brothers were "not" the first to fly.

Did the Wright brothers, Wilbur (1867–1912) and Orville (1871–1948), born respectively at Millville, Indiana and Dayton, Ohio, really fly into the history books with the first powered flight? Most aeronautical historians agree that the Wright brothers were the inventors of the world's first practicable airplane, but some skeptics denounce the Wright brothers' claim and the argument of who was first to fly has persisted for decades. There is what seems like incontrovertible evidence supporting an earlier flight by Gustave Whitehead, which is most compelling and should be given its due.

The evidence suggests that Gustave Whitehead (1874–1927), who emigrated from Bavaria in 1894, made a powered flight of a half mile or more on August 14, 1901, in Fairfield, Connecticut. The *Bridgeport Sunday Herald* even published a photo of Whitehead's flight in his *No. 21. Scientific American*, the New York *Tribune*, and the *Boston Transcript* all carried reports of the historic 1901 flight. The Wrights' *Kitty Hawk* (they referred to it as the *Flyer I*) flight did not take place until

December 17, 1903, more than two years after Whitehead's momentous flight.

Additionally, there are newspaper accounts chronicling the words of eyewitnesses to Whitehead's flight, with one eyewitness vividly recounting the flight, and even commenting that he had seen the Wright brothers in Whitehead's shop prior to their flight. Several books have even been written supporting Whitehead's claim. However, the preponderance of evidence has not been enough to convince the Smithsonian and the historical establishment at large that Whitehead was the first to fly. But why? It seems that duplicity might be the answer.

A previously undisclosed 1948 contract between the Smithsonian and the estate of Orville Wright has since surfaced to shed some light on the whole dispute. It disclosed an astonishing stipulation in the institution's obtainment of the famous Wright brothers' *Flyer I*, now the centerpiece of the nation's National Air and Space Museum.

Apparently, the agreement specified that the Smithsonian could not display any flying machine or model of such that predated the Wright brothers' flight in 1903. In effect, even if the Smithsonian were presented with incontestable evidence to demonstrate that someone flew before the Wright brothers, they could not recognize such an occurrence without forfeiting their most prized possession, *Flyer I*, since rechristened the *Kitty Hawk*, which reposes as the centerpiece in the National Air and Space Museum.

The Smithsonian has not recognized Whitehead's flight, saying that it was little more than a hop, and they flinch at the mention of any such deal with the Wright brothers' heirs being anything but forthright. They contend that the stipulation in the contract was accepted to settle a long-standing dispute between the institution and the Wright family.

During the time of the Wright brothers' experiments with manned flight, Samuel P. Langley, then secretary of the Smithsonian Institution, was hard at work on his own flying machine. He made two flights in October of 1903, both ending in crashes. Some eleven years after his death, a replica of his plane was constructed and flown, after which the Smithsonian put it on exhibit, claiming it was the first machine capable of manned flight.

By 1942, with the Wright brothers' reputation as the first to fly a powered aircraft accepted the world over, the Smithsonian finally conceded that the Langley replica had been significantly altered and that the Wright brothers did indeed achieve the first legitimate controlled, powered flight. Six years later, the contract was signed with Orville Wright's heirs and the *Kitty Hawk*, which had been on exhibit in London for the previous twenty years, was transported to the Smithsonian.

Even the French, whose forays into flight, beginning with hot-air balloons, are well documented, claim that their Clement Ader became the first to fly, gliding across the lawn of a chateau in his batlike flying machine called the *Eole*, in 1890.

As for Gustave Whitehead, he died in 1927, of a heart attack, taking dreams of his *No. 21* (also known as the *Condor*) with him. Whether he will receive the recognition many insist he deserves is in doubt, but what is not in doubt is that the controversy over who really was the first to fly has not ended . . . until now!

As a postscript to the saga of the "first in flight," the historical record has finally been set straight by none other than *Jane's All the World's Aircraft*, the world's foremost authority on aviation history. In March 2013, the publication officially certified "an August 1901 flight by Gustave Whitehead as the 'first' successful powered flight in history!" That's more than two years before the Wright brothers!

Well, there goes another cherished myth. The history books now need to be rewritten to reflect the truth, yet again. That said, the issue of who was the first to fly will probably never be resolved because there are those who have too much to lose.

Dynamite begot the grandest of prizes.

In 1860, the Swedish father-and-son team of Immanuel and Alfred Nobel demonstrated the commercial possibilities of nitroglycerin, but it was Alfred B. Nobel's (1833–96) invention of dynamite in 1867 that brought him fame and fortune beyond his wildest dreams, and with it, enough money to establish the most cherished of all prizes, the Nobel Prize.

It was Alfred's desire to endow a prize that would reward those who, each year, bestowed "the greatest benefit on mankind," and thus the Nobel Prize was born. The prizes, primarily monetary in nature, have been awarded since 1901 by the Nobel Foundation in Stockholm. They are awarded to recipients in the fields of physics, chemistry, medicine or physiology, literature, economics, and peace.

It seems most ironic that Alfred Nobel's invention of dynamite (the word is derived from the Greek *dynamis*, meaning "power") was the genesis of the Nobel Prize, with the prize for peace being arguably the most revered today. From the money generated from the sale of an extremely violent and powerful explosive, capable of decimating man and machine, comes the Nobel Prize for peace.

The microscope came from the land of Rembrandt.

The simple magnifying glass, comprised of a single converging lens, was known to the ancients. In the first century A.D., the Roman savant Seneca made mention of the simple magnification, probably from rock crystal, of letters. Rudimentary microscopes of this type allowed the ancients to explore the fundamental nature of insects, but that was about all. Moreover, because these magnifying lenses were usually chunks of impure glass, distortion was unavoidable. What was needed was a device that could magnify, without distortion, an object, oftentimes invisible to the unaided eye.

The credit for invention of the microscope elicits some controversy. Although the single-lens microscope was in use since the 1400s, many associate Galileo with the invention of the compound microscope, for by 1612, he had designed and constructed several models: a mechanism equipped with two separate lenses, the objective, which was convex, and the eyepiece, which was concave. However, the Dutch lens maker, Hans Jansen, along with his son, Zacharias, and Hans Lippershey, are credited by most as the fathers of microscopy. Between 1590 and 1608, they produced several examples of the microscope with very simple lenses.

Enter another Dutch inventor, Anton van Leeuwenhoek (1632–1723), a biologist and microscopist. By 1674, he had made microscopes of such precision (over four hundred in his lifetime, some of which are still extant) that many in the world of science recognize him as the father of microbiology. His single-lens models were more powerful than the compound examples of his day: his masterpieces of magnification could enlarge objects up to 270 times. This feat allowed him to become the first person to examine and record microscopic life, single-celled animals such as protozoa, as well as to identify red blood cells and bacteria that live within the human mouth and stomach.

By the dawn of the twentieth century, the compound microscope had achieved prominence, with the electron microscope of today able to magnify objects up to several million times, thus opening yet another door into the world of the unknown. And to think, it all started in the land of Rembrandt.

No one knows for sure who invented the telescope, but it wasn't Galileo.

The invention of the telescope is arguably the greatest boon to astronomy since Nicolaus Copernicus (1473–1543) spoke of the planets revolving around the Sun, for most of the knowledge about the universe beyond our Earth has come to us by means of this instrument. We know this to be fact, but what we do not know is who actually invented the telescope.

Numerous admirers of Galileo believe he was its inventor. This misconception comes to us by way of a treatise he published in 1610, *Nuncius siderius*, in which he talks of discovering the telescope for himself and understanding the universe like no man before. He did not say he invented the telescope, though he did improve upon its mechanics. What he can be credited with is being the first to utilize the telescope for astronomical purposes, to study extraterrestrial bodies. As for who invented the telescope, well, it's really up in the air, but here are the particulars.

The practice of using basic magnifying lenses—telescopy—was known to various civilizations throughout the centuries. Even the ancient Egyptians were aware of the characteristics of glass, and many precursors to lenses have been uncovered in both Asia Minor and Crete, which date back nearly four thousand years. Given a little help from serendipity, any one of the ancients could have stumbled upon the concept of combining lenses to produce the telescope. Even several British pedants, including Robert Grosseteste and Roger Bacon, were aware of the optical properties of glass and experimented with lenses in the eleventh and twelfth centuries, but with no success. Then, during the fifteenth and sixteenth centuries, two British mathematicians, Leonard Digges and John Dee, tested several multiple lens configurations in an effort to increase magnification, but once again, they had no luck. However, serendipity was to play a part in the invention of the telescope.

Most historians give the credit for its invention to Hans Lippershey (c. 1570–1619). Lippershey was a spectacles-maker, of Middelburg, in the Dutch province of Zeeland, who, like others before and since, had an uncontrollable propensity for usurping the work of others and taking credit for it himself.

It seems one day an assistant of Lippershey's was peering through combinations of lenses he had been tinkering with while his mentor was absent. In a moment of unexplained brilliance, the assistant took two lenses, placing one near his eye and the other one at almost arm's length. To his amazement, a faraway weathervane looked to be closer and larger than it really was.

Upon Lippershey's return, his assistant demonstrated his finding to him. Lippershey, a man of acute awareness, understood the significance of the finding. Realizing that holding the two lenses to produce the effect was not practical, he quickly fashioned a metal tube into which the two magnifying lenses could be placed in the appropriate positions. He called his new device a "looker." In time, it came to be known by various names: an optic tube, optic glass, or perspective glass. In 1612, its present name was coined by the Greek mathematician, Ioannes Dimisiani, and derives from the Greek words *tele* and *skopein*, meaning "to see at a distance."

In the most liberal sense then, it can be said that Lippershey invented the first telescope in 1608. It was the same year that he applied for a patent, but he was turned down because several others had demonstrated knowledge of the invention. One such fellow was Zacharias Jansen, one of the fathers of the microscope, who, in 1604, claimed to have built a telescope.

Despite being rejected by the patent office, Lippershey can be said to have invented the telescope, if for no other reason than he was the first to make the world aware of the telescope's importance and value. He suggested the Dutch government might find value in it as an instrument of warfare during the bloody war of independence against Spain. What a coup it would be for the navy to be able to see and move in on the enemy long before the enemy was aware of what was happening.

Lippershey took orders from the Dutch Republic for a binocular version of his telescope, but by the next year, 1609, a truce was signed with Spain and the Dutch were out of harm's way. Nevertheless, the secret weapon went on to make its way throughout the capitals of Europe, thanks to Lippershey and a host of others.

Seat belts and Wild Bill Hickok are connected.

Raymond T. Hickok (1918–92) was the head of a family business started in 1909, when his father, Stephen R. Hickok, purchased, for the sum of $350, a small jewelry business that manufactured nameplates. When young Raymond assumed the presidency of the business in 1945, at the tender age of twenty-seven, he was instrumental in expanding the family business into a major manufacturer of men's accessories, which included wallets, cuff links, suspenders, clasps, jewelry, and of course, belts.

Raymond Hickok was an enterprising individual who was both professionally and civically active throughout his entire adult life. During his time as chairman of the family business, he helped develop a device that has proven to be one of the greatest contributions to the modern automobile. Raymond Hickok is responsible for the development of the seat belt, and in the process, he is indirectly responsible for the countless lives saved yearly because of his invention.

But what of the connection between the seat belt and James Butler "Wild Bill" Hickok (1837–76), the legendary Old West character? He was the inventor's great-great uncle.

CHAPTER FOUR

SCIENCE AND TECHNOLOGY

A Midwest farm boy discovered a planet.

In 1930, a twenty-two-year-old farm boy from Illinois, Clyde Tombaugh (1906–97), became a member of the most select club in all of astronomy: he is one of only three individuals who were the first to see a "new" planet. Mercury, Venus, Mars, Jupiter, and Saturn are visible to the unaided eye and were sighted by ancient people. The outer planets did not come into view until the invention of the telescope (1608).

It seems Clyde Tombaugh's incredible discovery started out as nothing more than a curious amateur astronomer's gaze into the nighttime sky. In 1928, Tombaugh sent the Lowell Observatory in Flagstaff, Arizona, renderings he had made after studying Mars and Jupiter through a telescope that he had constructed himself from parts salvaged from a 1910 Buick, a mowing machine, and a straw spreader. The observatory was so fascinated by Clyde's efforts that he was immediately offered a job.

Percival Lowell (1855–1916), founder of the observatory, was partially responsible for Clyde's searching the skies for the mysterious "Planet X." Lowell proffered the existence of the planet based upon the irregularities found in both Uranus's and Neptune's orbits. Some mass large enough to affect these irregularities had to exist out there. The observatory was in financial straits and a find of this magnitude would attract the much-needed funding to keep its doors open. Clyde pointed the observatory's thirteen-inch telescope toward the heavens to search for the proverbial needle in a haystack.

Many intolerable nights were spent searching the dark sky for the elusive planet. Clyde would take side-by-side photographic plates of the same point in the sky every few days. He would then compare the 400,000 black specks on each snow-white plate with the assistance of a machine that shows first one plate and then another in an eyepiece. The process is called *blinking*. Normally, the stars' positions would remain constant. However, if two dots did not match up, that would indicate a moving object.

Although Percival had predicted where the planet might exist, Clyde was skeptical of searching just one area, so like the legendary nimrod of old, Clyde decided to search the entire sky. After establishing a routine that would continue for six months, the afternoon of February 18, 1930 was to prove a historic moment. While examining the plates from previous days, the machine made an annoying clicking sound that was heard across the room. Finally, the noise abated, and Clyde reexamined plates made on January 23 and 29. Among the countless dots on the plates, one had shifted about an eighth of an inch over the six-day period while the Earth had traveled some 600,000 miles. The dark planet had been illuminated by Clyde's relentless pursuit and for about forty-five minutes he was the only man on Earth who new that "Planet X" existed: Pluto was his to claim!

The announcement of this Earth-shattering finding was withheld for several weeks. Clyde wanted to make one more plate to verify his finding. After waiting a few days for the sky to clear, he again photographed his planet. The world was told of his discovery of Pluto on March 13, 1930.

Although Clyde wondered if he was up to the task of facing the media, his immediate concern was what to name his discovery. After much deliberation, he named the planet Pluto (from *Pluton*, a Greek alternate for Hades) inspired by the underworld god of the dead. Pluto is a planet of many oddities: it makes only one revolution around the Sun every 248.4 years in an eccentric orbit, it is nine times as distant from the Sun as the Earth, and its surface temperatures are greater than four hundred degrees below zero Fahrenheit.

Even with the discovery of Pluto, Percival Lowell's belief that a mass existed beyond Uranus and Neptune that affected their orbits was not proven by Pluto's existence. The mass of Pluto is too small to alter the orbits of Uranus and Neptune, therefore, in truth, Pluto is not Percival's "Planet X." Possibly another planet may hang in an orbit far beyond Pluto, but Clyde Tombaugh believed the hunt for the elusive "Planet X" would be a massive undertaking. Until then, the farm boy from Illinois is only one of three men to have ever been the first to discover a "new" planet.

In recent years information has come to light that has challenged Clyde Tombaugh's discovery. Finally, in 2006, the International Astronomical Union reclassified and redefined Pluto as a "dwarf planet" (a plutoid) and not a classical planet.

The abacus is the first hand-held computer.

Although the Chinese take credit for its invention and use, the abacus (in Chinese *suan pan*, meaning "counting board") was used daily by the ancient Greeks (they called it the *abakos*) and Romans, though it most likely originated in ancient Babylonia. The actual word derives from the Semitic word *abg*, meaning "dust." The earliest form of the abacus consisted of a board covered with very fine dust. The Hindus improved upon this by employing a wooden board covered with pipe clay. The clay was then dusted with a purple sand and the numerals were inscribed with a stylus. This type was used by both the ancient Greeks and Romans. The most frequently used form of the abacus in primitive times consisted of a board with beads that would slide on wires or grooves in a wooden frame.

Today, the abacus is used in India, the Middle East, China, Japan, and many of the former republics of the now defunct Soviet Union. To watch one experienced in this ancient counting-board's use is to marvel at the speed and accuracy with which the abacus can produce results. It can be said that the abacus is the world's first hand-held computer.

We need air pollution.

As difficult as it may be to believe, we need air pollution. Tell the people in Los Angeles or New York City that, and you will be deemed a prospect for a mental institution. But in scientific terms, and in real-life terms, the statement makes absolute sense.

Raindrops will not form unless there is what meteorologists refer to as hygroscopic or condensation nuclei, that is, minuscule particles floating in the air around which water droplets will form. These particles consist of salt from ocean spray, dust, and chemicals produced mostly by automobiles and factories.

Thus a pollution-free atmosphere would turn the Earth's surface barren, for rain, with a little help from snow, fog, hail, dew, and frost, is the only supply of fresh water. There would be no bodies of water such as rivers, streams, and lakes without rain, and there certainly would be no rain without air pollution.

A dry cell battery is not "dry."

Everyone has used them at one time or another; Christmas just wouldn't be the same without them; most flashlights need them. Yes, the ubiquitous dry cell batteries (Leclanché cells) are a godsend, but what they aren't is dry. They are wet inside; if not, they would simply not work.

The dry cell battery derives its name from the fact that it is a primary cell in which the contents (electrolytes) are in the form of a moist paste and thus are not allowed to flow.

Milk is not good for every "body."

Yes, that's the truth. Milk, thought to be the perfect food, is not good for every "body." It has been known for centuries that many people lack the ability to digest milk and milk products, all of which contain lactose, a sugar present in all mammalian milk. However, it wasn't until the latter part of the twentieth century that the problem began to appear in medical literature. It was then that medical science began to recognize just how widespread the problem is throughout the world. In fact, lactose intolerance is thought to be the number-one cause of chronic intestinal symptoms in patients who do not have critical ailments.

Countless people lack the necessary and unique intestinal enzyme, lactase, which permits the digestion of milk and milk products. Without this essential enzyme, the ingestion of milk or milk products can cause these people to experience chronic diarrhea, bloating, gas, and cramping pain. It must be said that lactose intolerance is not a disease in the real sense: no microorganisms have infected the body, nor have any cells malfunctioned. It's simply a matter of the body slowing down its production of lactase. The degree of lactose intolerance varies from one race of people to the next, but any way you look at it, the numbers are staggering.

It must be said that there are people who are lactose tolerant. They include people, whose ancestors came from Western Europe, Scandinavia, Great Britain, and certain areas of North Africa. However, an overwhelming number of people just cannot effectively deal with milk, or anything made from milk. Though the figures are only a barometer, they do tell a compelling story. West African blacks are almost 100 percent lactose intolerant, while Native Americans exhibit 80 to 100 percent intolerance. North American blacks are said to be about 75 percent intolerant as are Mexican Americans, with percentages among Jews, Arabs, and most Mediterranean Europeans ranging between 60 and 90 percent.

Given these astonishing numbers, it seems painfully obvious that milk, nature's perfect food, is definitely not good for every "body."

Yes, you can fool Mother Nature.

As much as we'd like to think that you can't fool Mother Nature, medicine does it all the time, and must. Vaccines against many once fatal diseases work by tricking Mother Nature, the body, into producing the necessary safeguards against a disease before it actually strikes.

In essence, the vaccine for a specific disease causes the body to produce disease-fighting substances known as antibodies, but does not actually cause the disease. These antibodies protect the vaccinated person should he or she be exposed to the deadly agent that causes the disease.

Many present-day vaccines are produced from disease-causing microorganisms that have been weakened or killed. They are then given orally or injected into the body where they do their work, fooling Mother Nature.

The first computer was not an Apple or IBM.

Even the ancients grappled with the concept of constructing a machine that would process numbers faster and more accurately than a human being. The abacus served them well, as it has others for five thousand years. Then, between 1623 and 1624, a German named Wilhelm Schickard built the first mechanical calculator capable of performing the basic functions of arithmetic: addition, subtraction, multiplication, and division. Others continued to advance the concept of machine calculating, and in 1833, a quantum leap was made.

In that year, English mathematician and scientific mechanician Charles Babbage (1792–1871), the inventor of the speedometer and locomotive cowcatcher, after having abandoned his work on his difference engine, conceived of his analytical engine. He envisioned this engine, or computer, as having a memory bank, analyzing results, and printing out necessary data. He even imagined 'it capable of revising its own program, processing data as a result, and using punch cards as input (the first computer program was written by Babbage's associate,

Augusta Ada Byron, Countess of Lovelace, the only legitimate daughter of the inimitable Lord Byron). The entire engine was designed to function automatically, requiring only one operator.

Babbage spent the last thirty-seven years of his life and a great deal of his own money building experimental models of his analytical engine, replete with gears, levers, cogs, wires, and cams, but to no avail. He lost government support, received little recognition from his peers, and was discouraged by his inability to put his ideas to work. He died an embittered man, only to be vindicated more than a century later.

Although Charles Babbage was never able to construct a working example of his analytical engine, his design concepts and beliefs were correct. His efforts have earned him the sobriquet of "father of the modern computer," long before there was an Apple or IBM.

To drink old wine can be a risk.

To drink old wine can be risky business. Connoisseurs of fine wines are attracted to wines whose vintages are older than yesterday. Actually, they usually measure the age of fine wines in terms of decades. Although these wines are aged purposely, as it is believed to enhance taste and body, there is no guarantee of quality.

The alcohol in wine is a by-product of the fermentation process, wherein yeast changes the sugar in grapes into alcohol. After a specific amount of alcohol has been produced, it kills the yeast and terminates the fermentation process. From that moment on, aging serves to improve the wine only up to a certain point. When wine is finally sealed in glass bottles, all the positive changes have essentially ceased. Poor quality in wines is more often caused by drinking them too late rather than too early.

Bottles are not always airtight, so wines will often turn rancid following a period of time. Maybe that extremely costly bottle of Chateau Lafite-Rothschild, Chateau Latour, or Chateau Margaux you've just purchased to drink with old friends is truly the nectar of the gods, or maybe it's really good for nothing more than an ingredient in a salad dressing—a very expensive salad dressing.

It is interesting to note that the French were not the first to produce wine. Archaeologists have unearthed evidence that the finest grape species for making wine, *Vitis vinifera*, was being grown in the Near East as early as 4000 B.C.

The first computer program had the woman's touch.

IBM, Apple Computer, and dozens of other computer firms were all founded by men. Today, it is understood that no computer can function without the software programs that permit them to perform given tasks. What is not known is that the development of software was born out of a woman's touch. The aristocrat, Augusta "Ada" Byron King (1815–52), Countess of Lovelace (aka Lady Byron), the only child of the celebrated poet George Gordon, the sixth Lord Byron, was the first computer programmer.

In 1815, Lord Byron abandoned his wife and infant daughter Augusta just thirty-six days after his daughter's birth. Lord Byron left Britain, never to see his family again. Ada never knew her father, although he always inquired about her whereabouts. Raised by her mother, a talented mathematician in her own right, Augusta was given a rigid classical education in the confines of the family home, never attending any formal school or university.

As Augusta entered her teen years, she demonstrated a unique facility for mathematics, but with the social customs of the time being what they were, she acquiesced and married Lord William King, the first Earl of Lovelace, in 1835. She assumed the life of the landed gentry and the title of the Countess of Lovelace. However, she couldn't ignore her love of numbers, nor could she forget first meeting Charles Babbage in June 1833, when she was but a mere teenager; he was to deeply influence the rest of her life. She was fascinated by his concept for an analytical engine, the precursor to the modern computer.

By 1842, she had completed a French to English translation of the Italian mathematician L. F. Menabrea's paper discussing the analytical engine. She made myriad additions to the original paper and developed the concepts of loops and subroutines, which are integral to modern computer programming. Unfortunately, it took a hundred years before anyone could make use of Augusta's programming theories.

As fate would have it, the countess grew to like working with Babbage and the two developed an intimate and long lasting professional relationship. The lamentable aspect to Augusta's life work was that she was sidetracked by a gambling addiction and her antifeminist attitudes, both of which caused her considerable angst. Because of this, she was never able to finish the engine nor run her program. She was also never able to see the fruits of her labor and died of cancer at the young age of thirty-six. She is buried next to her illustrious father in Nottinghamshire, England.

All was not lost, however. In 1982, the U.S. Department of Defense recognized Augusta "Ada" King's vital contribution to computer science by naming a new Pentagon computer language ADA.

Lightning can indeed strike more than once in the same place.

Lightning, the visible flash of light related to an electrical release (a stroke) between two clouds, within a cloud, or between the Earth and a cloud, is the result of thunderstorms. Lightning, of which there are several types, has remained somewhat of a mystery throughout the ages, with the ancient Greeks and Romans believing it to be a weapon of the gods. Yes, it can and often does strike twice in the same place. After all, lightning strikes the Earth about six thousand times per minute, with each strike generating one hundred million volts of electricity and heat rated at over sixty thousand degrees Fahrenheit. Lightning can be deadly, killing more than one hundred people and causing over ten thousand forest fires each year in the United States alone.

If lightning has struck a certain object, it is likely to strike it again if it happens to be in the same vicinity in the future. The mast of the Empire State Building was hit by lightning sixty-eight times during the first ten years of its having been completed, and it continues to be struck by lightning each year. As far back as 1723, John Pointer wrote in his book entitled *A Rational Account of the Weather*, "Various flashes of lightning followed the same track." He also says that "The first flash rarefies the air and makes the path for the succeeding ones."

Logic would dictate that if something attracted lightning once, wouldn't lightning be attracted to it again?

7UP was once a tranquilizer.

It is no secret that early production of Coca-Cola contained trace amounts of coca leaves, which when processed, render the drug cocaine. What is not known to most lovers of soda, however, is that Coke's biggest rival, 7UP, once included in its recipe lithium carbonate, a powerful and effective drug used in psychiatry and administered to individuals as a treatment for manic-depression.

Just days prior to the October crash of 1929, C. L. Grigg, a Saint Louis entrepreneur, began selling a beverage called Bib-Label Lithiated Lemon-Lime Soda. The timing couldn't have been better. His slogan for the drink was, "Take the 'ouch' out of grouch," and many victims of the Depression were somewhat sedated by Grigg's concoction.

Ultimately, the drink was changed to 7UP: the 7 was for its seven-ounce bottle, the *up* for "bottoms up" or for the bubbles rising from its dense carbonation. The carbonation was subsequently lessened and the lithium was discontinued by the mid-1940s. Presently, 7UP is made from carbonated water, sugar, citric acid, sodium citrate, lemon oil, and lime oil, but no lithium.

The apple inspired one of science's greatest moments.

Generally accepted as pure fantasy is the story of Sir Isaac Newton (1642–1727) observing the falling apple which led to his discovery of gravity. It was conjured up by none other than one of Newton's friendly admirers, Voltaire, in his work, *Elements de la Philosophe de Newton*. It seemed simply too good to be true, but Reverend William Stukeley (1687–1765), an acclaimed antiquary, was an eyewitness (*Memoirs of Sir Isaac Newton's Life* by W. Stukeley) and reported the Newton-apple story. He said that he was taking tea under the apple trees with Newton and during their conversation, Newton had confided to him that it was just such a circumstance that gave him cause to ponder the question of gravity. It was the observation of a falling apple that gave birth to many of his brilliant discoveries.

William Stukeley was a man of the cloth, the essence of veracity, and a dedicated scholar. He would have had no reason to falsify such an event. Furthermore, ever since the age of twenty-four, Newton had been struggling with how to resolve the motion of the Moon until he accepted the influence of gravity.

A descendant of the original tree in Newton's Woolsthrope is now thriving in Wellesley, Massachusetts, on the campus of the Babson Institute (Babson College). Roger K. Babson, the consummate Newtonist, thought it logical to add the tree to his collection of Newtonian artifacts. The tree was a Flower of Kent variety, whose fruit is not crisp and succulent like a McIntosh and thus not very edible. Maybe that's why Newton observed it instead of eating it.

Not only is the falling apple story true, but we know what kind of apple it was.

Bullwhips break the sound barrier.

Bullwhips, and most types of whips, when properly snapped, can achieve speeds in excess of 700 miles per hour, thus breaking the sound barrier, which is approximately 740 miles per hour at sea level (it declines with altitude). The cracking sound that is heard is, in fact, a mini sonic boom, just like the ones created by jet aircraft or the thunder produced by a lightning stroke.

A sonic boom is the result of an object moving through the air at the speed of sound or greater. Contrary to common belief, a sonic boom does not just occur at the moment the object breaks the sound barrier, for an aircraft flying faster than the speed of sound generates sonic booms that are continuous, so long as the aircraft is exceeding the speed of sound.

There are invisible beams that can pass through concrete walls.

Although invisible, radio and TV beams can pass through solid concrete walls much the same way that X-rays pass through the body. These beams actually bend as they penetrate a concrete wall. This is often to blame for poor TV reception indoors when using a standard indoor antenna.

What is baffling is just how these invisible beams pass through barriers as dense as concrete and leave no visible signs. More impressive yet are high-speed, subatomic particles known as neutrinos, which can pass through the Earth itself. Cosmic rays can do much the same, achieving speeds near that of light, and leaving absolutely no sign of entry or exit. In fact, these rays from outer space pass regularly through our bodies, without us even so much as saying ouch!

The blue sky is really "black."

The sky is the stretch of space, some one hundred miles thick and composed of numerous gases, that envelops the Earth. The color of the sky during daylight hours in clear weather is caused by the dispersing of sunlight. If it were not for this scattering of sunlight during the day, the daytime sky would appear as black as the nighttime sky. The higher up in the sky, the darker it gets.

The amount of dispersion, or scattering, caused by atoms and molecules is a function of the wave length of light: the shorter the wave, the more scattered the light. Since blue, purple, and violet rays are significantly shorter than red rays, they are scattered many times more than the red rays and therefore dominate the sky.

So the sky, which would otherwise be black during the day, looks blue because some of the blue light traveling through the atmosphere is strewn about toward onlookers on the surface of the Earth.

Sound travels through air slower than through steel.

Common sense dictates that since air is less dense than water, wood, or steel, sound would naturally travel faster through it. But common sense is mistaken.

The earliest documented, orderly study of sound was made by one of the ancient world's most prominent figures, the Greek sage and mathematician, Pythagoras (c. 580–500 B.C.). He noted that by plucking the shortest string of a lyre, it would produce a higher-pitched sound. The Roman architect Vitruvius Pollio (first century B.C.) recognized sound to be more than simply a motion in the air; it was a vibration. The Austrian physicist and philosopher Ernst Mach (1838–1916) contributed much to the understanding of the velocity of sound through a specific medium. The study of sound is as important today as it was in ancient times. What is fascinating about sound is its ability to travel at great speeds through very dense objects.

Sound travels through air at approximately 740 miles per hour, through water at 3,240 miles per hour, through steel at 11,200 miles per hour, and through glass at up to 13,400 miles per hour! Why does sound travel through air slower than through other mediums? Because air molecules are not as tightly packed as water, steel, or glass molecules, sound waves lose a significant amount of energy while passing through it. This energy loss significantly reduces their velocity.

Dry ice is produced from gas.

Dry ice is a solid form of carbon dioxide (CO_2). The gas is compressed until it reaches a state of liquefaction. At this point, it is then frozen into standard fifty-pound blocks. Its unique property of passing from solid to gas without ever becoming liquid makes dry ice ideal as a refrigerant.

There was medicine before Dr. Spock.

The practice of medicine is both an art and science. It deals with health care through diagnosing, treating, and hopefully preventing diseases. The early ancient Babylonians (pre-3000 B.C.) were consumed by the mysteries of medicine. Just like their counterparts, the Egyptians, their need to develop ways to care for the sick and prevent further disease was paramount to their very existence, since the establishment of villages and cities and increased farming caused man-to-man transmission of disease to multiply at an alarming rate. Something had to be done.

The famous Code of Hammurabi mandated that any physician who failed to save his patient would have both his hands amputated. This was obviously far too drastic by today's standards, but the idea of some sort of more direct accountability by doctors is not without some merit.

In Babylonia, patients who could not be successfully treated by a doctor were placed in the street so that any passerby could try his hand at healing the poor fellow. Egyptians thought this a bit primitive and recognized only licensed physicians. In about 3000 B.C. Imhotep, the minister of state for King Zoser, was granted the first degree in medicine. Sometime between then and 1200 B.C. the Egyptians produced the first series of medical papyri (books): they discussed treatments for skull fractures and magical potions to fend off evil spirits.

The first true breakthrough in medicine came in the fourth century B.C. when the noted Greek physician Hippocrates (460–370 B.C.) recognized that medical diagnosis should be the result of experience and observation. Although the physician's Hippocratic Oath was most likely not the writing of Hippocrates, it has nevertheless furnished the medical community with a standard of medical ethics to be upheld by all physicians the world over.

In the sixteenth century, physicians began experimenting with the physical exploration of the human body by dissection. Andreas Vesalius (1514–64) is the Flemish physician who fundamentally changed the study of biology, and hence, medicine, by his meticulous description of the anatomy of the human body in his monumental work *De Humani Corporis Fabrica*, regarded as the beginning of modern surgery.

Soybeans were the first antibiotics.

Antibiotics are chemical substances made by very minute cells called microorganisms, which generally cause disease. These antibiotics are able to kill off or suppress the growth of other cells. The Chinese created the first primitive antibiotics sometime between 1500 and 500 B.C. They made them from the moldy and fermented curd of soybeans, and they were used to treat wounds and superficial swellings such as boils and carbuncles. For the next two thousand years, the world sought to find a group of drugs to fight bacterial infections, but no one thought to follow the lead of the ancient Chinese.

In the late 1800s, notables such as William Roberts (1830–99) of England and Louis Pasteur (1822–95) and Jules F. Joubert (1834–1910) of France experimented with the issue of molds and their benefits as antibiotics. After the German physician Robert Koch confirmed the germ theory of disease, the door was open for what was to prove to be perhaps the single most important medical discovery up until that time.

Enter the renowned Scottish bacteriologist Sir Alexander Fleming in 1928, and his fortuitous observation of the *Staphylococcus aureus*, a common bacterium that is responsible for numerous infections. It had been contaminated with an airborne mold. In the area where the mold was multiplying, the bacteria were dead; something in the mold had secreted a substance that eradicated the bacteria. Although the substance would not be isolated for another decade until Chain and Florey did so, Sir Alexander Fleming named it *Penicillium notatum*, hence, penicillin. By 1940, The United States led the world in the commercialization of penicillin, and so began the golden age of chemotherapy.

The disease smallpox is a lifesaver.

The history of the development of vaccines to save lives was long and arduous, but the end result proved to be one of medicine's greatest contributions to mankind.

Smallpox, one of the most dreaded diseases of mankind—for if it didn't kill you, it would most certainly scar you for life—was the reason vaccines became possible. The early Chinese understood that smallpox resistance could be brought about if scabs on one victim were removed and ground into a powder, then blown up the nostrils of an individual who had not contracted the disease. It was a gamble, but sometimes it worked, and the individual became immunized.

By the seventeenth century, the Turks and Greeks were experimenting with taking the pus from the blisters of smallpox victims and then using a needle to scratch the skin of a healthy person, thus transferring a small amount of the disease, which would hopefully cause a minimal reaction.

Lady Mary Wortley Montagu (1689–1762), wife of the English ambassador to Turkey, heard of the practice and upon her return to England in 1721, she introduced the practice of immunization when, in a public demonstration, she had her son inoculated. The idea spread very quickly throughout the whole of Europe during the eighteenth century. Even the Colonists followed her lead when George Washington had his army inoculated for smallpox, which was prevalent in New England at the time.

The notion of a smallpox vaccine, based upon scientific experimentation, was the product of the English doctor Edward Jenner (1749–1823) in 1796. He was aware that farmers who caught cowpox from cattle were immune to the dreaded smallpox. If this was the case, why not use cowpox, a much less dreadful disease, to immunize people against the deadly smallpox? On May 14, 1796, Jenner tried his theory by injecting an eight-year-old boy, James Phipps, with the substance taken from a cowpox pustule on the hand of the dairymaid Sarah Nelmes. James Phipps developed the expected cowpox disease. Six weeks later, he was inoculated with smallpox and it failed to affect him; he was immunized. Jenner was right. He named his technique *vaccination*, derived from the Latin *vaccinia*, meaning cowpox. Jenner went on to be applauded by King George III and the whole of the British monarchy.

All of today's most important immunization policies owe a debt of gratitude to Edward Jenner, for it was his scientific discovery that made it all possible.

Doctors do not find the cures for what ails you.

Contrary to popular belief, advances in medicine are most often not made by doctors. When one must go to the doctor's office to seek medical help because of some ailment, the credit for the cure should go in large part to others who provide the doctors with the tools by which they heal you.

From digestive and heart problems, to the vicious maladies of cancer and the like, salvation comes at the hands of the invisible warriors against disease. On January 18, 1918, Professor W. Bulloch, M.D., of the London Hospital, lectured to the Hospital Officers' Association on the subject. It was Bulloch's firm belief that research, discovery, and experimental work are the basis of most medical advances, and are and have been generally performed by pathologists, bacteriologists, botanists, anatomists, and physiologists, as well many others laboring in laboratories, and not by doctors, nor at the patients' bedsides.

The evidence is undeniable: penicillin, X-rays, inoculations, diphtheria serum, insulin, and even diagnosis of diseases are the work of the invisible warriors against disease. These men and women, who toil away day after day, ensconced in laboratories around the world, who go unrecognized by the masses, and who make doctors look like they can walk on water, are in fact the ones to whom high praise is long overdue.

Some genes are suicidal.

Many people are aware of the miraculous research being done in the science of genetic engineering. The gene, a natural element of the hereditary material that is the physical essence of the transmission of characteristics of living organisms from generation to generation, is the foundation upon which this research is based. Each gene is made up of the essence of life, DNA (deoxyribonucleic acid). What is less known is the very specialized research being performed with some very extraordinary genes.

Genetic research and engineering have given birth to a new discipline of science wherein living gene-modified microbes are able to perform their work, then commit suicide, thus eliminating the possibility of any unwanted microbes escaping into the environment. This technology is based on the contemporary understanding that numerous species of bacteria are endowed with "suicide genes" that assist in controlling the life spans of their microscopic hosts. These suicide genes can be programmed to turn on at different light levels, temperatures, or in the company of certain chemicals, thus destroying unwanted bacteria.

This ability of some genes, which are often called "kamikaze" genes, has some biotech companies looking toward supplanting toxic pesticides and chemical-based fertilizers with benign microbial products. These genes might conceivably be able to destroy dangerous chemicals in toxic wastes, as well as provide the means of controlling any undesirable life forms that would threaten man's very existence.

Julius Caesar was not born by cesarean section.

It is conjecture at best to purport that the much practiced medical procedure known as cesarean section, the delivery of a baby through an incision in the mother's abdomen, was named after the illustrious Roman leader Gaius Julius Caesar (100–44 B.C.), who was, by the way, a general, a statesman, and the dictator of Rome, but never the emperor. When one ponders the minimal sanitary practices of ancient times, it seems almost impossible that Julius Caesar could have been born by way of a caesarean section without his mother dying of septic shock (she lived on well past his birth).

The specific facts are lost to history, but probability suggests that the seventh century B.C. practice of *lex caesarea*, which mandated that a woman dying close to the child's due date should be delivered abdominally to insure the life of the newborn, is closer to the origin of cesarean section; *lex caesarea* means "the law of incision."

If this be the case, nothing suggests with certainty that Caesar was delivered by this means or that his name was the inspiration for the medical procedure so common today.

Albert Einstein was not the first atomic scientist.

Democritus (c. 460–370 B.C.) was born into a wealthy family in Abdera, Greece. He inherited enough money from his father to spend his life traveling. It was during his travels that he began to formulate his radical new theory of the universe. Consumed by the problem that faced Thales, this prolific thinker believed that every material object was comprised of a finite number of atoms. These atoms were unchangeable and indestructible and made up the whole of the universe. He also posited that some atoms were physically different than others and this accounted for the variety of types of matter throughout the universe.

Although a pre-Newtonian, Democritus stated that atoms could neither be created nor destroyed, but could be rearranged in various combinations. A rationalist to the end, he insisted, against the advice of his contemporaries, including Socrates, that nature was governed not by the wishes of gods, spirits, or demons, but rather by a series of basic natural laws.

Unlike John Dalton, who conceived of the modern atomic theory of matter, or even Albert Einstein, whose theory of relativity ranks near the top of scientific accomplishments, Democritus did not have the tools of science: experimentation and observation. He reached his conclusions the old-fashioned way, through reasoning and intuition. His work was overshadowed by the celebrity of one of his contemporaries, Socrates, who had rejected his views in a wholesale manner. But Democritus was to be vindicated centuries later when modern science verified his profound genius and proclaimed him the first atomic scientist.

The bark of the willow tree can cure a headache.

Whether it is a headache that troubles you, or inflammation, or a high fever, just ingest the bark of the willow tree (*Salix alba*) and all will be right again. Seems so simple. It is almost just that simple. For you see, the bark of the willow tree contains a most miraculous substance known as *salicylic acid:* the ancient aspirin. Acetylsalicylic acid, modern aspirin, is a man-made derivative of salicylic acid, and is more effective.

Acetylsalicylic acid was first synthesized in 1853 in France by Charles Frederick von Gerhardt, but was all but ignored for almost half a century until 1893. It was then that Felix Hofmann, a chemist in the employ of the Bayer Company in Germany, in an effort to reduce the ill effects of the rheumatoid arthritis that was crippling his father, hit upon the idea of using the synthetic form of salicylic acid, based upon Gerhardt's research, which had proven effective as a pain reliever. He prepared a sufficient amount of acetylsalicylic acid and it was administered to his father by Heinrich Dreser, a young medical student. The results were nothing short of astonishing. The new drug, a nonnarcotic analgesic, had cured his father.

The Bayer Company realized the commercial potential in this wonder drug and quickly set about producing the new drug from the meadowsweet plant (*Spiraea ulmaria*) for worldwide use. They called the new product Aspirin, from the A in *acetyl*, the *splr* in *Spiraea*, and *in* because it was a widely accepted suffix for medications.

The Bayer Company began marketing the product in 1899 as a loose powder, and by 1915, the company offered Aspirin in tablet form. The Bayer Company trademarked the name Aspirin, but following World War I, and a well-known court ruling in 1921, the name Aspirin, now spelled as "aspirin," became recognized as a generic name. As such, no manufacturer has a claim to nor can the Bayer Company derive any royalties from the use of the name.

Since before the days of Hippocrates, who correctly prescribed the use of the bark of the willow tree for the alleviation of fever and pain, to almost a century since the first aspirin dosage was administered, scientists and chemists alike have not thoroughly understood just how aspirin relieves pain and reduces fever and inflammation.

Ponder for just a moment: if the lowly willow tree can yield the most widely used drug in the world with virtually no ill side effects, what other plants hold the cures for what ails mankind?

CHAPTER FIVE

ORIGINS AND FIRSTS

The croissant is not a French creation.

Although the croissant (crescent) is synonymous with all that is French, it is not French in origin. It was created in 1683 in order to celebrate Vienna's successful stand against the onslaught of the Ottoman Turks, led by Kara Mustafa. The starving populace of Vienna was ultimately rescued by Charles de Lorraine and the king of Poland, John III Sobieski. The Pole, Kulyeziski, helpful in the overall win, was awarded the cache of coffee abandoned by the defeated Turks and was permitted to open a cafe in Vienna. Kulyeziski then directed a baker to create the crescent-shaped delicacy that would go well with the coffee. The delicacy, the *kipfel* (the Viennese name for crescent), was conceived to represent the resolve against the Turkish invasion and was inspired by the crescent emblem on the Turkish flag. When a croissant was consumed, it symbolized Austria swallowing up the invading Ottoman army.

When Marie Antoinette, then Princess of Austria (1739–93), married Louis XVI of France about a century later, she brought with her the recipe for the *kipfel*. Croissants were soon accepted in the gastronome's paradise, and were ultimately produced in over fifty varieties. They became a mainstay of the Frenchman's diet. During the Roaring Twenties, the croissant made its way from Paris to America, and by 1970, commercial bakeries began production of the Viennese—not French—delicacy.

The first Frisbee was a discarded pie tin.

It was 1939, and several Middlebury College undergraduates were traveling through Nebraska when their car suffered a flat tire. While two undergrads were changing the flat tire, one of the other undergrads found a discarded pie tin along the roadside with the imprint: Frisbee Pie Company. Suddenly, the youth had a sunburst of inspiration and tossed the tin into the air, yelling, "Frisbee!" The rest is history, so to speak.

Many others around the country lay claim to the dubious discovery of the Frisbee, but Middlebury College in Vermont, in 1989, commemorated fifty years of the fabulous Frisbee, unveiling a bronze statue of a dog jumping to catch a Frisbee. Middlebury College believes that it all began that inauspicious afternoon in Nebraska.

Today's Frisbees (Frisbee is a trademarked name) come in a variety of sizes, with most being made out of plastic. They are used for both play and sport, with competitions reaching the international level. Also, it is calculated that more Frisbees are purchased each year than the combined total of all baseballs, basketballs, and footballs.

Lindbergh was not the first to fly "nonstop" across the Atlantic Ocean.

Between May 20–21, 1927, Charles "Lone Eagle" Lindbergh (also known as "Lucky Lindy," 1902–74) wrote himself indelibly into the history books when he flew nonstop across the Atlantic Ocean, landing at Paris's Le Bourget airport. Upon his return to America he was received by a zealous crowd of well-wishers and a ticker tape parade;

he was an instant sensation; he received a $25,000 prize and the country's highest honor—the Congressional Medal of Honor. Despite the personal tragedy in Lindbergh's life—the horrific kidnapping and murder of his infant son, Charles junior, and his own questionable Fascist sympathizing and isolationist views—he remained a genuine national hero.

Nevertheless, Lindbergh was not the first to make the treacherous trans-Atlantic crossing. Eight years prior to Lindbergh and his *Spirit of St. Louis* crossing, Captain John Alcock and Lieutenant Arthur Whitten Brown had co-piloted a Vickers Vimy twin-engine aircraft (biplane) on June 14–15, 1919, to a successful nonstop trans-Atlantic crossing.

Alcock and Brown were themselves renowned British aviators who did indeed make the "first" nonstop flight across the Atlantic Ocean. John W. Alcock (1892–1919) was the pilot and Arthur W. Brown (1886–1948) acted as navigator. They left Lester's Field near St. John's, Newfoundland, in their aircraft and set the plane down in a swampy bog near Clifden, County Galway, Ireland, after having traveled nearly 2,000 miles in 16 hours and 12 minutes—15 hours and 57 minutes were over water—at an average speed of 118 miles per hour. Their efforts earned the two daredevils knighthoods that were bestowed upon them by King George V. They also received a cash prize of £10,000 posted by the London *Daily Mail*.

It must be noted that there were two previous dirigible crossings of the Atlantic that transported a total of 64 persons, thus making Lindbergh the 67th to make the trip.

However, to his credit, Lindbergh's effort is both noteworthy and unique because he made the journey "solo," flying a much greater distance (approx. 3,600 miles), in over twice as many hours, but he was not the "first" to fly nonstop across the Pond.

The bagpipe did not originate in Scotland.

Yes, the inimitable icon of Scotland and all that is Scottish, the bagpipe, did not originate there. The bagpipe (it's *bagpipe*, singular, not *bagpipes*) traces its origins back to the first century A.D. in Asia. Although it most likely originated in Asia, its first historical appearance was probably made during early Roman times. The Romans called it *tibia utricularis*, an instrument first made famous by the nefarious Emperor Nero. The Greeks referred to it as the *askaulos* or *symphoneia*.

The bagpipe made its way across Europe in the Middle Ages and is documented in illustrations and sculptures of the period. The medieval bagpipe was referred to as the *symphonia, musa*, and *chevette*. It is said that even Henry VIII owned a bagpipe or two.

Apparently the bagpipe ended up in Scotland (the Romans called it Scotia) sometime in the fifteenth century. The best known bagpipe is the Highland variety, followed by the union pipes of Ireland, and the Arabic ghaita.

As much as the bagpipe is a curious looking instrument, it is nevertheless one of proud Scotland's greatest treasures.

The French did not create French fried potatoes.

That delicious everyman's delicacy, made from the lowly potato, revered by the French as one of their creations, is in fact, from Liege, Belgium. What is it, you say? Why, it's French fried potatoes. It seems that one Rodolphe de Warsage made mention of encountering such potatoes while walking home one day. He would stop in at small shops that prepared them for passersby, who would then take them home.

Initially Belgian fried potatoes were to be found only in such shops. Soon their indisputable popularity spread to France, especially Lille, and now the entire world enjoys that little Belgian delicacy, French-fried potatoes, called *pommes frites* in France and *chips* in Britain. The origin of the term *French-fried potato* appears to be wholly American, attributed to American writer O. Henry, in his work *Rolling Stones* (1912). The term *French frieds* appeared in America sometime in the 1920s, with French fries making an arrival during the 1930s.

An interesting note as to the origin of French fries in America: it seems that none other than Thomas Jefferson, while ambassador to

France, was a fan of the potato delicacy popularized in France. Upon his return to America, he brought the recipe with him and subsequently served it to friends at Monticello, thus introducing Americans to the world of fast food.

Mercedes never made a car.

Emil Jellinek, a well-mannered individual and consul general in Nice for the Austro-Hungarian Empire, was a race fanatic, who used his daughter's name, Mercedes (*mercédès* is Spanish for "mercy") as his racing pseudonym. In 1900, he commissioned the Daimler automotive works to develop a car for him to race. He offered to place an order for thirty-six cars if he was given the exclusive rights to sell the car in the Austro-Hungarian Empire, France, and Belgium. He also insisted on naming the car after his beloved eleven-year-old daughter. Daimler agreed, and automotive history was made.

Jellinek did much to help Daimler make a mark in the world of cars and when the separate firms of Daimler and Benz united (Misters Gottlieb Daimler and Karl Benz never met) in 1926, they opted to keep the name, hence, Mercedes-Benz. Daimler died before the car was introduced, but his name lives on in the German global automotive corporation Daimler AG.

It should be noted that the three-pointed-star emblem found on the hood of every Mercedes-Benz is a derivation of the old chemistry sign for phosphorus, a highly toxic substance. Daimler was obviously unaware of this, when, on a postcard to his wife, he drew a guiding star over his house and said that the star would one day signify the greatness of his work. Today, the three pointed star is also emblematic of the three modes of motorized transportation: land, sea, and air. The star was registered in 1923, while the name Mercedes was registered back in 1902.

The Civil War is known for many firsts in modern warfare.

The Civil War (1861–65) was called the first modern war, because it changed the ways in which wars are fought. It produced many firsts in warfare, both in tactics and weapons. It was the first war where soldiers fought under a unified command, battled from trenches, and waged a primary cordon offense.

In terms of weapons, some of the more interesting Civil War firsts are railroad artillery; a snorkel breathing device; land mines; flame throwers; aerial reconnaissance; repeating rifles; a submarine of modern design; a steel ship; a torpedo boat; income tax; hospital ships; the U.S. Secret Service; withholding tax; American conscription; the Medal of Honor; and the bugle call, TAPS. Telegraphy and railroads were also first introduced in warfare during the Civil War.

It was a total war, whereby one side's resources were completely exhausted. It was also the first war to see the assassination of an American president and the end of slavery.

Salt was once used as a currency as well as a seasoning.

When man changed from hunter-gatherer to farmer and began consuming mainly vegetables he could grow, he soon recognized the need to add some taste to otherwise tasteless foods. Salt, he discovered, added that something that was missing naturally in most vegetables.

Historically, salt has been one of man's most desired mineral resources. It is found mentioned in writings by Hebrews, Greeks, and Arabs alike. Newlyweds used to be given wine, bread, and salt as the products that sustain life. The modern English word *salary* derives its name from the Latin *solarium*, which referred to the use of salt as a currency, a means of payment in ancient Roman times.

Initially, salt for seasoning was obtained by burning naturally salty plants and removing white crystals from the burnt remains. The process was time consuming and it took several plants just to obtain a small amount of the precious seasoning. As man began to live in more civilized surroundings and his desire to eat cooked meat increased, the need for a condiment to enhance the taste was paramount, since cooking destroys meat's natural salt. He also needed a way to preserve what he cooked; he needed a new and easy source of salt.

During the Neolithic Age, man discovered salt mines. Evidence exists to point to the mining of salt at mines in Hallstein and Hallstatt around 6500 B.C. in what is present-day Austria. Salzburg, a nearby city that means the "city of salt," was the focal point of salt-mining operations.

The Romans owe much of their eventual success as a republic to the merchandising of salt that began about 800 B.C. Tribesmen were converted from shepherds to merchants when they discovered they could extract more salt than they required from the surrounding marshlands of the Tiber River. They sold much of their excess salt to neighbors and created a trade route for salt, the *Via Solaria*, the "salt road" that reached to the Adriatic Sea. Salt mines are found throughout the world in great abundance, and today, salt permeates every facet of food processing.

The pencil is the most common writing instrument in the world.

The most common writing instrument in the world, the pencil, started out by accident. It is named so because it bore a striking resemblance to the brush known in Latin as a *penicillium*. This writing brush was made by placing a specially shaped cluster of animal hairs inside a hollow reed—a precursor to the mechanical pencil of today.

The discovery of graphite, also referred to then as *plumbago*, which means "acts like lead," in Cumberland, England, in 1564, led to the eventual development of the modern pencil. The English produced a crude pencil by tightly wrapping string around a stick of graphite. The string would then be unraveled to expose the graphite as needed. However, the Germans of the sixteenth century are universally acknowledged as the first to write with long, slender graphite sticks enclosed in wooden shafts and shaped to a point at one end.

By the 1700s, the Cumberland mine, which had been worked for over three hundred years, had all but played out and chemists began searching for alternative means of producing pencils without using 100 percent graphite. It was the Frenchman Nicolas-Jacques Conté who in 1765 came up with the answer. Because of a graphite shortage and poor relations between his country and England, Conté made a pencil out of refined graphite powder and clay, kiln dried it, and encased it in cedar. The basic process is still in use today. But what about writing mistakes?

In 1858, an American inventor, Hyman Lipman, patented what is probably the singularly most important improvement to the pencil: the attachment of a rubber eraser to one end. Thanks, Mr. Lipman!

The Hershey Bar was the first candy bar.

Americans happily claim the honor of creating the ultimate candy— the candy bar. It was Milton Hershey, the Lancaster, Pennsylvania, confectioner, who, in 1894, produced the very first candy bar. His creation was fashioned from sugar, cocoa, chocolate, and milk. It sold for a modest two cents and was called the Hershey Bar.

In 1896, Leonard Hirschfield followed with the first paper-wrapped candy, named after his daughter's nickname, Tootsie (Roll). After that came Mounds and Almond Joy, created by Peter Paul Halijian. The Babe Ruth bar made its appearance in 1921. It was not named for Babe Ruth, but most likely after the granddaughter of the owners of the Williamson Candy Company that produced the bar. The naming of candy bars never ends, nor does the insatiable craving for chocolate in any form.

Man first tasted chocolate as a bitter drink.

Chocolate, possibly the most loved food on Earth, started out as a bitter, sometimes sour, drink. It is a product of the cocoa bean, found in South America. The Mayas, Toltecs, and Aztecs all utilized chocolate as a ceremonial drink. These civilizations thought so much of the cocoa bean that it was also used as currency.

Hernán Cortés, in 1519, while at the court of Montezuma II, the Aztec ruler, was served *xocoatl*, meaning "bitter water." It was a bitter cocoa-bean concoction that he then introduced to Spain, although some historians give Columbus the credit. The Spanish sweetened and flavored the drink and served it hot. Chocolate made its way into Italy in 1606, and Spain lost its secret.

In 1657, a Frenchman opened a store in London to sell chocolate blocks for making the chocolate drink. Only the wealthy could afford to buy and enjoy this newfound pleasure. In 1700, the English made a major improvement to chocolate by adding milk. Still, chocolate was only for the wealthy. Finally, when the import duty and overall costs were reduced, the common Englishman began to enjoy the secret of the Spaniards.

By 1765, the American colonies began the manufacture of chocolate in Dorchester, Massachusetts, yet it wasn't until the nineteenth century that chocolate became something more than a drink. In 1828, a Dutchman named C. J. van Houten produced from chocolate powder the creamy butter of the bean. This chocolate butter was mixed with a chocolate liqueur and in 1847, an English firm produced the world's first solid (eating), sweet chocolate.

The Swiss confectioner Daniel Peter followed not too long after and came up with the first light milk chocolate by adding dry milk powder; and the world has never been the same since. Dentists smiled then as they still do now.

Blue jeans came from gold.

When one thinks of things that are exclusively American, the flag, John Wayne, apple pie, and of course, blue jeans come to mind. The blue jean material, a strong, twilled cotton cloth, originated in Genoa, Italy, where it was produced in the Middle Ages. A similar, but poorer quality material called dungaree, from the Hindu *dungri*, was also made in India since the seventeenth century to outfit British sailors and locals. The material has been used extensively for working clothes since the sixteenth century, but it was the "forty-niners" of the California Gold Rush who made jeans—blue jeans—world famous. Blue jeans derive their name from the color of the material and the French name for Genoa, *Gênes*.

In 1850, a dry-goods merchant, Levi Strauss (1829–1902), went out West to make his mark in the gold country of California. His original intent was to sell the miners jean material for tents, but what he found were miners who needed stronger, long-lasting pants, not tents. In no time at all, he began manufacturing "waist overalls" in San Francisco.

The next years saw Levi Strauss improve his product to such an extent that his Levi's became known throughout the world. He used rivets to reinforce the pockets and he replaced the original canvas material with a stronger, more durable cotton named *serge de Nîmes* (hence the name *denim*). His final improvement was the most successful; he dyed the material indigo blue, making the pants blue jeans. Levi Strauss ultimately built his company into the world's first and largest manufacturer of blue jeans.

Since the historic days of the California Gold Rush, blue jeans have become one of the ultimate fashion statements. People, rich or poor, from California to China, or from Russia to Romania, all wear Levi Strauss's creation.

Not everyone likes soap.

The history of soap is one of curiosity and oftentimes hilarity. Pliny the Elder (23 or 24–79 A.D.), in his *Natural History*, credits the ancient Phoenicians with the invention of soap about 600 B.C. They made it from goat's tallow and wood ashes. The enterprising Phoenicians used it as an item of exchange with the Gauls. They also introduced soap to the Greeks and Romans.

The Romans found it to be an ideal complement to their penchant for baths and fountains. The word itself is linked to the Celtic word for soap, *saipo*. It wasn't until the second century A.D. that the Greek physician Galen (A.D. 129–200) recognized soap's value in cleansing wounds and the body in general; he recommended its use to every Greek and Roman.

In the eighth century, the countries of Italy and Spain produced large quantities of soap, and five-hundred years later, the cities of Marseilles, Genoa, Venice, and Savonna became centers of the soap trade. It is interesting to note that soap did not meet with great acceptance during the Middle Ages, despite the increased production of the product.

In many European homes, there was a fear that bathing too often, more than a few times a year, could be perilous to one's health, even causing death. People resisted soap so much that the Duchess of Jülich in Germany, in 1549, was insulted by receiving a gift of soap from an admirer and had him removed from her presence.

England saw its first soapmaking facility erected in the twelfth century in Bristol. By the thirteenth century, soapmakers were found in London hawking their product. After the Napoleonic Wars, the tax on soap prevented most people from purchasing the product, so they bootlegged it themselves in clandestine soapmaking operations protected by the cloak of night, much like the moonshiners during the Prohibition era in America. By the nineteenth century, the tax was rescinded and the majority of people in Europe came to their senses (one of them was smell) and welcomed the benefits of soap with open arms.

Soap became such a rage—though not as ridiculous as the tulip craze—that the German chemist Baron Justus von Liebig even issued a proclamation stating that the quantity of soap a nation used was a reliable measure of its affluence and civilization.

Many of today's soaps have synthetic cleaning agents in them, but environmental concerns have forced numerous soapmakers to use biodegradable ingredients, and none too soon.

The first bathroom is ten thousand years old.

Ancient man was aware that human wastes were detrimental to longevity, for they carried toxic agents that would, if left unattended, cause disease and ultimately give birth to any number of plagues. He needed a way to purge his living quarters of sewage.

Man's first attempt at constructing a bathroom was found in excavations on the Orkney Islands, situated about twenty miles north of the coast of Scotland. Skara Brae, an underground burg (city) in West Mainland, is one of the most well-preserved European examples of the late Neolithic Period. Latrinelike devices, set into the walls of stone sheds, were connected by a sequence of primitive drains that led from the huts, and thought to be over ten thousand years old. No radical improvements were to be found until several millennia later.

It was the Minoan civilization (c. 2000–1400 B.C.), who thrived on the island of Crete, that developed an advanced sanitary system constructed with clay pipes, the counterpart of today's copper, steel, and plastic pipes. The series of pipes drained sewage from such places as the royal palace and the homes of the wealthy, while at the same time providing the user with a toilet that was linked to a reservoir of water that would flush out the wastes: the first flushing toilet.

Since the nineteenth century, most bathrooms are found indoors, despite early well-to-do people believing that such an arrangement was crude and offensive.

The windmill did not originate in Holland.

The windmill evokes a feeling of tranquility and tulips, and common belief is that it came from Holland, but in truth, the origins of the windmill date back to as early as the seventh century (A.D. 644) in Persia, which is present-day Iran. There the first primitive windmills, a most efficient means of producing energy, were constructed.

The earliest appearance of windmills in Europe was not in Holland, but in France around the twelfth century. By the end of the twelfth century, the windmill finally emerged as a viable means of lifting water and grinding grain in Holland, as well as other European countries.

The windmill, which taps the power of the wind by way of sails mounted on a rotating shaft, in its present form is capable of producing upward of 17 percent of the United States' electrical power needs by the year 2017—all from a renewable source of energy, the wind.

There is no Panama hat.

The Panama hat, ubiquitous in tropical regions of the world and the American South, where it is called the planter's hat, is hand-woven from fine, costly straw of the jipijapa plant, and is made in Ecuador, Peru, and Columbia, but not in Panama.

The hat had been worn for centuries by inhabitants of equatorial regions. In 1895, American soldiers brought the hats back in large quantities from the Isthmus of Panama, and they became a fashion rage in America during the early part of the twentieth century. The name *Panama hat* came about because the hats were marketed in Panama.

Tennis was not born at Wimbledon.

The venerable game of tennis, played by both amateurs and professionals alike, culminates in the yearly championships known the world over as the Wimbledon Championships, the grandest of the grand-slam events. The All England Lawn Tennis and Croquet Club at Wimbledon, England, is deemed to be the official home of tennis. But the truth of the matter is that tennis did not originate at Wimbledon, and in fact, the origins of the game are not even English.

The modern game of tennis (the name comes from the Old French name for the game, *tenetz*) finds it beginnings in an indoor game played in France sometime between the twelfth and thirteenth centuries. A game called *jeu de paume*, "game of the palm," wherein the ball was batted back and forth over the net with the palm of the hand, was fashionable with French royalty. It is believed that the French most likely learned the game from their Italian and Greek counterparts of the same period, for they engaged in a similar game. In time, rackets were used to increase the player's reach. It wasn't until about a century later that the British entered the picture.

It was then that British aristocrats fancied the same indoor game that had been a mainstay of French aristocratic life for sometime. Called real tennis in Britain and court tennis in the United States, the game, much like badminton, still enjoys a large following in both countries. Finally, in 1873, a country gentleman of Nantclwyd in Wales, Major Walter Clopton Wingfield, wrote the first book of rules for tennis and it is because of this that he is credited with fathering the modern game. He patented the game the following year.

Wingfield took the game outdoors, where it was played on an hourglass-shaped court, with a net placed much higher than it is today. He called his game *Sphairistiké*, Greek for "playing ball." The game's sobriquet was a mouthful to pronounce, so Wingfield settled on a less difficult but more appropriate name: lawn tennis.

By 1877, the game was more popular in England than croquet, and the All England Croquet Club (established in 1868) had added the words Lawn Tennis to its name. That same year, the club, now called the All England Lawn Tennis and Croquet Club, held the first major tennis tournament at its home in Wimbledon, a suburb just outside of London.

An American sportswoman, Mary Ewing Outerbridge, is credited with introducing the modern game of tennis to the United States. The year was 1874, and Mary was vacationing on the Island of Bermuda, where she watched British soldiers playing the game of tennis. Intrigued by this new game, she acquired two rackets and a set of balls. Upon her return home to Staten Island, she and her brother introduced the game to members of the Staten Island Cricket and Baseball Club in New York City.

It must be said that some historians give the credit to Dr. James Dwight for introducing the game to Americans around the same period. It seems that Dr. Dwight and a friend, Fred Seers, were preparing a court in Nahant, Massachusetts, the eventual site of the first U.S. tournament, for a social happening in 1876. The first official U.S. men's singles championship was played at Newport, Rhode Island, in 1881, the same year the United States National Lawn Tennis Association, now called the United States Tennis Association (USTA), was organized.

To be sure, the game of tennis has become the rage of the sporting world, with tournaments played yearly throughout the world; however, it owes its beginnings to the game that used the player's hand to bat the ball, not a racket.

India ink does not come from India.

To those in the know, Indian ink or preferably India ink, is called China or Chinese ink, for it originated in China. The ink is made from the soot of unusually hard woods such as olive or grape vines, or sometimes from the lampblack of the oil flame, then blended with a gum or glue that acts as a binding agent. In some cases, perfume is added to disguise the pungent smell. The resulting product is then pressed into sticks or cakes and is used principally for drawing.

So India ink does not come from the subcontinent of India, it never did. It is a misnomer. The name India ink first appeared in 1665, when the diarist Samuel Pepys (in his Diary) called the ink Indian incke. Later, luminaries such as Horace Walpole and William Makepeace Thackeray continued Pepys's egregious error.

The Scottish kilt originated in the Mediterranean Basin.

There are few things more synonymous with Scotland than the wearing of the kilt, a man's knee-length, wraparound skirt that displays his clan's tartan. Originally one piece, it is now distinctly pleated. Though it would be logical to believe that the kilt's origins can be traced back to the mystical highlands of this divine spot of land off the coast of the Continent, the truth of the matter is much different.

Of all the unlikely places, it is the area surrounding the Mediterranean that gave life to the kilt of old. The royal Egyptians of the Eighteenth Dynasty (sixteenth century B.C.) are depicted as having worn a detailed and luxurious costume, the royal haïk, which suggested raiment composed of a short kilt, tunic, and cloak. A garment resembling a kilt was also known to the Minoan civilization. The Persians of the sixth century B.C. displayed the use of kiltlike attire, as well. Even Roman soldiers wore a kiltlike skirt made of leather and metal. During the Louis XIV period, opera costumes featured men wearing a short kilt with various trappings.

Although the kilt has its origins in a time before there was a Scotland as we know it, the Scottish Highland version of the kilt has been around for many centuries and was probably introduced during the Roman occupation of the British Isles. Its modern version (seventeenth century), the *féile-beag*, is undoubtedly the most well-known of all the kiltlike attire, and the centerpiece of every Scottish Highlander's dress.

The rickshaw did not originate in China.

The rickshaw (also spelled *ricksha*) did not come from China, as many a movie would have you believe. It appears to have originated in about 1870, in Japan. That's why its true name is *Jinrikisha* (also spelled *Jinrickshaw*), from the Japanese, meaning "human-powered vehicle," and that's just what it is: a small, two-wheeled vehicle, door-less, with a collapsible hood, designed to carry one or sometimes two passengers, and pulled by a man. It was once a primary means of transportation in East and Southeast Asian cities.

Although the identity of its inventor is unknown, speculation has it that an Occidental clergyman was responsible for its design. The rickshaw was a modification of Western horse-drawn carriages and was also comparable in some ways to the old French *brouette*.

In the early twentieth century, the rickshaw fell into disuse upon the arrival of the pedicab, a rickshaw propelled by a bicycle, but not before American carriage manufacturer James H. Birch produced many such Japanese human-powered vehicles for export.

Golf did not begin in Scotland.

Although the last word in *golf* (from the German meaning "club") emanates from Scotland, home to golf's ultimate golf course, The Royal and Ancient Golf Club of Saint Andrews (established in 1754), I am sorry to say that the game did not begin there.

Several experts trace the origins of the game to ancient Roman times. Then they played a game called *paganica* ("the country game"), with a curved stick and a leather ball stuffed with feathers. It was most often played in the streets of cities throughout their empire, including those in both Scotland and England. Still others claim that golf originated with the Dutch game of *het kolven*, wherein the object was to hit a standing post in the least number of attempts. Some even assert that the French and Flemish should be given some credit for inventing the game. They enjoyed a sport called *chole*, a game in which the clubs favored modern-day design and took place over a large expanse of land. Even an English version called *cambuca* is linked to today's game of golf.

It must be noted that none of these games required the sinking of a ball, which became rubber-cored in 1898, into a hole—a task that makes the game about as frustrating as any sport known to man. Since the object of today's game of golf is to sink the ball into a predetermined hole in the least number of strokes, then the nod must go to the Scottish adaptation of the sport, once played by the ancients, as the game millions know today as golf.

Chop suey is not Chinese.

To the millions of gourmands and epicures alike, who relish a night of Chinese take-out and a good movie, the realization that one of their favorite dishes is not even of Chinese origin can prove somewhat disheartening. That's right; chop suey, as Chinese-sounding as anything could be, and cooked in the Chinese style, actually originated in the United States of America.

Chop suey is a mélange of small chopped bits of red meat, chicken, or seafood that is blended with diced vegetables, cooked slowly in sesame oil, then served over a bed of rice. The creation was concocted by a Chinese chef to please the American palate.

It seems that the origin of chop suey can be traced back to 1896. Then the distinguished Chinese statesman Li Hung-chang was on a diplomatic mission around the globe and had cause to stop over in New York City, where he entertained numerous American friends at various Chinese restaurants in Chinatown. One evening a stylish lady in Li's party remarked that she enjoyed a particular dish served during dinner and wanted to know what it was, not having been familiar with such a Chinese dish before. The Chinese chef, when asked by Li what it was, apparently answered that it was an original creation: chop suey.

Chop suey most likely derives its name from the Cantonese *shap sui*, which means a "mixture of various bits and pieces," although it has never been used to describe any authentic Chinese dish.

Soon other Chinese restaurateurs knew a good thing when they saw it and began offering several different combinations with such names as Li Hung-chang Chop Suey and Li Hung-chang Rice. These dishes were created for the same reason the first chop suey was, to please American patrons.

Chop suey today is a blend of various ingredients that have been used in China for centuries, although chop suey as a particular dish is virtually unknown in China, since the Chinese regard the mixture far too rich for their tastes.

CHAPTER SIX

LAWS AND TRADITIONS

The number "thirteen" is not just like any other number.

The moment one steps on an elevator and pushes the button for a specific floor, one notices that in most cases there seems to be something missing: the button for the thirteenth floor. Whenever Friday the thirteenth rolls around, people get edgy, and no one wants their address to be thirteen, nor does anyone want to be one of thirteen people at a dinner table or in a boat. Why the aversion to the number thirteen in all of its variations?

It seems that of all the superstitions that affect the majority of people today, the association of the number thirteen with something ominous is right at the top of the list. The number evokes feelings of something foreboding, deadly, evil, unknown, and just plain weird. This feeling of uneasiness is found worldwide: the Italians omit the number thirteen from their national lottery; a Frenchman won't live at a house whose address is thirteen; most high-rise buildings eliminate the thirteenth floor and simply label it fourteen; airlines rarely, if ever, have a row of seats numbered thirteen; the British believe that if thirteen people congregate in a room, one will die within a year, nor do they want to have a child born on the thirteenth day of the month; race car drivers feel to have the number thirteen on a race car is to court disaster; sailors won't set sail on the thirteenth day of the month; in black magic, thirteen demons were summoned; and occultists call it The Death. The list is endless and the superstitions surrounding the number thirteen are observed by young and old, and bright and simple people alike.

So how did this constant trepidation and phobia of the number thirteen come about? *Triskaidekaphobia* is the technical term for the fear of the number thirteen, and it seems to have its origins in Norse mythology in the years before the birth of Christ.

It all started at the god Odin's favorite home, Valhalla, wherein twelve gods were summoned to a banquet, when suddenly Loki, the specter of evil and turmoil, the Sly One, appeared, uninvited, thus making the thirteenth guest. In an effort to eject him from the festivities, the much-loved god Balder suffered a deathblow from a spear of mistletoe.

The myth surrounding the number thirteen began to gain believers as it spread throughout much of Europe, and it finally reached the Christian world when at the Last Supper, Christ and his apostles numbered thirteen. Within a day's time, Christ was put to death on the cross.

What about Friday the thirteenth? Is there anything more dreadful than what is already known about this horrific day? It seems so.

As much as the number thirteen is thought to be unlucky, should the thirteenth day of the month fall on a Friday, don't even think about leaving the house. Friday the thirteenth has been immortalized in both myth and movies as the ultimate day of horror. If things can go wrong where the number thirteen is involved, one shudders to think of the possibilities of having the thirteenth day of the month fall on a Friday.

Friday was named for Frigga, the Nordic goddess of married love, the clouds and sky, and housewives. In Norse mythology she is the primary wife of Odin and mother to Balder. When the Norse and Germanic clans were baptized as Christians, it was Frigga who was marked a witch and exiled to live out her days on a mountaintop. Shamed by what had happened to her, Frigga was determined to have revenge. It is said that every Friday, she would gather with eleven other witches and Satan, thirteen in all, and concoct devious schemes that would make the ensuing week most unpleasant for those who did her wrong. Thus, Friday has always been thought to be a day of misfortune (although in ancient Rome it was a lucky day). Superstition cautions never to marry on this day, begin a new job, launch a ship, or do just about anything else. In Scandinavia, Friday used to be called Witches' Sabbath. As for Friday the thirteenth, didn't Eve entice Adam with the apple on that day? The Tower of Babel was said to be overcome by a cacophony of tongues on the same day, as was the crucifixion of Christ. There's simply no denying it; to those who believe, Friday the thirteenth is unlucky, very unlucky.

However, as much as the number thirteen is generally associated with the worst of all possibilities, there are still those to whom the number thirteen is now and then good luck. It is the Mexican number of regeneration; a harbinger of unusual things to come; a bearer of blessings; and sometimes a number associated with new beginnings. Evidence the thirteen colonies that gave birth to the United States. Why weren't there twelve or maybe fourteen colonies? Was the number thirteen by accident or by design? However, as wonderful as that occurrence was, it might not be enough to convince most people.

Folklorists the world over agree that the number thirteen, in all of its various forms, is firmly entrenched in the human psyche as just plain unlucky. You'll notice that this entry does not have thirteen paragraphs!

Celebrating Christmas in Britain could land you in jail.

Whether you call it The Feast of the Nativity, Genethlia, Nöel, Navidad, or Weihnacht, the meaning is the same: Christmas. The most glorious of Christian festivals, Christmas celebrates the birth of Jesus Christ, and December 25 is a time of joy and reflection for all His believers. But things were not always so festive on this day in Britain.

It has been said that if the government of Britain chose to rigorously enforce all the laws on the statute books, Christmas Day in

Britain would be anything but joyous. Quite frankly, the police forces would be on full alert and pushed to their limits, as countless arrests for violations would fill the jails to overflowing with offenders. If one celebrates Christmas Day in Britain, the chances of breaking an antiquated law are about 100 percent.

The obvious question is: How could this happen? How could the celebrating of Christmas land you in jail? What are these moronic laws? It seems that in earlier times in Britain, particular Christmas laws were passed because of unique situations, and, as in most civilized countries, any laws on the books are valid: if they are not officially repealed, they remain so, even if the circumstances that justified their origin no longer exist.

In Britain, Christmas Day is a common-law holiday, and with this classification comes hundreds of years of legal rulings that make just about anything, including a policeman doing his job, illegal.

Take the Christmas dinner itself. It is unlawful to consume more than three courses at Christmas dinner, in your house or anyone else's. Cromwell's Long Parliament found Christmas pudding and mince pies to be repulsive and to be avoided by all practicing Christians.

The Holy Days and Fasting Days Act of 1551, passed during the brief reign of Edward VI (1547–53), the only legitimate son of Henry VIII, serves to demonstrate just how absurd these laws can be. Edward VI was a religious and obstinate monarch, who was plagued by poor health, all of which probably accounted for such Acts of absurdity. As such, the troubled monarchy of the time was hostile toward the celebration of Christmas Day. The Act of 1551 mandates that everyone must attend church services on Christmas Day. If that's not enough, one must walk to and from church. Should one take the chance and use another mode of transportation, the police are directed to impound any vehicle, sell it, and to dole out the proceeds to poor parishioners in the area where the violation was committed.

To further impede the celebration of Christmas, the Unlawful Games Act of 1541 permits only the sport of archery, with leaping and vaulting having been added at a later date, to be practiced on Christmas Day. An Act in 1625 even makes it unlawful for spectators to watch sports being played outside their own parishes.

Charles II in 1677 must have hit his head just before a law forbidding any worker from working at his normal job on Christmas Day was enacted. The law states that it is permissible to work at a job, so long as it's not your normal job. So what do the police do?

Another bizarre Act in 1831 makes it illegal for anyone to use any gun, dog, or other contrivance to kill game animals on Christmas Day. The only permissible use of a gun on Christmas Day is in defense of self or country. That pretty much takes care of it. So what else could be illegal?

Well, the Act for Better Prevention of Corruption of 1906 forbids businesspeople from giving or receiving gifts, or even agreeing to such exchanges. This Act was thought to prevent large companies from thanking customers who gave them business during the past year, thus eliminating payola.

Though the constables in Britain nowadays thankfully look the other way on Christmas Day, they do have the option, while breaking the law themselves, to take you in to the station. The penalties for those in violation of any of these Acts range from fines to imprisonment, and should you catch the sovereign at a bad time, who knows what the punishment might be.

Now that you know what awaits you on Christmas Day in Britain, enjoy a merry and unlawful Christmas.

The tomato is a fruit, but the U.S. Supreme Court says otherwise.

Botanically speaking, the ubiquitous tomato (*Lycopersicon esculentum*, meaning "edible wolf peach") is a fruit native to Peru, in South America, where it was viewed as a weed growing wild in maize and bean fields. In time, farmers realized that the weed thrived in high altitudes and was easy to cultivate. It ultimately made its way north to Mexico, where it was most likely carried by Spanish priests to Europe sometime in the early part of the sixteenth century.

The tender and savory tomato comes in over four thousand varieties, many of which are named after other fruits: cherry, currant, pear, and grape. For centuries, Northern Europeans and the British thought the tomato was unhealthy because botanists had identified the fruit as a member of the *Solanaceae* family, which consists of the virulent nightshade, black henbane, and the infamous belladonna—all poisonous. In fact, the leaves of the tomato plant are toxic. Because of this association, the tomato did not achieve popularity as a food until the first part of the 1800s, when it was discovered by cooks to be a delightful addition to a meal. The Italians of the sixteenth century were so enamored of the tomato that they referred to it as the "golden apple" (*pomi d'oro*). It took until the start of the twentieth century before the collective public appreciated the fruit as both tasty and healthful. Even Americans were skeptical at first, thinking tomatoes were carcinogenic and could also precipitate an appendicitis attack.

The simple yet luscious tomato, the humble fruit from Peru, has now gained worldwide acceptance, even though the United States does not recognize it as a fruit, despite its botanical classification. It is a vegetable, and the U.S. Supreme Court says so! Why would the highest court in the land be concerned with the simple tomato?

It all began in the late 1800s. That's when the Tariff Act of 1883 had fixed a 10 percent duty on "vegetables in their natural state," but permitted fruits, whether "green, ripe, or dried," to come into the country duty-free. Customs officials of the Port of New York jumped at the opportunity to increase revenues by proclaiming tomatoes to be "vegetables in their natural state," hence, they would not be duty-free.

In 1893, the importers and all concerned brought about a lawsuit that found its way to the United States Supreme Court in Washington, D.C. Justice Horace Gray delivered an opinion on behalf of a unanimous Court. Dispensing with much of the legalese, the essence of the ruling is: The Court understands that tomatoes are botanically classified as fruit of the vine, much like cucumbers, peas, squashes, and beans. However, in the vernacular of most Americans, whether sellers or consumers of foods, all these are vegetables, which are cultivated in home gardens, and regardless of how they are eaten, are much like potatoes, carrots, turnips, beets, celery, cauliflower, and lettuce, which are generally served at sometime during the main part of the meal, unlike fruits, which are usually served as dessert.

This is a sophistic deduction at best. Anyway, who's to tell the Court it's wrong? The next time you bite into a piece of fruit called a tomato—or as the French used to call it, the "love apple," because it was thought, if eaten, to make people fall in love—remember, the U.S. Supreme Court says you're eating a vegetable. Love apple sounds much better.

Popular elections "do not" elect United States presidents.

Every four years (on even-numbered years) the people go to the polls to elect the next President of the United States. Seems simple enough, but it isn't true. The people do not elect the president, the Electoral College does. In fact, five times in American history a candidate won the popular vote and ended up losing the election. In 1876, Samuel Tilden defeated Rutherford B. Hayes in the popular vote but lost in the Electoral College. Again, in 1888, Grover Cleveland defeated Benjamin Harrison at the polls, only to lose to him in the Electoral College. And yet again in the spectacle of 2016, Hillary Clinton won the popular vote, only to lose the presidency to Donald Trump in the Electoral College.

The Electoral College, an absolute mystery to the majority of Americans, is a body of electors that is empowered to choose both the president and vice president. Simply set forth in the United States Constitution, Article 2, Section 1, and Amendment XII, the selection of electors is left up to each state legislature, but their number must be equal in number to its senators and representatives in Congress. The normal selection of electors is done by party conventions, party organizations, or in primary elections.

Once selected, the electors meet in their particular state capitals to cast their votes on the first Monday after the second Wednesday in December in presidential election years. They vote separately for president and vice president. After the voting is completed, certified records of the votes for each office are sent to the president of the U.S. Senate. On the next January 6 (or the next day, should the sixth fall on a Sunday) the president of the Senate, before a joint session of Congress, opens the records and the votes are counted.

To safeguard against the possibility of having both a president and vice president from the same state, an elector is permitted to cast only one vote for one candidate who is a resident of the elector's own state. This is the only constitutional constraint. Moreover, there is no provision in the U.S. Constitution that prohibits an elector from casting his vote for someone other than his party's chosen candidate.

In order to be elected, a candidate for president and vice president must receive a majority of all the votes cast by the Electoral College. If in the event that a majority is not reached for the president, then the House of Representatives moves at once to choose the president from among the three candidates with the most electoral votes. At this point, each state has one vote (this occurred in 1801 and 1825) and to win, a candidate must get a majority of votes. If a majority is not reached for the vice president, then the Senate chooses from the two candidates with the most electoral votes (this occurred in 1837) and a majority of votes must be received by one candidate in order to win.

Why do we have this peculiar method of electing our presidents and vice presidents? During the Constitutional Convention of 1787 (May 25 to September 17) no problem vexed the delegates more than the method of choosing a President of the United States. The convention at large rebuffed the recommendation that Congress select the president, believing that the president would be a puppet of the legislature. The recommendation that the people elect the president was also turned down, thinking too much democracy was not in their best interests. To resolve the burning issue, the convention agreed that a system of indirect popular election was the answer, hence, the Electoral College.

The Electoral College has come under fire in recent years and changes are in the offing, most notably, doing away with it altogether, and establishing direct popular vote for the president, but that would take a constitutional amendment. Until then, the next time you vote for president, remember, your vote is merely an indirect way of electing the president. The Electoral College makes the real selection.

Ernesto Miranda changed the U.S. legal system forever.

Ernesto A. Miranda was a most unlikely character to be involved in one of the twentieth century's most celebrated legal cases, but he changed the U.S. legal system forever.

Ernesto A. Miranda was an unsavory character whose early years were spent as an incorrigible and whose adult years were spent as a criminal with a very impressive rap sheet. He was bad to the bone. In 1963, Miranda, a warehouse worker, kidnapped a teenage girl from a Phoenix movie-theater candy counter and took her into the desert where he savagely raped her. Miranda's criminal record made him a likely suspect and he was arrested in short order. After having been identified by the victim in a police lineup, Miranda confessed to the charges, acknowledging that he was informed of his legal rights, and he was found guilty. He was sentenced to incarceration for forty to forty-five years. However, during the trial, Miranda's court-appointed attorney contended that he had not been informed of his right to an attorney. The American Civil Liberties Union picked up the case of *Miranda v. Arizona* and argued it all the way to the highest court in the land. The Warren Court heard the case in 1966.

Essentially, in *Miranda v. Arizona*, the United States Supreme Court ruled on June 13, 1966, in a five-to-four ruling, that an arrested individual must be made aware of his or her right to silence, that should he or she talk, what he or she says can be used against him or her in a court of law, and that he or she has the legal right to an attorney during questioning, and if he or she cannot afford an attorney, one will be appointed for him or her.

This landmark ruling reversed the conviction of Ernesto A. Miranda and shook the law-enforcement community to its very foundation. In effect, the Supreme Court established a code of conduct for police interrogation of criminal suspects throughout the United States. It based its ruling on the Fifth and Sixth Amendments to the U.S. Constitution. The Fifth Amendment protects individuals from self-incrimination; the Sixth Amendment guarantees a defendant's right to an attorney.

The *Miranda v. Arizona* ruling has been amended since its inception to limit its scope. One such example (*Harris v. New York*) is the 1971 Supreme Court ruling stating that a voluntary confession obtained in direct violation of the *Miranda* decision can be utilized as evidence in a trial to establish that the defendant is lying.

As for Ernesto A. Miranda, he went the way of most malefactors. Because of new information, he was convicted once again of charges of kidnapping and rape, and sentenced to prison. He was paroled in due course and subsequently died, stabbed to death in a bar fight.

Ernesto A. Miranda did indeed change the course of U.S. legal history forever as the man behind the *Miranda* warnings.

You can be punished twice for the same crime.

Double jeopardy is a constitutional guaranty provided for by the Fifth Amendment. The amendment states in part: "Nor shall any person be subject for the same offense to be twice put in jeopardy of life or limb."

Double jeopardy is devised to guard an accused against the dangers of more than one trial and the likelihood of numerous convictions for an alleged offense. However, there exists no provision in the Constitution of the United States that prohibits a person from being tried and punished for the same offense by both a federal and a state court. This provision of the Fifth Amendment simply prevents the federal Government from punishing a person twice for the same offense. In essence, a state prosecution that comes after a federal prosecution for the same offense does not violate the guaranty against double jeopardy.

It does occur with some regularity that a person can be in violation of both a federal and a state law by a solitary act, thus precluding the defense of double jeopardy.

The Pilgrims "did not" eat turkey at the first Thanksgiving dinner.

What, no turkey at Thanksgiving? Hard to fathom, isn't it? But the traditional feast of turkey and all the trimmings at Thanksgiving was probably not what the Pilgrims consumed.

Although the turkey (the origin of the word *turkey* is thought to possibly come from the English guinea fowl that was imported from Turkey, and which resembled the American turkey) was in abundance, there is no official record of it at the Pilgrims' Thanksgiving table. The record does indicate a feast of fowl, venison (supplied by the Indians), eel, and side dishes, but not specifically turkey.

Not only was there most likely no turkey at the first Thanksgiving celebration, we also know there was no butter, milk, apple cider, nor cheese—no cows were available. It is also believed by some that there wasn't even any bread, for all the flour from the *Mayflower* had been consumed and it was sometime before wheat, barley, and peas could be successfully cultivated. Nevertheless, the Pilgrims did have pumpkin, which they ate boiled, for there was no flour to make a pie. Corn was also available, which they worked into dough, then fried in venison fat, to form an ersatz bread.

Thanksgiving came about out of a desire for the Pilgrims to celebrate the harvest, the glory of God, and other good fortunes of the past year, and to establish a rapport with the local Indians. Despite the fact that, of the original 102 Pilgrims that landed, only 55 survived the first winter, when spring arrived, the survivors pledged to make the new land their home.

It must be noted that the Pilgrims were not the first American settlers to set aside a day of thanks for a bountiful harvest. In 1578, English fishermen in Newfoundland celebrated a good catch, and in 1607, George Popham and his colonists in Maine had a day of thanksgiving. Even a small settlement of French Huguenots near Jacksonville, Florida, in 1564, had a day of thanks to God. Unfortunately, they were slaughtered by a band of marauding Spaniards in 1565, yet Florida's first Thanksgiving is commemorated by the Fort Caroline Memorial.

However, the day Americans hold sacred did originate with the Pilgrims.

The first Thanksgiving was in the autumn of 1621, when Plymouth Governor William Bradford summoned neighboring Massasoit Indians (about ninety in number) to partake of a three-day festival (more like an outdoor barbecue) that included feasting and recreation with the Pilgrims. There was even a show of power, when Pilgrim men fired shots from their English muskets to demonstrate their superiority. However, the Pilgrims were not ones to celebrate anything on a regular basis, and Thanksgiving was no exception, for prayer was their call to order. They had no intentions of establishing an annual holiday. It wasn't until November 29, 1789, that President George Washington proclaimed a national day of thanksgiving: a day of solemn prayer and thanks to God. Even that wasn't enough to make it an official holiday.

Thanksgiving became an official holiday due in large part to the efforts of Sarah J. Hale, editor and founder of the *Ladies' Magazine*, who began her campaign for an official holiday in 1827. She editorialized in her magazine about the need for a national holiday and she even wrote to President Lincoln pleading with him to make it official. Finally, Lincoln acquiesced, and on October 3, 1863, during the height of the Civil War, he set aside the last Thursday in November as Thanksgiving Day. In 1939, President Franklin D. Roosevelt moved the day to the fourth, but not necessarily the last Thursday, to stimulate holiday shopping. In 1941, a Congressional Joint Resolution made it official: Thanksgiving Day is to be celebrated on the fourth Thursday in November.

The eating of turkey on Thanksgiving was not part of the celebration in New England until the end of the nineteenth century. It did not become a national tradition until after World War II. The poultry industry helped champion the use of turkey as the main course at Thanksgiving and probably originated the presumed Pilgrim practice of eating turkey at the feast.

As for the Pilgrims feasting on turkey in 1621, no one knows for sure. What is known is that no mention of Ben Franklin's favorite bird, the one he proposed as the national symbol of the U.S.—fortunately, the magnificent Bald Eagle won out—exists. The eating of turkey on

Thanksgiving has, however, become one of America's most revered traditions.

You cannot be convicted of a crime without circumstantial evidence.

Easily one of our greatest misconceptions about the legal system is that to be convicted by purely circumstantial evidence is tantamount to a conviction based solely on suspicion of having committed a crime. In reality, all evidence, other than that given by a witness is circumstantial. It is recognized that spurious convictions are more apt to occur because of false testimony by a witness.

The fact is that there are only two admissible types of evidence: personal observation (direct) and circumstantial (indirect). Since our legal system has the onus of proving guilt and because the accused does not have to incriminate himself or herself, generally the only reliable method of conviction is by a preponderance of circumstantial evidence.

Confession is not sufficient to convict one of a crime, for false confessions abound. Eyewitness testimony is not enough, for that, too, is subject to the inconsistencies of personal observation. A man who stands accused of murder can be convicted only if there is overwhelming circumstantial evidence to support the accusation. Historically, most executions of criminals have been based solely on circumstantial evidence. So when one is convicted by circumstantial evidence, it is not evidence born out of suspicion, but rather the nonsubjective circumstances of the crime.

Warranties are meant to protect the seller, not the buyer.

Conventional wisdom would dictate that warranties are designed to protect the buyer of a particular item. On the contrary, they serve to limit the manufacturer's or dealer's obvious liability, and not to protect the buyer.

There are two types of warranties: one is the express warranty, which is predicated upon an explicit statement of coverage made by the seller of a product, very much like those used by automobile manufacturers: they indicate no guarantee of buyer satisfaction. The second type of warranty is that which is referred to as an implied warranty, which is much more inclusive in its coverage. Thus, reason holds that prudent manufacturers, such as automobile manufacturers, spell out the extent of the warranty: what they will be responsible for and nothing more. The warranty generally includes a declaration that states it stands in place of any other warranty of any kind, whether "stated or implied."

The Eighteenth Amendment did not prohibit drinking.

Throughout much of the nineteenth century, U.S. temperance movements beseeched Congress to enact a law of prohibition. The Prohibition Party made it a national issue, and in 1872, it even nominated presidential and vice-presidential candidates. The movement gained momentum, with several states passing their own prohibition legislation. During World War I, the cause for prohibition hit full stride and on January 15, 1919, the Eighteenth Amendment to the Constitution was overwhelmingly ratified, with Prohibition taking effect one year later.

What must be understood here is that the amendment did not prohibit the consumption of liquor, only its manufacture, sale, or transportation within the United States. It also forbade the import or export of such liquor. In essence, under the law, it was not illegal to drink an intoxicating liquor, possess, or for that matter to even purchase it, so long as it was purchased before the establishment of Prohibition. A case in point: the Yale Club legally served alcoholic beverages purchased prior to Prohibition.

The amendment was also unclear as to what constituted an intoxicating liquor. It was the charge of the Volstead Act of the same year to clarify what an intoxicating liquor was at the time. The law was championed by Representative Andrew Volstead of Minnesota and in October 1919, it defined an intoxicating liquor as any drink containing at least 0.5 percent alcohol by volume. It was enacted to enforce the Eighteenth Amendment by allowing for the investigation and punishment of violators.

But enforcement of the Eighteenth Amendment through the Volstead Act proved too much, as bootleggers and speakeasies circumvented the law, and anti-Prohibitionists insisted that the amendment caused crime to increase and loss of tax revenue. So, on December 5, 1933, the Eighteenth Amendment was repealed by the Twenty-first Amendment: Prohibition was over and the Eighteenth Amendment became the only amendment to the United States Constitution to have ever been repealed.

A jury does not have to be made up of twelve members.

Have you ever heard of a jury, or petit jury, comprised of less than twelve jurors? How about six or eight or even nine? It happens. It seems that convention mandates you must be tried by a jury of twelve of your peers, but the law does not say so. In fact, since about 1970, the number of jurors has varied a great deal, and in most states grand juries have as many as sixteen to twenty-three members.

There is nothing in the Bill of Rights or the United States Constitution that prescribes a specific number of members for a jury, nor does a verdict always have to be unanimous to convict in most courts.

Richard Nixon did not originate the "V" sign.

The V sign, synonymous with Richard M. Nixon, was not his own creation. Historically, the sign has meant many things to many people.

In logic, the V sign signifies the whole universe, or the logical idea of *or*. Even some meteorologists utilize the sign to denote frost or white frost. Numerous car manufacturers use the sign to represent victory or military supremacy: Buick, Cadillac, and Daimler.

The palm-forward V sign is fraught with meaning. It was often considered a variation of the European "cuckold" gesture. It sometimes rep-

of profit is increased while at the same time the publisher sells more books.

Yet another theory hints that the phrase may have found its beginnings once again during medieval times, when bakers were held in very low regard. Their reputations were often likened to that of the devil. Sometimes the names *baker* and *devil* were thought of as the same. In the vernacular of the period, a *devil's dozen* meant thirteen, the unluckiest of numbers; thus, the *baker's dozen* may have resulted from the baker's association with the devil and the number thirteen (also the number of witches in a coven).

In time, a *baker's dozen* came to denote thirteen of anything.

We didn't always eat three meals a day.

Imagine only eating two meals per day. This was the norm through the Middle Ages (c. 400–1500), mandated by the clergy. Only the infirmed, laborers, infants, and the elderly were allowed a third meal, for health reasons. This third meal was the breaking of the fast, hence, *breakfast*. The custom soon became the accepted practice by all individuals, regardless of their station in life.

St. Valentine died a terrible death, twice.

"When a young man's fancy lightly turns to thoughts of love," it must be Saint Valentine's Day, a celebration full of love, cards, and candy. But the man whose name is forever linked with this celebration died a most harrowing death. Although the holiday receives a lot of attention in America and Britain, the Roman Catholic Church removed the date from its calendar in 1969. Who was Saint Valentine, the patron saint of lovers, and why do we remember him?

There are two versions of who this legendary Christian martyr was. One version has a Roman physician and cleric as the object of outrageous torture during the oppression of the Christians at the hands of Emperor Claudius II Gothicus (c. 214–270). Apparently, the emperor felt that single men made superior soldiers, and thus they were not permitted to marry. Valentine went against the emperor's orders and married young couples. For his insolence, he was bludgeoned to death and beheaded on February 14, in approximately A.D. 269. He was laid to rest on the Via Flaminia. Pope Julius I purportedly erected a basilica over his remains.

The other version has a bishop of Terni, Italy, who befriended many children, imprisoned for not worshiping Roman gods. While in prison, children would write him loving missives and toss them into his cell. He was martyred in Rome and his remains were returned to Terni. This version may explain the practice of exchanging love notes on Valentine's Day.

The possibility exists that these two legendary figures were originally based on real individuals, but the stronger notion is that they are actually the same man. How Saint Valentine's life and name have become an eponym associated with love and romance has been perplexing to historians of all generations. Perhaps the answer may be linked to the ancient Romans.

Reaching far back into history, we find that one of the most prominent festivals celebrated by the ancient Romans was Lupercalia, February 15, a day marked by unconstrained frivolity and fertility rites. Upon the invasion of the British Isles by the Romans in A.D. 43, they introduced their beliefs and customs to the locals, who wasted no time in celebrating numerous Roman festivals. It was at this point that some observers believe that the festival of Lupercalia and Valentine's Day are connected because of a similar date and the practice of fertility rites. Yet others consider the association as nothing more than mere coincidence.

Some years later, in the thirteenth century, an effort was made to erase any evidence of Roman pagan rituals in Britain, and replace these idolatrous festivals with those of the Church. Hence, a celebration of Saint Valentine, who was martyred on February 14, the eve of Lupercalia, was to replace the licentious Roman festival with a celebration of the return of spring, "when a young man's fancy lightly turns to thoughts of love."

In the Old English tradition, February 14 also signaled the springtime mating of birds, and it is to this belief that this may be the most plausible origin of Saint Valentine's Day. In the works of both Chaucer and Shakespeare can be found references to the mating of birds on Saint Valentine's Day.

Many conventions are associated with the Saint Valentine's Day celebration, such as men drawing by lot the names of young ladies, children parading to houses of important people to receive wreaths of flowers and true-love knots, and the remuneration with halfpennies to children who would sing a special rhyme. None is more widespread than the exchanging of the popular valentine card between male and female.

Some believe that the first man to compose verses of love was the Frenchman Charles, Duke of Orléans. While held prisoner during a war with England in 1415, he sent romantic missives to his wife from his cell in the infamous Tower of London. It must be said that some question the truth of this story. However, the practice of exchanging missives was in full swing in Britain by the 1700s.

It seems that the first commercialized valentine cards appeared in the 1780s, most notably in Germany, where they were referred to *as friendship cards*. In the early 1800s, the British artist Kate Greenaway achieved much notoriety with her valentine cards depicting cheerful children and halcyon days. Esther A. Howland, a woman from Worcester, Massachusetts, is recognized as being one of the first U.S. producers of commercial valentine cards in 1847.

Whatever the origins of Saint Valentine's Day might be; whatever the reasons for the ritual of exchanging of cards by young and old alike, the observance of Saint Valentine's Day continues to be a much cherished ritual on every February 14.

The founder of Mother's Day was not a mother herself.

Despite the observance of Mother's Day as a recent event in the United States, the veneration of motherhood has existed for millennia. The oldest account of ritualistic mother worship dates back to ceremonies of Cybele or Rhea, the Great Mother of the Gods, in Asia Minor. The image of mother as a strong and majestic force was glorified, and this image ultimately made its way to Rome by way of Greece, some 250 years before the birth of Christ. The Romans called it the festival of Hilaria, and it was celebrated on the Ides of March (March 15), when worshipers made offerings in the temple.

With the birth of Christianity, pagan rituals celebrating motherhood became somewhat civilized; the Great Mother of the Gods festival became the Mother Church celebration. It soon became the practice of all believers that on Mid-Lent Sunday, the fourth Sunday in Lent, they would visit the church where they were baptized to place offerings on the altar.

It is not precisely known how this transition from worshiping the Mother Church to Mothering Sunday came about, but what is known is that during the Middle Ages (c. 400–1500) in Britain it became a time-honored tradition for young adults who left home to work, to return to visit their mothers bearing mothering cakes, and they would make this pilgrimage every Mid-Lent Sunday. However, it is certainly a stretch from these prosaic English observances of the Middle Ages to the celebration of today's Mother's Day.

Although the idea for a Mother's Day celebration in the United States was first proposed by Julia W. Howe in 1872, the modern celebration of Mother's Day owes its beginnings to American Anna M. Jarvis (1864–1948). She was a West Virginia schoolteacher, whose relentless reverence for her mother and the observation of the mistreatment of elders by their children led her to establish a special day for motherhood.

When Anna's mother, Mrs. Anna Reeves Jarvis, died on May 9, 1905, she initiated a letter-writing campaign to businessmen, clerics, and government officials to establish a national day to honor mothers. Her efforts were finally rewarded on May 10, 1908, as churches in both Grafton, West Virginia, and Philadelphia, then her place of residence, held Mother's Day celebrations, three years and a day after her own mother's passing. In 1910, the state of West Virginia became the first to declare a national day of celebration, and within twelve months, the rest of the states would fall in line. In 1914, when Anna Jarvis was fifty years old, President Woodrow Wilson recognized a joint resolution of

Congress declaring that Mother's Day would be observed by the nation on the second Sunday in May.

Miss Jarvis also initiated the wearing of a carnation, her mother's favorite flower, on Mother's Day to signify the beauty, truth, and fidelity of a mother's love. Sometime later, the practice became more specific: a colored carnation signified that a person's mother is living, while a white carnation indicated that a person's mother is dead.

A lamentable sidebar to this charming story is that Anna Jarvis herself never experienced the joys of motherhood.

A woman started Father's Day.

Father's Day, a day set aside to honor fathers, is celebrated in the United States on the third Sunday in June, in both church services and in the home. Gifts and cards are part of the celebration, as is the custom of wearing a red rose to signify a living father and a white rose for a deceased one. The ancient Roman Parentalia was a celebration most closely resembling Father's Day; however, it paid homage only to deceased parents and relatives.

Although there existed isolated celebrations that honored fathers in America, and despite Harry C. Meek, Mrs. Charles Clayton, and a few others having claimed credit for the origination of Father's Day, Mrs. John Bruce Smart Dodd, of Spokane, Washington, is generally credited as the originator of Father's Day.

She got the inspiration for this day while listening to a homily on Mother's Day, in 1909. Moved by her own father's tenacity and goodness—he had been a Civil War veteran who raised six motherless children—she was determined to establish a holiday that would honor her father, William Jack Smart, and all fathers. With the assistance of her minister, Dr. Rasmus, she drafted a letter to the Spokane Ministerial Association as well as the Spokane Ministers Alliance. Their response was one of excitement, and together with the support of the local YMCA, the first Father's Day was celebrated in Spokane on Sunday, June 19, 1910. Mrs. Dodd's own father was born on June 5. Even famed orator William Jennings Bryan complimented Mrs. Dodd on her desire to establish a day to honor fathers. Proclamations were issued by the mayor of Spokane and the governor of Washington, W. E. Hay, thus officially endorsing Father's Day, but a national day of observance was a long way off.

Despite having been endorsed by President Wilson, the same man who endorsed Mother's Day, Father's Day, nevertheless, languished in local city observances for over sixty years as an orphan holiday. It seems that Congress was hesitant to establish an official national holiday to honor fathers. Could it be some sort of act of false modesty, since most congressmen were fathers themselves? Several presidents and legislators labored for decades in an effort to make Father's Day a national holiday. At last, in 1972, they acted upon a request to approve Father's Day, as they had its counterpart in 1914. President Richard Nixon signed a Congressional resolution making the day a national day of observance for all fathers throughout the nation. Father's Day had finally achieved its well-deserved parity with Mother's Day.

Halloween was once a New Year's Eve celebration.

Halloween, which means "holy or hallowed evening," is celebrated on the night of October 31, and to the ancient Celts it was Old Year's Night, their New Year's Eve, the day before All Hallows or All Saints' Day, November 1, the Celtic New Year.

The ancient Celts were barbarian peoples who spoke Indo-European dialects and whose presence stretched over much of Europe from the second millennium B.C. to the first century B.C. Though endemic to central Europe, they also inhabited the mystical Highlands of Scotland, where they reached their zenith, as well as living in Wales, Ireland, and a portion of Britanny. The Celts were followers of the religion of the cabalistic Druids, and it is because of this association that Halloween is one of the most peculiar and bizarre holidays of record, and whose earliest observance is part of hidden history.

There were two significant feasts that the Celts observed: one, honoring Beltane (Bel's fires) on May 1, the start of planting, pasturing cattle, and warm weather, and the other, the autumn festival honoring their Sun god and Samhain, the Lord of the Dead, on October 31. This holiday signified the summer's end and the beginning of the hard winter; hence, the Celts celebrated their New Year's Eve on this day and the start of their New Year on the next day, November 1.

Since Halloween is not wholly English or Protestant in origin, it was slow to become a regular day of celebration in America. In fact, for the first two hundred years of American colonization, the celebration was observed mostly in isolated Irish Catholic villages. By the time of the horrific potato famine in Ireland in the 1840s, things had changed. Starving Irish fled across the Atlantic, seeking food and comfort in a free land. They brought with them, as did the Scots, their religious customs surrounding All Saints' Day and Eve, including their practices regarding the eve of Samhain, and all the prankishness associated with the eve before All Saints' Day. By the late 1800s, the celebration of Halloween had become a national celebration in America.

One of the most identifiable images of Halloween is the jack-o'-lantern, a wholly Irish creation. It was the custom of the Irish to use various large vegetables, usually turnips, rutabagas, and potatoes—since pumpkins were not readily available—hollow them out, and draw faces on their outsides. A lit candle was placed inside, and the hollow vegetables were used as lanterns to light the celebrants' way on Halloween.

Today's celebration of Halloween does have some connection to a Roman festival honoring Pomona, the goddess of fruits. American Halloween was once called Nutcrack Night and nuts and fruits were used in acts of divination. The harvest festival was celebrated on November 1. It was thought that by offering the previous winter's storage of nuts and apples to Pomona, this would cause the gods of fire and water to help in making the next year's crops abundant.

Wearing costumes and the tradition of trick-or-treating on Halloween also find their beginnings in the pagan traditions of the Celts. Ghosts were believed to fly about the houses of the living, so they were presented with a table full of food in hopes of distracting them from any ghoulish ideas. When the feasting was complete, villagers, dressed in masks and costumes that symbolized the souls of the dearly departed, led the ghosts out of town in a paradelike manner.

The actual origin of trick-or-treating is lost in the mists of history, but theories do exist to attempt to explain it. One theory states that there is a connection to the practice of souling or soul-caking. This was when Englishmen went about on both All Saints' and All Souls' Day, to beg for soul cakes, square buns with currants, in memory of the dead. The beggars vowed special prayers for the dead of those who gave.

Some link the practice of trick-or-treating to the Guy Fawkes celebrations honoring the scotching of the 1605 Gunpowder Plot to do away with King James I and blow up Parliament, which is celebrated November 5, and has been observed since the Renaissance in Britain. During these celebrations, children made themselves up to resemble the executed confederate and to beg "a penny for the Guy" from passersby.

The most logical theory states that the practice can be traced to an Irish custom on Halloween, when gatherings of peasants walked from house to house, entreating those within to give money for an elegant feast, sometimes requesting livestock from the givers. These generous contributions were usually asked for in the name of Muck Olla, probably a Druid god, who would exact a heavy toll on those who did not give freely, and who would guarantee future abundance to those who did. In time, these threats of Muck Olla became the tricks today's children play on those individuals who do not give treats.

Today, when children dress up in ghost costumes, wear masks or witches' hats, carry pumpkinlike lanterns, mark cars with the sign of the cross in soap, and decorate their Halloween parties with bats, black cats, witches, corn candies, and the like, they are only emulating many of the ancient customs that have come down to them from very early pagan times.

In some parts of the world, Halloween is a solemn and religious observance, but in America, Halloween, the New Year's Eve of the Celts, is a time of gaiety and pranks for children, and because of these customs, the holiday is one of the most beloved of today's celebrations.

Business cards once meant that you did not have to work.

In today's workaday world, everyone from panhandlers to chairmen of the board distribute their business cards with reckless abandon. It is almost incumbent on all classes of workers today to advertise their abilities and availability by way of the omnipresent and prosaic business card.

Oddly enough, today's custom of handing out business cards is a bastardization of the nineteenth-century social calling cards. In polite society of the time, possessing a calling card evinced that you were not concerned about forming business relationships, because you were of such old money, and therefore did not have to work for a living.

For those who were of the calling-card class, life was a cabaret and mornings were enjoyed riding around in carriages paying calls on one another, leaving or receiving calling cards. The use of such cards was strictly governed by etiquette manuals predating World War I. These rules mandated who could leave a calling card for a young damsel. They even dictated whether an unwed young lady of between fourteen and eighteen years of age was permitted to possess more than six or less than thirteen cards in her purse during the months beginning with a J. Rules also governed when it was appropriate and not appropriate to fold the edges of a calling card, the practice of which had very specific meanings. Leaving calling cards was one of the most complicated social codes of etiquette of the latter nineteenth century.

At the beginning of the twentieth century, the business card came into use as the difference between commercial and social functions became indistinguishable, except in diplomatic and military circles, and people saw no value in simply riding around visiting one person after another. The age of calling on someone and leaving your card for purely social purposes was fading fast. Even into the late 1960s, when both types of cards were still in use, there were those social pundits who warned people not to use calling cards for business purposes, but times have changed and so have customs.

The O.K. sign did not originate in the United States.

In America, the obvious sign of approval, that something is O.K., perfect, or all right, is when the forefinger and the thumb are joined in a circle. The expression, O.K., is inextricably associated with American popular culture. O.K. originated in the 1840s and is most likely an abbreviation of the appellation given to Martin Van Buren, Old Kinderhook, in reference to his birthplace in Kinderhook, New York. The sign created by joining the forefinger and the thumb together is much older. It can be traced back to the first-century rhetorician and teacher Quintilian (A.D. 35–96). In his essay on oratory, *The Training of an Orator*, a significant contribution to educational ideology and literary criticism, he gives the gesture as an indication of approval.

We know the origins of the sign and the phrase, but what of the use of the forefinger and thumb as a gesture of approval? One possible answer to this conundrum is that the ancients thought the association between the gesture and the thumb-to-forefinger precision grip to represent the fine points in human conversation. Another possible answer is linked to Buddhist and Hindu traditions wherein those who meditate seek the inner perfection that the circle has always symbolized. Whatever the origin of the sign, it is always universally understood.

Christians and non-Christians alike make the sign of the cross.

We cross our fingers in a futile attempt to summon the god of good luck or forgiveness in order that we may acquire good luck or to avoid bad luck, or even because we've told an untruth. This gesture is an obscure form of the sign of the cross, a symbol that was in use before Christianity.

Prior to the reign of Emperor Constantine in the fourth century, Christians were extremely hesitant about displaying the sign of the cross in public for fear of humiliation or even death. These early Christians often employed the technique of crossing their fingers to represent the sign of the cross in the presence of such pagans. Some say that the superstitious act of crossing the fingers is in effect tempting fate, especially when crossing fingers on both hands.

Through centuries of use, crossed fingers ultimately achieved a universal acceptance as an innocent social gesture, used by Christians and non-Christians alike.

CHAPTER SEVEN

GEOGRAPHY AND PLACES

A great city went missing for nearly five hundred years.

The immense Inca Empire (A.D. 1200–1538) extended from present day Quito, Ecuador, to Santiago, Chile, a distance of over three thousand tortuous miles. The Incas were a rich and industrious people, who achieved a level of civilization unmatched in South America. They were the largest native empire of the Americas.

In 1532, the Spaniards invaded the Incas, who quickly recognized that the invading Spaniards, led by Francisco Pizarro, were hungry for gold. It was their belief that if they gave Pizarro gold, he would take his soldiers and leave, but Pizarro stayed, and with just 168 soldiers and the help of internal strife, he defeated the Incas, who numbered 12 million persons. By 1538, the once spectacular Inca Empire was no more.

The Incas left behind splendid examples of their once prospering civilization, the most celebrated being Machu Picchu. Machu Picchu, meaning "old peak," was a city fortress that contained carved stone temples, houses, religious plazas, residential developments, and terrace walls miraculously constructed without mortar. Precariously perched two thousand feet above the Vilcañota River in the Peruvian Andes, fifty miles northwest of Cuzco, the once glorious city was surrounded by farming terraces joined by steps and irrigated by aqueducts. This agricultural system produced sufficient quantities of food, while at the same time controlling erosion. The city, whose age is unknown, was never entered by Pizarro, and by the time he had arrived in Peru, the Incas themselves had simply abandoned it.

Nearly five hundred years would pass before Machu Picchu, one of the most well-known archaeological sites in the world, would be discovered by the American explorer Hiram Bingham (1875–1956) in 1911. The precise purpose of the city is not truly understood, since the invading Spaniards never knew of its existence, thus, their records do not make mention of it. It can only be speculated, because of its site and architecture, that Machu Picchu served as a religious center, a place to worship Mother Earth, who was the embodiment of the divine. It was also speculated that it served as a border outpost.

Not only did the Incas leave behind a mysterious and magnificent city high up in the Andes that remained unknown for centuries, but they also built an extensive system of royal roads connecting all the cities of the empire. These roads traversed a mountainous terrain stretching thousands of miles, yet for all their greatness, the Incas never discovered the wheel. In fact, they never even discovered writing.

Saudi Arabia is not located in the Middle East.

Although Saudi Arabia is known as one of the world's largest suppliers of oil, home to wealthy sheiks, and the love of T.E. Lawrence, it is—as well as the other countries of southwest Asia, which include Iraq, Jordan, Syria, Israel, Lebanon, Turkey, and other smaller countries of the Arabian Peninsula—not in the "Middle East!"

I hear it said on the evening news and read it in the newspapers on a regular basis that Saudi Arabia is located in the Middle East. Sorry, but the Middle East is an area made up of southwestern Asian countries that include Afghanistan, India, Pakistan, Iran, and Burma (Myanmar).

To be blunt, this insidious misnomer and classic example of misinformation must be stopped, for although most insist on placing Saudi Arabia, Israel, Lebanon, Iraq, etc., in the Middle East, the United States Department of State does not officially recognize the term when referring to these countries. By the way, Saudi Arabia is in the Near East.

Greenland is white.

Greenland (in Danish, Grønland), with about four-fifths of its surface covered by a white ice cap, is anything but green. It is located northeast of Canada, and with an area of 840,000 square miles, it is the world's largest island that is not a continent. Its ice sheet is second only to Antarctica's in overall size, with an average thickness of five thousand feet. If it's so white, why call it Greenland?

Historically, Greenland was first inhabited by the Inuit people some three thousand to four thousand years ago; they continued their migration until A.D. 1000. Then, in 982, Eric the Red (died c. A.D. 1000), a Viking banished from the Norse colony of Iceland for murder and various other nefarious dealings, set out with his crew to find a better place to make a life. He ultimately chanced upon a large island teeming with fish and game, an abundance of birds, and with a coastline that reminded him of his homeland. Eric remained in his adopted land for three winters. Finally, returning to Iceland in 985, Eric called the island he had lived on Greenland, in hopes that it would excite people to colonize the ice-covered land.

In 986, Eric was successful in establishing two settlements on Greenland, but because of the island's increasing coldness and with only 5 percent of the land inhabitable, the advertising ploy that he had devised was short-lived. The island never achieved the population hoped for, but it was successfully converted to Christianity by way of Leif Eriksson in the eleventh century.

In 1721, the Danes appeared on the island when Hans Egede established a trading company and Lutheran mission. By 1815, Greenland had become part of the Kingdom of Denmark and remained so until 1953. Self-rule was realized on May 1, 1979, but the island still remains a Danish dependency.

For a brief period, from 1940 to 1945, when Denmark was occupied by the Germans during World War II, Greenland was a protectorate of the United States. After the war, it was returned to Denmark. The land that Eric the Red named Greenland, in a moment that would make any ad copywriter envious, in truth, should be called Whiteland.

California is a fantastic place.

California, the Golden State, is the only state to be named for a fantastic place that existed in the mind of Spanish novelist Garcí Ordóñez de Montalvo. De Montalvo's novel, *The Exploits of Esplandián* (c. 1502), is an early sixteenth-century romantic work depicting a black Amazon kingdom called California.

Esplandián, the praiseworthy knight, journeys to an island called California, in close proximity to Terrestrial Paradise. California is populated by black women, and is flush with pearls, precious stones, and gold. There Esplandián encounters Queen Calefia, the island's monarch, and battles her for possession of the island. The island becomes Christian. End of story.

In all fairness, the origin of the name is of questionable derivation. Other theories do exist. In 1862, Edward Everett, the man who spoke prior to Lincoln in Gettysburg, and author of *The Man Without a Country*, stated that the name *California* was probably the result of Spaniard Fortún Jiménez's visit to Baja California in 1533–34, when he mistook it for an island. Jiménez was familiar with de Montalvo's book and named it so.

Yet another theory states that in 1552, the name California first appeared in Juan Cabrillo's memoir as an entry written after his landing at Point Loma Head, San Diego.

It is also thought that the name may have derived from the Greek words *kalli ornis*, meaning "beautiful bird." Even historian Hubert Howe Bancroft, while hearing testaments from pioneers in the last century, heard about an Indian expression that might be interpreted by Spaniards as *kali forno*. It translates as "native land" or "high ground."

Whatever the origin of the name *California*, it certainly qualifies as a fantastic place.

A Greek poet conceived of geography.

Eratosthenes of Cyrene (c. 276–195 B.C.), an ancient Greek mathematician, philosopher, astronomer, and poet, was also the father of geography. In fact, he was the first to use the word *geography*, from the Greek, meaning *ge*, "the Earth," and *graphe*, "to describe."

Many of Erastosthenes' forbearers attempted to describe the world and its characteristics, but he was the first to measure the Earth's circumference with any definitude, and his method is still considered theoretically accurate. Erastosthenes, who knew the Earth was round, also sought to measure the distances of the Sun and Moon from the Earth. His classic work, *Geography*, served as a prototype from which others were to advance the discipline.

Lake Malaŵi is the world's largest aquarium.

Envision a body of water with thousands of species of fish found nowhere else on Earth—the world's largest aquarium. Lake Malaŵi (Lake Nyasa), the ninth largest and fourth deepest lake in the world, 360 miles long, bordered by Tanzania and Mozambique to the north and east, with most of the lake in the country of Malaŵi, is indeed the world's largest aquarium. David Livingstone, of "Dr. Livingstone I presume?" fame, is credited with the discovery of the lake in 1859, although Gaspar Boccaro, a Portuguese trader, saw the lake 250 years before him.

Lake Malaŵi is a cornucopia of fish that is world famous among aquarium traders and biologists alike. Known for its unmatched diversity of fish, Lake Malaŵi is the most species-rich lake in the world. There exist more varieties of fish in Lake Malaŵi than in the Atlantic Ocean from Greenland to Brazil. What is most astonishing is that nearly all of the species are indigenous to the lake and found nowhere else in the world. The cichlids (similar to American sunfishes, with over one thousand species in the lake) of Lake Malaŵi, during their life cycle exhibit every possible form of fish behavior. This makes the lake a virtual font of information for studying the intricacies of evolution.

Because of the lake's extreme scientific importance and unique characteristics, ninety-four square kilometers, comprising inland waters, three mainland forest reserves, and twelve islands at its southern end, together with most of the Cape Maclear peninsula and its bay, were designated in 1980 as the Lake Malaŵi National Park, the world's first freshwater national park. Some four years later, Lake Malaŵi, the world's largest aquarium, was chosen as a UNESCO World Heritage Site.

Washington, D.C., is unique.

Washington, D.C., is the capital of the United States of America; it is also one of the only national capitals established exclusively as a seat of government. Moreover, it is situated in and conterminous with the District of Columbia, a governmentally owned enclave sixty-seven square miles in area.

It is the masterwork of the French engineer, architect, and American Revolutionary War veteran, Major Pierre Charles L'Enfant, who designed the city in 1791, making it one of the very few cities anywhere that was designed before it was built. The federal government relocated from its temporary capital in Philadelphia to Washington, D.C., in 1800.

Washington, D.C., is designed with the Capitol building as its focal point and the various streets and avenues radiating from it, much like the hub and spokes of a wagon wheel. The city is replete with countless majestic government buildings, august monuments, superb museums, picturesque parks, and splendid public walkways, and it is thought by many to be the most architecturally perfect city in the world. Washington, D.C., also has the distinction of being the only city in the

United States that is not part of a state, and as such, throughout much of its history its citizens have lacked certain liberties common to other citizens of other cities.

To begin with, since 1961, thanks to the Twenty-third Amendment, residents of the district now have the privilege of voting in presidential elections, and it was not until 1970, that the district was accorded the right to elect a nonvoting delegate to the House of Representatives. Moreover, the city only became self-governing in 1974, yet Congress still has a hand in local decisions and oversees the city's budget.

Washington, D.C., the center of world power, was named after both George Washington and Christopher Columbus, but is that its real name?

From early in the City's history, legislative and executive branches of the federal government failed to make a distinction between the City of Washington and the District of Columbia. Subsequently, the city was called everything from "The Federal City," and "Washington, D.C.," in its early years, to "The City of Washington, Territory of Columbia," and "the Capital of the United States." In 1871, Congress sought to clear things up by decreeing that as far as government and legislation were concerned, Washington and the District of Columbia were one and the same. However, the name of the city continued to change until in the 1920s, an Executive Order proclaimed that the official name of the capital of the United States of America would be forevermore The City of Washington. It sounds simple enough. What took so long? It seems that there's just no accounting for government bureaucracy.

Hong Kong is not a city.

There is no such place as the city of Hong Kong. Hong Kong, although thought of as the ultimate destination for serious shoppers the world over and a manufacturer's paradise, is a hilly and mostly volcanic rock island—that's right, not a city, but an island—off the southern coast of Kwangtung (Guangdong) province, China. It has been an official

British crown colony since 1842, when China ceded it to Britain after its loss in the first Opium War, also called the Anglo-Chinese War of 1839–42.

Present-day Hong Kong (meaning "fragrant harbor"), and its islands, with one of the world's highest population densities (over fourteen thousand per square mile), is comprised of 1,126 square miles, of which only 410 square miles of the entire area is land: Hong Kong Island, Kowloon Peninsula, Stonecutters Island, numerous incidental islands, and a small portion of the mainland.

As for the city itself, it is called Victoria, named after Queen Victoria, the girl queen. Victoria, founded in 1843, is also the capital of Hong Kong Island. It is situated on its north shore, and is one of the world's most magnificent natural harbors, a major reason for early British interest in the area. As the administrative and commercial center of Hong Kong Island, Victoria remains one of the Orient's most important trading centers, but that changed in 1997.

In 1997, Britain's lease expired, and Hong Kong reverted back to its original owner, mainland China. Insofar as both China and Britain wish to maintain Hong Kong's unique commercial success and stability, an agreement between the two countries was signed in December 1984, mandating that Hong Kong would become a Special Administrative Region (SAR) of China on July 1, 1997, thus retaining most of its basic freedoms until 2047, it is hoped.

The Sun does indeed rise in the Pacific Ocean.

Persons on specific portions of the Isthmus of Panama witness the Sun rising in the Pacific Ocean and setting in the Atlantic Ocean.

The Isthmus of Panama, a serpentine land formation 450 miles long, twists and turns in such a way that the terminus of the Panama Canal (opened in 1914) farthest east meets the Pacific Ocean while the terminus farthest west meets the Atlantic Ocean. (The name *isthmus*, which is a thin strip of land that links two larger bodies of land, was first assigned to the Isthmus of Corinth, between the Peloponnesus and the mainland of Greece.)

The concept of the Sun rising in the Pacific on the Isthmus is made difficult by virtue of the fact that most people expect that the canal (approximately fifty-one miles long) runs east and west, when in reality it runs in a northwesterly-southeasterly direction. To illustrate the point, Cristóbal, at the Atlantic terminus, is farther west than Balboa, at the Pacific terminus. By using the canal and avoiding the trip around Cape Horn, ships save about seventy-eight hundred miles between the ports of New York and San Francisco, making the distance traveled some fifty-three hundred miles.

Rest assured; if you live on the east coast of the United States, the Sun will most assuredly rise tomorrow morning in the Atlantic Ocean.

The Spanish Steps are not Spanish.

The famed Spanish Steps, or Scala di Spagna, soar up from the piazza to the French-built church and convent of Trinità dei Monti in Rome. This magnificent work of art was started in 1495 by the beneficence of King Charles VIII of France. The Spanish Steps were designed in the baroque style and gifted by the French, not the Spanish, to the city of Rome in the eighteenth century. The thought was to glorify the approach to the church, which served the interests of the French community.

As for why the steps are named after the Spanish and not the French, it is because they are located in the Piazza di Spagna, home to the Spanish Embassy, which was founded there in the early seventeenth century and is still the Spanish Embassy to the Vatican.

There's a bridge with a heart.

Often called a bridge with a heart, the 29.2-mile Lake Pontchartrain Causeway (twin causeways), built in 1956–69, which spans Lake Pontchartrain in Louisiana, is the world's longest bridge and over-water highway (continuous), with 23.9 miles completely over water. Made of precast, prestressed concrete, it is also one of the world's longest bridges, and the pride of New Orleans. Police officers relentlessly patrol the bridge, aiding stranded motorists. Should a motorist have a flat, an officer will change the tire; should overheating occur, an officer will add water to the radiator.

The bridge carries about twenty thousand vehicles daily (at a minimal charge) and occasionally babies are born on the bridge. One time an airplane in distress even landed on it. Since land is not sighted at one point for over eight miles, some motorists are overcome with panic and stop abruptly on the bridge. For those motorists who must travel the bridge to work daily, but are afraid of the journey, a psychologist conducts therapy classes to help deal with this phobia.

So, should you find yourself stranded on the longest over-water bridge in the world, never fear, for a patrolman is always near.

To the Turks, there is only Istanbul.

Istanbul is a city and seaport in northwest Turkey, situated on the Bosphorus and spanning two continents, Europe and Asia. The early Greeks called a previous settlement on the same site Byzantion and the Romans called it Byzantium. In A.D. 324, Constantine the Great (280–337) started to expand Byzantium and decreed it to be his capital, and on May 11, 330, he declared it the seat of the Eastern Roman Empire. The city was officially called New Rome, but most referred to it as Constantinople, "City of Constantine," in honor of its ruler. It quickly became the heart of the world of Christendom.

The city was built to resemble Rome. It is situated on seven hills, and rises from both sides of the Golden Horn, an inlet of the Bosphorus that is the gateway to the Black Sea. In 1453, the Turks took control of the city and made it the capital of the Ottoman Empire. From then until now, the Turks have called it Istanbul, from the Greek *eis ten polin*, which translates "into the city." In 1930, the city's name was officially changed to Istanbul.

The Turks do not recognize the name Constantinople, and haven't for over five hundred years. If any mail, whether official or private, is sent addressed to Constantinople, and not Istanbul, it is returned to sender.

Once there was "no" summer.

The year was 1816, and there was no summer. Across the expanses of northern Europe and the eastern United States, daytime temperatures rarely, if ever, exceeded fifty degrees Fahrenheit. On June 6, a snow-storm left a foot of fresh snow on sections of New England and for a prolonged period of time, it blanketed much of the area. The cause of the missing summer, known as the Little Ice Age, was a volcanic erup-tion on the other side of the world.

On April 5, 1815, one of history's most stupendous volcanic erup-tions took place on Sumbawa, an island of present-day Indonesia. The eruption blew off the uppermost four thousand feet of Mount Tam-bora, (approximately eighty cubic kilometers of Earth) thus ripping a seven-mile-wide crater in the peak and killing twelve thousand people. An additional eighty thousand died of starvation because the ash decimated countless farmlands. The explosion was heard almost one thousand miles away on Sumatra and is rated eighty times greater than the Mount Saint Helens eruption.

By the summer of the following year, a tremendous cloud of volcanic dust and debris traveled around the world and lay suspended over the Northern Hemisphere, deflecting the sun's radiation. The nights were often below freezing in normally sweltering Savannah, Georgia. The city posted a daytime high temperature of only forty-six degrees on July 4.

Crop failures were common and numerous people died of winter-time ailments the year there was no summer.

New York City's Central Park is not the largest city park in the world.

We're all familiar with New York City's famed Central Park—that sprawling expanse of greenery, walking paths, and park benches—that is a symbol of what the city is all about. To most of us, Central Park is big at 843 acres, but to the people of Phoenix, Arizona, it is but a mere spot of green grass. Phoenix is home to not only the largest city park in the United States, but in the world as well: South Mountain Park.

When the park was obtained by the city in 1924, during the presidency of "silent" Calvin Coolidge, Phoenix was not yet considered a major city, for it had less than thirty thousand people. It was growing, though, and the city fathers thought the citizens should have a place to enjoy the outdoors close to the city. South Mountain Park was purchased through passage of a bill in Congress that allowed the city to acquire it for a dollar an acre.

It is surrounded by a flat cosmopolitan area presently occupied by over two million people. It is an authentic mountain island, a place to beat a retreat from all that is civilized, yet maddening. It is a place to recharge the batteries, to commune with nature. It is a last vestige of the upper Sonoran Desert in the middle of a major metropolis.

Just how big is South Mountain Park? It is gargantuan by anyone's definition. It comprises sixteen thousand weather-beaten acres replete with forty miles of trails, seasonal streams, three springs, and it is dry virtually 99 percent of the time. South Mountain Park is just a short jaunt from downtown Phoenix. At nearly nineteen times the size of New York's Central Park, it is the largest city park in the world.

There is more than one Kremlin.

Yes, the Kremlin (Russian, *kreml*) in Moscow is not the only kremlin, just as Athens is not the only city with an acropolis, for numerous Greek cities possessed an *akropolis* (meaning "highest point in the city") from which to defend against intruders. The term *kremlin* is a medieval word meaning the "walled-in centermost district of a town," whose function is to protect the inner city from intruders. Many Russian cities possess a kremlin or fortress; it's just that Moscow's is the most well-known.

The Kremlin in Moscow is not simply one building, but rather a series of various buildings, most of which are architectural masterpieces. It is spread out over ninety acres. The crenellated walls were completed between 1485 and 1495, and are accented by twenty different towers. Numerous cathedrals, palaces, and museums are protected by the walls. It was the tsar's official residence until Saint Petersburg became the capital in 1712.

Since the U.S.S.R. is now a fading memory, the fate of the Kremlin is in question, but its history is one of survival since the fifteenth century, and odds are that it will survive for many centuries to come.

Rome is not the oldest city.

Rome, the home to Caesar and the Colosseum, is often believed to be the oldest city in the world, but Rome, the Eternal City, established in 753 B.C., is surpassed by Damascus, Syria, established around 3000 B.C. It was a vital center of trade during the ancient Assyrian, Greek, Roman, and Byzantine empires.

Most historians believe Damascus (*Dimashq* in Arabic) is indeed the oldest continuously occupied city in the world, surpassing Rome by many centuries.

The Gulf Stream is an invisible giant river.

The Gulf Stream is an invisible—that is to say, unseen—giant river that flows north in the western North Atlantic Ocean some ten to five hundred miles off the east coast of the United States. In the sixteenth century, it was believed that its current originated in the Gulf of Mexico. Today we know this is not the case; however, the misconception persists.

The Gulf Stream is a very narrow current that flows from the Straits of Florida to the Norwegian Sea. It is about sixty miles wide, often as deep as thirteen thousand to sixteen thousand feet, and one thousand times larger than the mighty Mississippi River. Its current velocity is four miles per hour, and it transports water (average temperature seventy-five degrees) at the astonishing rate of twenty-two billion gallons per second.

As the Gulf Stream (named by Benjamin Franklin in 1762), the giant undersea river, continues to bring warmth and abundance to those in its path, the study of its benefits is never ending.

The largest freshwater lake in the world is in North America.

The largest freshwater lake in the world is situated between the United States and Canada, in North America. Lake Superior, the grandest of the Great Lakes, covers 31,800 square miles and at its greatest length is 350 miles long. It is 160 miles across at its widest, 1,333 feet at its deepest, and represents 53.8 percent of the Great Lakes' total water content.

Lake Superior ranks second only to the Caspian Sea as the largest lake in the world.

Surfers had a great year in 1933.

The highest ocean wave in recorded history occurred in 1933. While traveling from Manila in the Philippines to San Diego, California, the American tanker U.S.S. *Ramapo* sighted a wave measuring a staggering 112 feet high. This is about ten times greater than the average ocean wave. Waves of this magnitude are produced by winds scudding over great expanses of water at speeds in excess of fifty knots. Cowabunga dude! Note: In 1958 a tsunami hit the coast of Alaska measuring 1720 feet high.

The oldest city in the United States is not in New England.

No, the oldest continuously settled city in the United States is not Jamestown or Plymouth; it's not Lexington, Concord, or even Boston, though they all seem like reasonable choices. The truth of the matter is, it's way down south, located in the northeastern portion of Florida. It's called Saint Augustine.

Saint Augustine is the seat of Saint John's County, and it faces

Matanzas Bay on the Atlantic Ocean. Juan Ponce de Léon, the famous Spanish explorer, in search of the fabled Fountain of Youth, landed there in 1513 and claimed the area for Spain.

In 1564, the French constructed Fort Caroline about twenty-five miles north. The Spanish viewed the French actions as a threat to their rule in the area, and the following year they summoned Admiral Pedro Menéndez de Avilés, who arrived on August 28, the feast day of Saint Augustine. Under his leadership, the Spanish destroyed the French settlement and in 1565 founded the city of Saint Augustine, named for Saint Augustine, Bishop of Hippo.

Mount Everest is not the world's tallest mountain peak.

The most celebrated, romantic, and poetic mountain peak in all the world is Mount Everest. As sublime and magnificent a work of nature as one can envision, Mount Everest is a peak of the Great Himalaya (Sanskrit for "Abode of Snow"), where peaks of twenty thousand feet or greater are commonplace and number well over a thousand.

Mount Everest grandly bestrides the boundary between Nepal and Tibet. Few can agree on its present height, but most sources place it at 29,028 feet and growing, about one centimeter per year. Mount Everest is said to be the tallest peak in the world, and on May 29, 1953, Sir Edmund Hillary, a beekeeper by vocation, and the Sherpa, Tenzing Norgay, were the first men to successfully climb the mountain and stand on its summit.

The peak, once known as Peak XV by mapmakers, was named after Sir George Everest (1790–1866), who was the surveyor general of the Great Trigonometrical Survey of India from 1830 to 1843. Oddly enough, he most likely never saw the peak named after him. Locals call it and its surrounding area Chomolungma, or Goddess Mother of the World, which sounds much more appropriate.

No doubt Mount Everest is the big kid on the block, but not by much. It is in a neighborhood, the Himalayas, populated by eight more of the ten highest peaks in the world. However, there's more to mountain peaks than meets the eye.

If you measure a mountain peak from its place of origin, then Mount Everest is easily surpassed by Mauna Kea, a volcano in Hawaii. When measured from the Pacific Ocean floor, this semiactive volcano rises to a height of approximately 33,500 feet (only 13,796 feet are visible from sea level), making it the world's highest mountain island, if not the world's highest mountain peak.

The first dinosaur was not discovered at the La Brea Tar Pits.

The *Iguanodon*, a relative of the duckbill, achieved worldwide prominence as the first official dinosaur introduced to science. It was unearthed from gravel quarries in Tilgate Forest, Sussex, England, in 1822, by the English physician and paleontologist, Gideon A. Mantell (1790–1852).

England was not destined to be the land of the dinosaurs, but it does boast of the first find of its kind.

The world's longest drivable beach is not in Hawaii.

Much to the amazement of beach bums and car enthusiasts the world over, the longest drivable beach in the world is not in Hawaii. In fact, it is not even in the tropics, as one would expect.

On any given day you can literally drive up and down a beach that stretches for twenty-eight seamless miles in one direction. It is called Long Beach and is located, not in the Caribbean or even California, but in the southwest corner of the state of Washington (the only state named after a U.S. president).

MARKO PERKO

The Burgess Shale is unique to paleontology.

Ensconced eight thousand feet up in the majestic Canadian Rockies, at the eastern border of British Columbia, sits the most significant fossil find ever. A small limestone quarry formed 530 million years ago, the Burgess Shale is less than a city block long and barely ten feet high. But tightly packed into this small area are the remains of a prehistoric sea that gave birth to more varieties of life than can be found in all the modern oceans combined. This prehistoric sea was home to dozens of creatures that were unknown until its discovery. Tens of thousands of complete examples, many in startling detail, with soft bodies intact, were evidently buried by submarine slumping of sediment. Some fossils even contain remains of a creature's last meal. Included in this wellspring of fossils are the five-eyed Opabinia and the circular mouthed Anomalocaris.

The fauna was discovered in 1909 by Charles Doolittle Walcott (1850–1927), America's most distinguished paleontologist and then secretary of the august Smithsonian Institution. Walcott, saddled with the antiquated beliefs of his time, set forth to misinterpret these fossils in a very systematic fashion: he identified every fossil as belonging to some modern group, when nearly twenty Burgess Species cannot be affiliated with any known group. In short, Walcott charted no new territory, when just about everything he discovered was new, truly new.

Walcott's work went unchallenged for more than half a century. Then, in 1971, Professor H. B. Whittington of Cambridge University published a treatise that reexamined Walcott's findings and concluded with a drastic reinterpretation of the Burgess Shale. Professor S. J. Gould of Harvard University, who has written extensively about the Burgess Shale, believed that the invertebrates found there are the world's most significant animal fossils.

The Burgess Shale is a storehouse of answers to many of the riddles of our very own existence, and there is still much to learn from it.

The Caspian Sea is the world's largest lake.

That's right, the Caspian Sea is a lake, the world's largest. Known in ancient times as Caspium Mare, it is located on the border between Europe and Asia, and duly qualifies as a lake. In geographical terms, any large body of inland water, whether fresh or salt, is called a lake.

The Caspian Sea is landlocked and dominates an incredible area of 149,200 square miles—larger than many countries. It is approximately 750 miles long and averages about 200 miles in width. The greatest recorded depth is 3,209 feet at its southern end (Lake Baikal in Russia is the world's deepest at 5,710 feet). It's so immense that different sections experience quite different climates. There are more than fifty islands within its boundaries. At about 92 feet below sea level, it is also the lowest point in Europe.

Though it is a leading transport route for the region, its claim to fame is the giant sturgeons that yield the world-famous Beluga caviar.

The world's smallest continent is also its largest island.

Traditionally, a landmass larger than an island is a continent. A continent is one of the Earth's two primary geographical components and the ocean is the other. Just 29 percent of the Earth's surface is land area, while the overwhelming percentage, 71 percent to be specific, is covered with water.

The land of kiwi birds and kangaroos, and, oh yes, Crocodile Dundee himself, Australia, is the world's smallest continent and its largest island. It is also the only country that is a continent. As a member of the Commonwealth of Nations, it lies undivided in the Southern Hemisphere. Australia is immense, with an area of 2,966,200 square miles; it is the sixth largest country.

Australia's discovery is claimed by many nations, but the overall credit for its discovery and initial colonization goes to the Dutch. It was originally called New Holland by its Dutch discoverer, Captain Willem Jansz, when in 1606 he first sighted its coast. James Cook declared it a British possession in 1770. The British, after recovering from the loss of the Colonies, decided to seek other lands to place their prison convicts. Called New South Wales by its British sovereign, Australia was the logical choice. In 1778, the first prisoners arrived and continued to do so for the ensuing half century.

By 1801, cartographers had taken a serious look at this gargantuan island, with its lesser islands, and realized that it was truly the sixth continent (for most of man's history there were only three continents: Europe, Asia, and Africa). Christened Australia that same year, and named after the mythical land, Terra Australis (Southern Continent), it was a place thought to have existed in theory since the age of the ancient Greeks.

Once the mighty Mississippi River flowed backward.

The mighty Mississippi River, the third largest and fourth longest river in the world, stretches for 3,710 miles from its headwaters in Minnesota to its final destination, the Gulf of Mexico. Its drainage area covers 40 percent of the United States. Much of the colonization of America occurred on or near this immense river. It's the main artery that flows through the very heartland of the country, an area that has for centuries been a place of beauty and tranquility, or has it?

Between 1811 and 1812, something happened on the Mississippi River that literally changed its course. That's right, the river was moved, not by damming it or diversion by some other means, no, an earthquake did it. Hard to imagine, but the greatest earthquake to strike the continental United States occurred in New Madrid, Missouri, on December 16. Actually, there were three quakes over several weeks. Admittedly, the casualties were very few, less than a dozen, since the area had a low population density. Nevertheless, the results of the earthquakes were profound.

Three quakes caused the ground to heave, jerk, and convulse. The sound of wrenching earth, together with darkness, ear-shattering explosions, and even the earth throwing up vast amounts of sulfurous vapors, water, sand, and organic matter were the result. Whole groves of trees were decimated and many a giant oak was split up the middle like a man splitting firewood with and ax. Houses went up in flames and looked as if they were giant campfires. Tremors were reported more than eight hundred miles away in Washington, D.C. The town of New Madrid itself collapsed into the river.

There were reports of the Mississippi River reversing its course and flowing backward as men tried to escape on boats, only to find themselves tossed about by giant waves and beached. The river swallowed up sandy bluffs as if they were scoops of ice cream devoured by a hungry child. The mighty Mississippi River continued to respond to the quakes for the next several weeks by even changing its course. This peaceful river of dreams, a giver of life, was moved by a force unimaginable at the time.

Just how powerful was this series of quakes? The logarithmic Richter scale that measures earthquake activity was not developed until 1935; therefore it could not be utilized to determine the magnitude of the quakes. However, the revised (Modified) Mercalli scale, which measures the strength of quakes in terms of physical damage (houses demolished, quantity of sand and mud ejected from the earth, etc.), could be applied to determine intensity. This evidence can be analyzed using current descriptions.

The scale's range is depicted in Roman numerals, I through XII. At the top end of the scale, XII represents complete destruction and is equivalent to the high "eights" on the Richter scale. The three quakes that rocked New Madrid between December 1811, and continuing into February of the next year are rated from XI to an astonishing XII! And you thought it only shakes in California!

The White House is the oldest public building in Washington, D.C.

The site of America's most revered residence and possibly the most recognized building in the world started out as cold, windy, and mucky. The area around the Potomac River was just that, everything one would imagine a marsh to be—not the most likely place to build a house of such prominence.

Nevertheless, Pierre C. L'Enfant was put to work designing the new City of Washington, and James Hoban, an Irish-American architect (c. 1762–1831) won a prize of five hundred dollars in 1792 for his design of the President's Mansion, also initially called the President's Palace, or Executive Mansion. Although it became known as the White House early on, it was not officially deemed so until 1902, when Theodore Roosevelt placed the words "The White House" on his letterhead and Congress passed a resolution affirming the fact.

The White House has the distinction of being the oldest public building in Washington, D.C., as it was the nascent government's first order of business. The White House of today is but a reproduction of the original, for only a section of the outer shell, along with the third floor, remain. The building has been entirely gutted and rebuilt on new foundations with steel reinforcing by the Army Corps of Engineers.

The basic architecture of the White House is a copy of manor houses found in Ireland, England, and France. It wasn't uncommon for architects to copy others because the country was not old enough to have established its own architecture. The 132-room mansion stands resplendently among eighteen beautifully manicured acres.

James Hoban lived to build the White House twice; the second time after the British burned it in 1814, requiring an entirely new interior. Strange as it may seem, the only interior object to survive is a portrait of George Washington by Gilbert Stuart that now hangs in the East Room.

Moreover, the house that was built for George Washington never had him as a resident. For you see, George Washington is the only president who never slept in the White House; he died before it was finished. President and Mrs. John Adams became the first residents in 1800.

The Supreme Court Building is a unique American landmark.

The United States Supreme Court Building, designed by Cass Gilbert, is arguably the largest man-made marble structure in the world. The highly polished marble, together with its massive size, give the building a brilliant and powerful presence. As the focal point of the American judicial system, the Supreme Court Building is also America's finest example of colonial and federal architecture, inspired by ancient Greek architecture.

The interior is entered through two massive bronze doors weighing more than six tons. Once inside, the main hall displays busts of former chief justices and the courtroom itself is adorned with allegorical friezes, fine mahogany furniture, and velvet drapes. The oddest room in the building is found on one of the upper floors. It contains a basketball court. Some call it the "highest court in the land."

Often referred to as the judicial Vatican, the building and its environs are policed by its own autonomous constabulary, whose duties are to protect the building and environs, receive writs at night, and to keep tourists and visitors in order.

When in session, the Supreme Court uses no court reporters; instead, a tape recorder tapes every session. Transcripts are rarely if ever done, inasmuch as there is no appeal. The Court's decisions can only be reversed by itself, when it deems it necessary.

Even the location of the Supreme Court Building is unusual and curious at the same time. Sandwiched in between the Capitol and Maryland Avenue, NE, its approach is less than would be expected for such an auspicious structure. Even its view of the Capitol is obscured. It's unfortunate that L'Enfant's recommendation to locate the Supreme Court Building in Judiciary Square was never followed, for a building of such presence and solemnity deserved a better location.

The building is the Court's first permanent home, because from 1789 to 1935, it was a roving branch of the government, convening in such sites as over a market in Manhattan, in a room in the Capitol basement, and even in a tavern. The Court never had a permanent home until William H. Taft, the only man to hold the office of president and serve as chief justice, insisted that Congress authorize the building of a permanent home for the Court. The Court's official home was completed in 1935, but Taft never lived to see it finished.

In 1977, the Supreme Court Building was officially proclaimed a National Landmark.

There is no place called Scotland Yard.

Scotland Yard is the headquarters of the London Metropolitan Police and the Criminal Investigation Department (CID). Scotland Yard's name came about because it once stood on the site of a thirteenth-century medieval castle that was the home to Scottish royalty during their official visits to London. By the seventeenth century, Scotland and England were ruled by James I and Scotland Yard was divided into two areas: Greater Scotland Yard and Middle Scotland Yard. Then, in 1829, the Metropolitan Police Force was formed by Sir Robert Peel, hence, the sobriquet *Bobbies* or *Peelers*. For the next sixty-one years, the force was headquartered at 4 Whitehall Place, not Scotland Yard. In 1890, the Metropolitan Police Force moved to the New Scotland Yard located on the Thames Embankment, and then again in 1967, to a new building just off Victoria Street at 10 Broadway. Therefore, today Scotland Yard as an address has no significance, for nothing is located at the original site.

Scotland Yard officers are any officers of the Metropolitan Police Force, from the commissioner to the lowliest Bobbies. They are not a specific, elite unit of police specialists. Moreover, Scotland Yard is the headquarters of the police force that supervises all of metropolitan London (except for the City of London, which has its own separate police force), with no jurisdiction beyond its environs.

The Colosseum in Rome was the first domed stadium.

The Colosseum is arguably Rome's most visited and most famous tourist attraction, immortalized in both print and film. The actual structure, originally known as the Amphitheatrum Flavianum (the Flavian Amphitheater), was a marvel in its time. Emblematic of an-cient Rome's power and one of the world's wonders of antiquity, it was constructed under the aegis of the Emperors Vespasian and Titus on the site of Nero's renowned Golden House. It was opened to the pub-lic in A.D. 80—after some six to eight years of construction—with a ceremony that consisted of one hundred days of games. Subsequently, it was renamed the Colosseum because the Emperor Hadrian situated an immense statue (colossus) of Nero at its entrance.

It is a freestanding structure made of travertine blocks set on a thick foundation of concrete. Elliptical in shape, the Colosseum could hold somewhere between forty-five thousand to fifty thousand spectators on marble and wooden seats bolstered by an arched substructure. It was some 159 feet high, with a total area covering about six acres. The first three floors exhibited the various Greek column designs known to architecture as Doric, Ionic, and Corinthian, in that order, and the fourth floor was a windowed wall.

The main arena floor was made of timber, and beneath its surface were a series of chambers that quartered wild animals, as well as passageways and drains. Before the dome covered the stadium, the entire Colosseum might have been covered by a gigantic canvas awning, called a *velarium*, suspended from wooden poles on the fourth floor, to shield spectators from inclement weather.

Because of its architecture under the flooring, it was apparent that it could be filled with water to accommodate mock naval battles. However, its primary use was one of entertainment for the privileged. It included gladiatorial contests between men and exhibitions of wild beasts fighting to the death.

Although the Colosseum has been remembered as the place where numerous Christians were martyred, simply thrown to the lions and such, the truth seems to be otherwise. Modern-day academics seriously question this belief, since the ancient Christian writings do not even suggest any such martyrdoms took place there. No verifiable proof exists that such heinous acts ever occurred in the Colosseum, although the Circus Maximus, often confused with it, may have been the site of such spectacles.

The Colosseum of today has deteriorated, mostly because it was used as a stone quarry during the Middle Ages—it was the source of the travertine for Saint Peter's Basilica—and because of the effects of earthquakes, but it still stands tall, a symbol of what was once the glory of Rome.

There was once a wall at Wall Street.

Tourists and New York City residents alike often surmise that Wall Street, America's financial center, was named so because it is walled in by a succession of very high buildings. Actually, the street is named after the wall that actually divided Manhattan Island. The short and narrow street travels the same path as the old earthen wall that was constructed across the lower portion of Manhattan, the oldest borough of New York City, in 1653, by the Dutch settlers to keep anticipated invaders such as the English and Indians from entering the small city on the tip of the island.

Peter Minuit, governor of the New Netherland colony of Dutch settlers, purchased the island from the Indians in 1626, for the paltry sum of twenty-four dollars' worth of trinkets, beads, and cloth. It was possibly one of the greatest real estate deals in history.

The North and South Poles are quite different.

Both polar regions are to most people just giant masses of ice and snow, but in reality, they are just as their names suggest, opposite each other. Although essentially unknown to the classical world, they have for the past several centuries lured explorers to their inhospitable landscapes.

The Arctic is the northernmost area on Earth, centralized around the North Pole and consisting primarily of an ice-covered ocean. The Arctic is the smallest of the oceans, and some scientists wonder if it can truly be called an ocean basin because it is smaller than some seas. It is doubtful if the region ever supported a native population. Flora and fauna are plentiful, but there are no penguins in the Arctic, although it does boast a rather significant lemming population. You've heard of the suicidal lemming, but maybe you never thought it was a real animal. Well, it does exist, and it resembles a mouse. Contrary to popular belief, it is an excellent swimmer.

In contrast, Antarctica is an immense ice-covered landmass that surrounds the South Pole and measures approximately 5.5 million square miles, making it the world's fifth-largest continent. Enveloped by a cold and unfriendly ocean that is populated by countless icebergs, the region supports no native population nor is it the possession of any nation. Because the temperatures rarely rise above freezing, the region is basically a zoological and botanical wasteland, and is regularly the coldest place on Earth. In fact, the coldest temperature ever recorded anywhere on Earth was at the former Soviet Union's Vostok station in Antarctica, thirteen thousand feet above sea level. On August 24, 1960, a world-record low reading of -126.9 degrees Fahrenheit (-88.3 degrees Celsius) was recorded. The mean average temperature of the six-month Antarctic winter is minus 70 degrees Fahrenheit. Mean temperatures are normally 20 degrees colder than those in comparable areas of the Arctic. It should be noted that Arctic temperatures during the warmer months can exceed 60 degrees above zero Fahrenheit, which is not too bad for an area made of ice.

The reason for the differences in temperatures between the two polar regions is that land is generally colder than water because of its greater density. Therefore, Antarctica is usually much colder than the Arctic Ocean because it is a landmass that is ice-covered while the Arctic is just ice.

If penguins are not at the North Pole, then where are they? They are found only in the colder waters of the Southern Hemisphere that include the Galapagos Archipelago, South America, South Africa, Australia, New Zealand, numerous islands, and of course Antarctica.

Antarctica is for the taking.

Just imagine if you could own Antarctica, a snow-covered landmass surrounding the South Pole, you would possess the world's fifth largest continent, which has an area of approximately 5.5 million square miles. In a peculiar way it's possible, for nobody really owns Antarctica in a legal sense; therefore, it is anyone's for the taking. But would you really want a place that contains 90 percent of the world's ice and is the windiest, coldest, and driest continent of them all? It seems that many nations do.

Antarctica has no indigenous population, or for that matter, no permanent population. It doesn't even have flowering plants, grasses, or mammals of any appreciable size, but it is populated by a variety of birds and sea life. Between 1772 and 1775, British Captain James Cook made several voyages that approached the continent, but he never actually sighted land. Then, on November 18, 1820, American Nathaniel Brown, in his sloop *Hero*, discovered Orléans Strait and eventually made landfall. A Russian excursion led by Admiral Fabian von Bellingshausen soon after circumnavigated the landmass. Another American, John Davis, captain of the vessel *Huron*, is credited with having been the first to set foot on land. Yet another American, this time Lieutenant Charles Wilkes of the U.S. Navy, during an expedition in 1838–42, determined that Antarctica was a bona fide continent.

As for who owns Antarctica now, the answer is still no one. Argentina established the first weather station on Laurie Island in the South Orkney Islands in 1904, and by 1908, they had claimed a portion of it as their own. Britain, as well as other nations, followed suit and attempted to establish ownership of at least some portion of this mammoth continent. However, if anyone can justifiably lay claim to Antarctica, it should be the Americans, for they have discovered and mapped more of the continent than all other nations combined. Yet they have neither claimed nor recognized any other claims of any part of Antarctica.

In May 1958, the United States recommended that the eleven nations of the International Geophysical Year establish a program to preserve the land just as it is. On December 1, 1959, agents of the twelve original nations agreed to the Antarctic Treaty that prohibits the use of the continent for warlike purposes and mandates it remain a nuclear-free zone. It permits only scientific research and overall peaceful use of the continent.

So, if you've the mind to withstand all that Antarctica can throw at you, it's yours for now.

There are more than seven seas.

First of all, is there a difference between an ocean and a sea? Well, in the general sense, no, for the two words are used interchangeably, but scientists attempt to make a distinction. Traditionally, the ocean, from the Greek *Oceanus* (eldest son of the Titans), is an interconnected body of salt water that has been split up, and covers seventy-one percent of the Earth's surface. This one giant ocean is divided into several major oceans and smaller seas. A sea refers to a large body of oceanic water that has its own characteristics and is partially enclosed by land—a subdivision of the oceans. There are exceptions, however. What about the Sargasso Sea, which lays in the middle of the North Atlantic Ocean?

What about the seven seas? Actually, there are many more than the proverbial seven seas; the real number is nearer to seventy-seven than seven. The ancients referred to the seven seas as the Indian Ocean, the Red Sea, the Persian Gulf, the Black Sea, the Sea of Azov, the Adriatic Sea, and the Caspian Sea. The designation became fashionable when Rudyard Kipling published a book of poems entitled *The Seven Seas*. Today, the term, though rarely used, stands for the Arctic Ocean, Southern Ocean (Antarctic), Indian Ocean, North Pacific Ocean, South Pacific Ocean, North Atlantic Ocean, and the South Atlantic Ocean.

As for how many seas there are, it's a matter of what definition you accept, but we can start by naming a few: the Mediterranean Sea, the Scottish Sea, the Adriatic Sea, the Sargasso Sea, the Arabian Sea, the Caribbean Sea, the North Sea, the Weddell Sea, the Sea of Azov, the Red Sea, the Yellow Sea, the Black Sea, the South China Sea, the Philippine Sea, the Coral Sea, the Irish Sea, the Bering Sea, the Norwegian Sea, the Sea of Japan, the Baltic Sea . . . you get the idea.

CHAPTER EIGHT

ART AND MUSIC

The most valuable work of art in the world mysteriously disappeared.

The Amber Room, the single most valuable work of art in the world, mysteriously disappeared, by order of Hitler, at the end of World War II.

Of all the exquisite objects that man has created, perhaps none has had a more curious or intriguing history than the famous *Amber Room*. The British Ambassador to the Court of Peter the Great once remarked that the room was "the eighth wonder of the world." Very few individuals were ever granted permission to see the room, and those who did were overwhelmed by a feeling of warmth and grandeur, as if they were in a dream or fantasy.

It all started in 1716 in Königsberg, Prussia. King Friedrich Wilhelm I of Prussia (1688–1740) and Tsar Peter (I) the Great of Russia (1672–1725) confirmed their anti-Swedish alliance by exchanging gifts to demonstrate their mutual respect and solidarity. Peter's gift was a company of Russian soldiers, each one at least seven feet tall, as recruits to complement the celebrated Prussian regiment of giant-sized grenadiers. In return, Wilhelm I gave Peter a yacht that would fit well in Peter's newly formed Russian navy. Wilhelm also gave Peter a set of panels, meticulously carved from selected true amber, which is fossilized tree resin from now-extinct conifers at least sixty million years old. Approximately one hundred square yards in area, and destined to line the ceiling, doors, and walls of a palace chamber, the architectural wonder was called *The Amber Room*, and it was one of the most magnificent and dramatic examples of the carver's art.

The astonishing *Amber Room* was baroque in character with amber mosaic panels depicting Roman landscapes showing, allegorically, four of the five basic senses. There were precise carvings of flowers, shells, trees, garlands, and tiny figurines. Immense mirrors, framed in gilt, set off each end of the room. Between the mirrors were chandeliers sparkling with hundreds of faceted amber drops. The various colors of amber in the room attested to its chilling impact: brilliant hues of red, gold, yellow, and brown. *The Amber Room* even contained dishes, vases, candlesticks, snuff boxes, powder boxes, and cutlery made of amber. Countless architects and craftsmen labored twelve years to complete the room.

After Tsar Peter took possession of this magnificent gesture from Wilhelm I, it was taken by sleigh to Saint Petersburg, where it was assembled in the Tsar's winter residence. By 1755, Tsarina Elizabeth (1709–61), daughter of the Tsar, had the entire room relocated to the Catherine Palace at Tsarskoe Selo, outside Saint Petersburg, where she continued to add exquisite amber objets d'art to the room as late as 1763.

Six tons of select, exceedingly rare amber were taken from the Baltic Coast to build the room, and when it was appraised in 1985, by way of drawings that survived Hitler's men, the amber panels were valued only in terms of weight to be worth an astounding one hundred million dollars. But when all the components needed to finish the room are considered—the carved, gilded woodwork that frames the amber panels; the selection, cutting, polishing, matching, joining together, and fitting of the numerous panels to create the end product; and the artistry of the carving—then the legitimate worth of *The Amber Room* is said in one word: *priceless!*

There were numerous people who fell victim to the mysterious *Amber Room*'s "300"-year history in Eastern Europe, and the room's present whereabouts continues to puzzle historians and laypersons alike. One theory has it that the room was taken apart and hidden during the Russian Revolution in 1917. Another postulates that the room was destroyed by fire during the Allied assault of 1944. Still another theory suggests that *The Amber Room* is entombed somewhere below ground in Kaliningrad, in present-day Russia. The most arresting theory has it that the room was dismantled sometime between 1941 and 1943 and moved to the Prussian Fine Arts Museum in Königsberg by order of Hitler himself. Then, in April 1945, just prior to the Soviet Army's taking control of the Prussian capital of Königsberg, the Nazis packed the panels, supervised by *The Amber Room*'s guardian, Dr. Alfred Rohde, onto a convoy of trucks and transported it out of the city. Rohde never revealed the whereabouts of the room and just before he was to be questioned by Soviet officials after the war, he, along with his wife, met with an untimely death.

In November 1991, *The Amber Room* once again became the center of a worldwide media blitz when Russian President Boris Yeltsin declared that the whereabouts of the room had been located: in Weimar, Germany, to be specific, buried in crates. If found, *The Amber Room* would be returned to Russia. However, many find the hunt for the room nonsense; it only revives bad memories of a time that most are trying to forget. At the same time, Hans Stadelmann, a retired German construction foreman, has made it his life's work to find *The Amber Room* and to this extent, he has added yet another interesting chapter to the history of the room.

Stadelmann will gain nothing financially if he finds the room. He is motivated by wanting to expiate for the sins of Nazi Germany. Armed with Nazi-era blueprints of the buildings in and around Weimar's main square, information from secret informants, and volumes of notes, photographs, and maps, Stadelmann is positive that the catacombs beneath Weimar will someday reveal the world's greatest art treasure.

Nevertheless, whatever the outcome, it's been three centuries since *The Amber Room* was given as a gift to Peter the Great and over seventy years since the room, the most valuable work of art in the world, mysteriously vanished.

Seeing great works of art can drive you crazy.

Since 1978, specialists and psychiatrists have counseled over 110 foreign visitors to Florence, Italy, for what has come to be known as Stendhal's Syndrome. These experts believe that exposure to great works of art in the city leads those with the propensity for psychological problems to be overwhelmed with bouts of mental turmoil such as suicidal urges, confusion, and panic.

Apparently the reaction is not modern, for this Renaissance city has overwhelmed travelers for centuries with its great works of art. French novelist Marie Henri Beyle (1783–1842), whose pseudonym was Stendhal, succumbed to the beauty of Florence almost two hundred years ago. He chronicled his emotional reaction in his book *Rome, Naples, and Florence.* The syndrome seems to occur in other cities that arouse one's emotions: Venice, Jerusalem, and Athens, to name a few.

It appears that it's not a city such as Florence that causes the problem, but rather the exposure to great works of art that can trigger dramatic reactions in an already unstable individual.

Even authors Henry James and Marcel Proust, along with psychoanalyst Sigmund Freud, admitted to being under the spell of Stendhal's Syndrome.

The famous Whistler painting is not called *Whistler's Mother*.

James Abbott McNeill Whistler (1834–1903) was an American painter and etcher who was influenced by Gustave Courbet and deeply moved by Japanese art. He took his first drawing lessons in Saint Petersburg, Russia, while his father built a railroad to Moscow. In 1851, he was appointed to the United States Military Academy at West Point, but was asked to leave after failing a chemistry class in his third year.

1855 found young Whistler in Paris, destined to be an expatriate. By 1863, he made London his primary home, becoming president of the Royal Society of British Artists in 1886. His most famous work, a painting of his mother done in London in 1872, which hangs in the Louvre, is called *Arrangement in Grey and Black, No. 1: Portrait of the Artist's Mother*, not *Whistler's Mother*. But why not just call it *Whistler's Mother?* Everybody else does.

As a proponent of art for art's sake, Whistler thought art should be abstract, simply responding to the artist's imagination. Accordingly, he resorted to obscure titles, influenced by music, the most abstract of arts. Such works as *Caprice in Purple and Gold, No. 2: The Golden Screen* (1864); *Symphony in Grey and Green: The Ocean* (1866–67); and *Old Battersea Bridge: Nocturne—Blue and Gold* (1872–75) demonstrate his need to remain abstract, holding that a painting should be a "joy to the artist."

Whistler produced a massive body of work that included over four hundred plate etchings, many of which are every bit the equal of Rembrandt, but none were ever called *Whistler's Mother*.

Great works of art are being destroyed.

A Turner, a Whistler, a Rothko, a Courbet, and even a Rembrandt, are all gone because there are no laws to protect them. It's natural to think that art is destroyed by forces beyond our control, such as natural disasters, wanton acts of individuals, or soldiers pillaging a town. Sad to report, there is a little-known, but well-established history of reckless and wholesale destruction of art by persons or institutions who are the guardians of such art.

Owners of works of art or their heirs hold sway over the fate of the art they control. One eccentric American collector invited his friends to play darts using a Rembrandt portrait as a target. The collector neither violated any public law nor was he the subject of any private restraint.

Owners and caretakers often destroy great works of art. The most regularly destroyed works are usually murals, portraits, nudes, and large-scale sculptures.

The case of the celebrated artist J. M. W. Turner, who died in 1851, and art critic John Ruskin, is most fascinating. Turner left the body of his unsold creations, about 19,300 drawings, watercolors, and oils, to the British nation, naming his confidant John Ruskin, as one of the executors of his estate. Ruskin was mortified by the sexual explicitness in much of the art and took it upon himself to decide its fate.

After great deliberation, Ruskin decided to burn Turner's erotic art. In actuality, Ruskin did not possess the pluck to commit such an unforgivable crime so he directed staff members at London's National Gallery of Art do the despicable deed in 1858.

Five years after the Turner fiasco, Gustave Courbet painted *Return from the Conference* (1863), a somewhat unappealing view of drunken clerics. Courbet was known as an anticleric and as such, the painting was never fully appreciated. The fate of this painting ended up in the hands of a devoutly religious individual who purchased the painting and then destroyed it in short order.

James McNeill Whistler, the painter of *Arrangement in Gray and Black, No. 1: Portrait of the Artist's Mother* (incorrectly called *Whistler's Mother*), was president of the Royal Society of British Artists in 1886. He painted a signboard for its meeting rooms, but two years later, after Whistler had distanced himself from the Society, it had his sign effaced and repainted by someone else.

Yet another wholesale destruction of art involved a Diego Rivera mural commissioned by Nelson Rockefeller to hang in the RCA Building. It was demolished by Rockefeller Center workmen in 1934 after Rivera, a devout Communist, declined to paint over a portrait of Lenin from the work entitled *Man at the Crossroads Looking with Hope and High Vision to the Choosing of a New and Better Future*.

In 1980, Donald Trump became a member of the much abhorred list of destroyers of art when he ordered several art deco sculptures by E. J. Kahn demolished after he had promised them to the Metropolitan Museum of Art.

Even the New York Historical Society, founded in 1804, is an accomplice in the needless destruction of art. They've had to destroy numerous works of art because they were stored in two substandard warehouses where they were victims of neglect and were permitted to mildew.

One can only speculate as to what other great works of art have fallen prey to some people's need to destroy beauty.

Caves were the first art studios and galleries.

The exact origins of painting are lost to history, but art historians theorize that painting began sometime in the latter part of the Old Stone Age (Upper Paleolithic Period—50,000–10,000 years ago) with evidence to be found in both France and Spain.

The most renowned cave paintings are in south central France at Lascaux, and in Altamira, Spain, dating back some ten thousand to thirty thousand years. These ancient cave paintings are most pleasing to the modern eye; both exhibit universal qualities. These paintings also depict reindeer, bison, ibexes, and other animals of the epoch in impressive detail.

The Altamira paintings were discovered by chance in 1869, when a little girl accidentally strayed into the cave while playing. The walls abound with gigantic paintings of bison, various other animals, and figures of men hunting for game. These paintings date back about fifteen thousand years while the Lascaux examples may even be another fifteen thousand years older.

The Lascaux paintings seem to follow an architectural scheme, with a main atrium adorned with wall frescoes and ceiling murals that give the room real presence. Additional rooms are adorned with depictions of animals produced by an advanced blowing technique: applying pigment blown from a reed or hollow bone. The various techniques used to execute these paintings are astonishing, given the painters' lack of experience and primitive materials.

It is interesting to note that evidence suggests people of the era did not inhabit the caves, but instead used them as primitive art studios and galleries.

Two sisters wrote "Happy Birthday to You."

As ubiquitous as the air we breathe and traditionally sung before the birthday boy or girl blows out the candles on the cake, "Happy Birthday to You" is the song that signifies one's celebration of one's birth. Written in 1893 by two unassuming sisters, the song is the most widely sung tune throughout the world.

Mildred J. Hill (1859–1916), an organist and concert pianist, and her sister Patty Smith Hill (1858–1946), composed, or rather arranged the elementary melody and lyrics in order that young children could sing it with confidence. It is interesting to note that the song's original title was "Good Morning to All."

The English horn is not English.

The sorrowful and mute-toned English horn is not English; it's not even a horn. The instrument comes from Vienna, (c. 1760), and it is a woodwind instrument of the oboe family, actually an alto oboe. The bassoon and the oboe d'amore are also members of the oboe family. The famed composer Johann Sebastian Bach used the English horn, then called an *oboe da caccia*. Today's English horn is long, thin, and straight in shape, while its earlier counterpart had a curved or horn-like shape.

Any explanations as to the origin of its name are most certainly conjecture, though some say its French name, *cor anglais*, "angled horn," was ultimately misinterpreted as English horn.

The painting of Washington Crossing the Delaware does not exist.

Arguably the most well-known painting ever done of George Washington, Founding Father of his country, and one of the true American icons, depicts his famous crossing of the Delaware: *Washington Crossing the Delaware*. This world-famous painting was done by the nineteenth-century artist Emanuel G. Leutze (1816–68). He was born in Gmünd, Germany, and by the age of nine he moved to Philadelphia with his parents. There he began to study painting, and in 1841, Leutze made his way to Düsseldorf, Germany, where he continued his studies for the next twenty years, refining his abilities in various other cities on the Continent. His last ten years were spent painting in his second country, the United States. Despite painting one of America's most revered works of art, he has always been a rather obscure figure in the world of art history.

Leutze did the painting of this historic moment in Düsseldorf, utilizing the Rhine as his representation for the Delaware. It began as a twelve-by-twenty-one-foot canvas in 1849, but in the latter part of 1850, he was forced to cut the painting from its frame so that he could save it from a fire that had engulfed his studio. In the process of heaving the large canvas through a studio window, it was ripped into about a half-dozen pieces. The insurance company actually reimbursed Leutze for his costs ($1,800) and took possession of the mutilated painting. They had it restored and it was entered in a Berlin art festival where it took a gold medal in 1852. The fate of the Leutze painting did not end there, for it was subsequently sold to the Bremen Museum, and in 1943, an Allied bombing raid destroyed it. The painting that very few Americans had ever seen no longer existed.

If this is so, what is the painting that many of us have seen? After Leutze was compensated for the loss, he was allowed to keep the painting for several months in order that he could make a copy of his original work. It is said that Leutze was inspired by Washington's crossing of the Delaware and that he had created the painting to inspire his fellow Germans to revolt, just as Washington and his comrades had done.

It is interesting to note that there are several rather significant historical errors in the painting. The boats depicted in Leutze's work are incorrect. The boats actually used were Durham craft, each forty to sixty feet long, while the boats in the painting are somewhat smaller in size. Moreover, the flag seen in the foreground has thirteen stars and stripes. What is important to note here is that the crossing took place on Christmas night in 1776; the flag of this type was not adopted until June 14, 1777.

The errors do not stop here. The soldiers in the painting are holding their arms in an upright position, something that would not have been done in a downpour of sleet, as the barrels would rust. Even Washington's position is questionable. Why would he have stood up in an overcrowded boat in such inclement weather? Old George had to be smarter than that.

As for the painting that we see in the Metropolitan Museum of Art in New York City, it is the 1851 replica that was purchased by a gentleman lover of art in 1897, and then donated to the Met.

Although whether Leutze's allegiance lay with the United States or Germany is not known, he is, nevertheless, buried in Washington, D.C.

The Impressionists did not coin the word "Impressionism."

Much to the dismay of lovers of art and artists themselves, the word *Impressionism*, as it applies to art, was not the invention of French painters. Though the painters associated with this era (1867–86) were bent on breaking with the French Academy School of Painting, they were, nevertheless, more wanderers than a focused group of painters. Much of the time they used unmixed, pure colors and small, loose brush strokes to produce paintings that demonstrated the visual reality of a scene, playing with light and color. They were arguably the first to take art out of doors and capture landscapes in a vague manner.

Monet and a coterie of his peers exhibited their "new art" in April 1874 at the studio of photographer Felix Tournachon, also known as Nadar. Included in this exhibition was a Monet piece entitled *Impression-Sunrise* (1872). Present at the showing was the noted art critic, Louis Leroy, who wrote for the satirical publication *Le Charivari*. On April 25, Leroy reviewed the exhibition and his response was less than favorable. He entitled his review "L'Exposition des Impressionistes," which he thought would hopefully demonstrate his contempt and dislike for what he saw. Thus it was Leroy, not the painters, who coined the epithet that today describes their style of work, a style that conveys an overall impression produced by a scene or object to the exclusion of minutiae. Leroy likened Monet's brush technique to something resembling "black tongue-lickings."

Subsequently, the painters of this style did embrace the moniker *Impressionists* for themselves, despite its original pejorative connotation, but in 1879, they renamed themselves the Group of Independent Artists. Other memorable Impressionists were Renoir, Pissaro, Degas, Sisley, Morisot, Bazille, Cézanne, and Manet.

The Spanish painter El Greco signed his paintings in Greek.

El Greco (1541–1614), the renowned Spanish painter, was a skilled draftsman and highly schooled in the art of the brush. His paintings demonstrated refined elegance, religious intensity, and penetrating dramatic style. El Greco's use of the distortion of form, space, and light often served to underscore the spiritual aspects of figures and events.

Since El Greco did most of his greatest work in Spain, the Spanish conferred upon him the title of El Greco, meaning "the Greek," for he was born a Greek, in Candia, Crete. His real name was Doménikos Theotokópoulos, and this was the name he routinely affixed to his paintings using Greek letters, sometimes attaching the name Kres, "the Cretan," to the end of it. During his years spent in Italy, he was called II Greco, also meaning "the Greek."

El Greco died in Toledo, Spain, and was buried there, yet no evidence of his final resting place survives.

The Emmy Award is not named after a person.

Unlike the movie industry's highest accolade, the Oscar, or the theater's most coveted award, the Tony, the Emmy was not named after any individual.

Feeling that the fledgling industry of television needed its equivalent of the Oscar or Tony award, Charles Brown, then president of the burgeoning National Academy of Television Arts and Sciences (NATAS), formed a panel in 1948, to recognize the most outstanding achievements in TV that year and to select a name and symbol for the award.

The initial choices were rather prosaic, even by scientific standards. One of the top contenders was Iconoscope, a large orthicon tube, actually an early TV camera tube. That idea was nixed because of the possibility of referring to the award as the Ike. Ultimately, it was a pioneer TV engineer, Harry Lubcke, soon to become president of the academy (1949–50), who proffered the name Emmy, a variation on Immy, a nickname for the image orthicon tube, which was state of the art at the time. The choice won the day and now the academy had an Emmy. Next they had to decide what it was to look like.

The statue itself was created by Louis McManus, who was awarded a gold lifetime membership in the academy and one of the six statuettes presented at the first awards banquet on January 25, 1949. By 1955, the awards ceremonies were nationally televised, and from that point on, they became an annual event, attended by a long list of celebrities.

The largest painting in history is missing.

In 1846, artist and writer John Banvard (1815–91), a native New Yorker, displayed the world's largest painting. Measuring an enormous twelve feet high and reputedly an unbelievable three miles long, his *Panorama of the Mississippi* depicted twelve hundred miles of the Mississippi River valley from the embouchure of the Missouri to New Orleans, and everything in between.

Banvard, inspired by his father, who was an architect, spent the 1830s as a portrait painter. It was odd training for an artist who was soon to embark upon the greatest project of his life and the greatest example of panoramic art. He spent much of 1840 traveling by boat up and down the Mississippi River, drawing landscape after landscape, some four hundred in all. He then constructed a makeshift studio in Louisville, Kentucky, to begin his masterwork, which was to occupy the next five years of his life.

In 1841, the first section of his work in process was displayed. Upon completing a section of the work, each one had to be stored in an enormous cylinder. Finished in 1846, Banvard took the "largest painting in the world" on a whirlwind world tour, achieving his greatest success in England, helped by the generosity of Queen Victoria, where it was exhibited at Windsor Castle. Audiences from New York to Paris were held spellbound as they watched Banvard unspool his canvas showing an authentic view of America, with riverboats, Indian encampments, and forts all represented in precise detail. Amazingly enough, he duplicated this enormous painting so that one version could be viewed in England, while another copy could be seen in France. Banvard's painting was the rage, enlisting kudos from the likes of Dickens, Longfellow, and Thoreau.

Regrettably, Banvard's complete panorama no longer exists. After all, a painting of its size was not easily preserved. From constant use, the immense canvas began to disintegrate and could only be preserved in sections. Some sections were removed to be utilized as scenery in the opera house of Watertown, South Dakota, the final home of the Banvard family.

Banvard died in 1891, and the whereabouts of the majority of the largest painting in the world, the *Panorama of the Mississippi*, died with him.

Music did not come from Nashville or London.

It is often postulated that early man created the first concept of music by striking two objects, generally sticks, together to scare off intruders. Early man obviously found some sort of enjoyment out of the sounds he created and soon began striking one object after another in an effort to create new sounds: music.

The denizens of ancient Mesopotamia, the region between the Tigris and Euphrates Rivers, are said to have been the originators of western music. The Fertile Crescent, occupied by the Assyrians, Babylonians, and Sumerians from 2500 to 500 B.C. left behind crude examples of almost every class of musical instrument: idiophones, devices that resonate as a whole; aerophones, devices that resonate a column of blown air; cordophones, devices with strings to be struck or plucked; and membranophones, made of animal skins pulled over a resonating body. A hymn etched in stone and dating from 800 B.C. is evidence enough that the Mesopotamians had even produced a rudimentary system of musical notation.

The Greeks supplied the most direct connection with musical development in western Europe. They literally dominated the evolution of music, giving the world an elaborate system of music theory. Two fundamental Greek religious sects, one faithful to Apollo, the other, acolytes of Dionysus, became the paradigms for the two aesthetic poles, Classical and Romantic that have been dominant throughout Western cultural history.

Drama was created by one man.

Drama, or tragedy, as some students of the stage call it, was the accomplishment of one man. Aeschylus (c. 524–456 B.C.) is acknowledged to be the creator of drama. As the first of the three most distinguished ancient Athenian writers of tragedy, he changed the format of the play forever.

Previous to Aeschylus's time there was only one actor, the poet himself, in the play. He would assume numerous roles by changing his mask and costume, but was only able to carry on dialogue with the chorus. What Aeschylus did was to create drama; he introduced a second actor. In time, the duties of the chorus were diminished until their function became nonexistent, as the actors assumed all the responsibilities for action and thought.

Aeschylus, the father of drama, is with us today in his seven plays (he wrote about ninety) that exist in complete form: *Agamemnon, The Libation Bearers, The Furies, The Persians, Seven Against Thebes, The Supplicants*, and *Prometheus Bound*.

CHAPTER NINE

PLANTS AND ANIMALS

Dinosaurs invented flowers.

Presently, flowering plants, known as angiosperms, are easily the most abundant of land foliage, numbering countless species, and most play an important role in the survival of mammals. The variety of angiosperms range from oaks, birches, maples, and all other broad-leafed trees to just about every berry-producing bush and shrub, grasses, palms, and dandelions, along with tulips, leeks, lettuce, spinach, and innumerable other plants. Virtually every plant utilized for food, raw materials, and beauty, save the conifers and a few other nonflowering plants, is an angiosperm. How did dinosaurs invent flowers?

It all came about at the dawn of the Cretaceous Period (144–65 million years ago) as herbivores began consuming vegetation low to the ground. Low-growing shrubs and seedlings were now confronted with extinction by herbivores. The response by the early angiosperms was to adapt quickly. Some would grow as fast as possible to reach a height so that low-browsing herbivores could not endanger them. Yet other angiosperms took a gamble: they attempted to spread enough seeds, with the help of animal pollinators (insects, birds, bats, etc.), onto yet undiscovered areas of bare Earth to reproduce a group of shrubs immediately. It worked! This reproduction by way of seeds guaranteed that another generation of seeds, hence plants, would survive to once again reproduce in yet another area where herbivores had yet to go. These primitive angiosperms were able to do this where the conifers and other nonflowering plants had to rely on the wind, a less efficient means of spreading their seeds.

A symbiosis occurred between the low-feeding beaked dinosaurs and flowering plants. As the Cretaceous Period produced more varieties of beaked dinosaurs, countless more angiosperm families evolved. By the Late Cretaceous Period, angiosperms counted more species as their own than the conifers and other nonflowering plants combined. At the end of the Cretaceous Period, enormous extinctions were the order of the day. Most nonflowering plants disappeared, yet the mutable angiosperms continued to evolve and their ancestors live to this very day.

Today's angiosperms are not dependent upon low-feeding herbivores for their superiority over conifers and other nonflowering plants. Nevertheless, in the early years of the Cretaceous Period, square-snouted and pincer-beaked herbivores were crucial in assisting the flowering plants to overcome the other floral competition. Angiosperms soon became the fastest growing plant group.

In this way, dinosaurs were paramount to the survival of flowering plants. You could even say that they invented them.

The porcupine does not shoot its quills at its attacker.

Here we go again. Is this a fabulous factoid or what? A porcupine shoots its quills at its attacker. Never happens. They simply can't do it because they have no way of launching the quills, which are long, sharp bristles of hairs that are fused together.

The porcupine defends itself, if running away doesn't work first, by striking its attacker with its quilled tail. The quills are attached very loosely, and when touched they stick into the attacker because most have barbed ends. If you should accidentally touch a sleeping porcupine, the result would be the same, a hand full of very sharp quills that are hard to remove. The quills may even cause infection and eventual death in certain animals.

As an aside, some people mistakenly refer to North American porcupines as hedgehogs, which is incorrect, because they only exist in the Eastern Hemisphere.

So the next time you run across your local porcupine, you won't have to dodge flying quills, but just don't touch it.

The beautiful ladybug is deadly.

The gentle, beautiful ladybug (*Coccinellidae*), or as the eminent zoologist Miriam Rothschild preferred to call it, a ladybird beetle (in honor of "Our Lady" the Virgin Mary), is quite poisonous, in fact deadly.

Ladybugs, of which there are over forty-five hundred varieties, are friends of gardeners and farmers the world over. They are voracious predators that can devour troublesome insects with miraculous efficiency.

However, despite their usefulness, Miriam Rothschild discovered that one ladybug egg, when injected into a cat's bloodstream, will render a cat dead in short order. Remember, one minute egg, just one, can kill a feline! And we thought they were so lovely and innocent.

There's more to the human skin than meets the eye.

The human skin, the body's largest organ and one of its most complicated, is made up of three principal layers, with the paper-thin epidermis visible. Beneath the epidermis is the dermis, and then the subcutaneous tissue.

What makes human skin so absolutely complex is that in one square inch of the average adult there exists an elaborate network of 20 blood vessels and 78 nerves; together with 65 hairs and muscles; 78 sensors for heat, 13 for cold, 160–165 for pressure; 650 sweat glands (facilitates the elimination of wastes and cooling of the body, and on very hot days the skin can release over 2,500 calories); some 1,300 nerve endings; and almost 20 million cells!

As the body's largest organ, the skin measures about 18.5 to 21 square feet in the average adult, and it has a weight of between 8.5 to 10 pounds. The skin is continually shedding and replacing itself, and during an average lifetime a normal-sized man or woman will shed about 105 pounds of skin, making for about 900 new coats of skin in all.

The skin is virtually waterproof and effectively protects against bacteria and chemicals invading most parts of the body. It also regulates internal body temperature, contributes to the body's immune system, cushions the body's internal organs and bones from injury by outside forces, and does a host of other invaluable duties.

The dinosaur is a "terrible lizard."

It wasn't until 1842 that anyone had a name for these gargantuan creatures from a very distant time. Then the world's most distinguished zoologist and anatomist of the Victorian era, Sir Richard Owen (1804–92), coined the name *Dinosauria*, from Greek origins meaning "terrible lizard."

Until Owen—who vehemently opposed the Darwinian theory of evolution—gave the world a name for these curious creatures, the nascent science of paleontology didn't know what to call them.

French zoologist Baron Georges Cuvier (1769–1832), the father of paleontology, had originated the methodology of reconstructing form and function in fossil creatures less than a half century earlier. Although the study of the Earth's crust had only gone on for about one generation, the naturalists of 1840 had been aware that the reptilian epoch preceded the mammalian epoch. Owen created a term to describe the gargantuan land animals that roamed the Earth in prehistory.

Now scientists were confronted with a new science, paleontology, and they had a new method to study a new fossil find, the dinosaur, or "terrible lizard."

The largest shark in the world is harmless.

This leviathan of the deep blue, *Rhincodon typus*, is second only in size to the whale. This gentle giant, also known as the whale shark, is unique to the family of sharks (250–300 species). A loner by nature, the whale shark, is neither aggressive nor generally a threat to man, yet it is the largest of all sharks and the largest of all living fishes.

The biggest whale shark measures forty-five feet and weighs about fifteen tons, although some specimens have been sighted in the sixty to eighty-foot range. The whale shark is generally brown or gray in color and is uniquely marked with small white or yellow spots and thin vertical lines of white and yellow. It is a lethargic creature that swims slowly near the surface of the water, sometimes colliding with ships. When swimming—mouth agape—it takes in thousands of gallons of water, all the while feeding on large amounts of plankton, small fishes, and squid that are strained through its gills. Unlike most sharks, this enormous fish neither consumes nor desires large fish or other large vertebrates such as humans.

The whale shark is also unique to most other sharks in that its mouth is spread across as opposed to under the front of its face, and it is several feet wide. The nostrils are between four and five feet apart, and they resemble eyes. Thousands of scarcely visible, minute teeth apparently serve no logical purpose in catching its food, although it is believed that sharks were the first living creatures to develop teeth. What's more interesting is that the whale shark has the singular ability, should it accidently swallow large objects, to eject them by turning its stomach out of its mouth, then drawing it back into itself.

As for the shark's reputation for being a notoriously violent and aggressive animal that attacks humans at every turn, the whale shark is an exception. In fact, stories abound of skin divers hitching rides on these gentle giants, who appear to enjoy the company, because they are usually such solitary creatures.

Because of the shark's near perfect physiology, it has all but defied evolution for well over two hundred million years, staying basically the same, and is possibly the most proficient of all predators. Yet the whale shark is an enigmatic creature, who neither relishes confrontation nor the taste of humans, something to be thankful for.

Not much is known about the whale shark; it still remains much of a mystery. When it is finished feeding for several days, it then descends to depths unknown, to places unknown, and in numbers unknown.

The mistletoe is a vampire.

For centuries, the European mistletoe plant (*Viscum album*) and its American cousin have been synonymous with numerous traditions and holidays, the most famous of which is the Christmas season. It is said that the ancient Druids and their contemporaries regarded it as a sacred plant. They cut the mistletoe that lived on oak trees and gave it to others as charms. Teutonic legend speaks of an arrow fashioned from mistletoe causing the death of Balder, the son of the goddess Frigg. Mistletoe was a ceremonial plant in early European civilizations. The custom of kissing underneath a sprig of mistletoe during Christmastime most likely comes from its history as such a plant.

However, this harmless looking evergreen plant, of which there are many varieties, is anything but harmless. It's often referred to as the vampire plant. Members of the mistletoe family are considered parasites. They live by attaching themselves with roots to various types of trees. These roots, actually called bark suckers, are used to suck nourishment from the host plant, which can sometimes be one of its very own kind, often weakening the host plant and ultimately killing both plants, since it will only live as long as its host plant does.

Mistletoe plants also produce berries that are so toxic to animals and humans that death can be the result, so should you find yourself underneath the mistletoe, pay close attention to what you're kissing.

Bats are the only mammals that really fly and much more.

Dracula is arguably one of the most loathsome creations of any writer's imagination. The Dracula legend was created in 1897 by the English novelist Bram Stoker (1847–1912). It was replete with all the necessities of a good horror novel: a villain of epic proportions, vampires, a European setting, and suspense, all inspired by the abominable vampire bat. However, the image of the vampire bat, one of at least eight hundred species of bats (*Chiroptera*), who mercilessly sucks blood from its victims, unforgiving in its relentless pursuit of its next victim, is grossly undeserved.

The diminutive vampire bat of Latin America, about the size of the common sparrow, with a wingspan of seven inches, and weighing less than two ounces, looms large in the minds of those who fear its evil power. Probably hated more than any other animal on Earth, save the shark or snake, the vampire bat's true story is not that of a merciless killer.

New field research demonstrates that the vampire bat shares blood meals with hungry mates who actually beg for food: such generosity is all but unheard of in the animal kingdom. Moreover, medical researchers have now found a link between the anticlotting substance in the bat's saliva and the development of a new heart drug that could save countless lives.

The vampire bat's feeding habits require it to suck blood from mostly cattle and horses; on rare occasions it will nibble on a human, but it does not kill its victims. Other bat species feed primarily on insects and plants. After making a minute bite, the vampire bat then sucks up about one tablespoon of blood in about a half hour. The process is basically painless because the vampire bat's saliva also contains an organic anesthetic. An anticoagulant can keep the blood flowing from an opening in the victim for up to six hours, which permits several vampire bats to feed simultaneously.

The anticoagulant found in vampire bat saliva is up to twenty times stronger than any substance manufactured today, and the medical implications are tremendous, for blood-clotting problems are ever-present in heart patients. Many of the most prominent pharmaceutical companies are investigating the prospect of utilizing the vampire bat's saliva to save heart patients, since the drugs now in use have a most deleterious side effect: life-threatening bleeding.

The vampire bat defies the myths that surround it. Like all bats, it is a mammal, not a bird, but unlike other mammals, it can fly. It is useful in medical research, it navigates by echolocation, and is even capable of walking, running, and hopping.

It must be said that although the vampire bat became a paradigm for the story of *Dracula*, it lives only in Latin America, not in Europe.

Plants and animals have always been at war with each other.

The British naturalist Charles Darwin (1809–82), whose theory of evolution, along with Alfred Wallace's, revolutionized the science of biology, established evolution by natural selection. It became increasingly apparent to Darwin that plants and plant eaters coevolved. As plant eaters (herbivores) met plants head-on in a war to survive, plants began to build up resistance to such unsolicited acts by developing methods to thwart plant eaters. Some plants kill their attackers with deadly alkaloids, while others fend them off with thorns and spines, and still others produce plant tissue that is simply unchewable.

Don't think for one moment that plant eaters have no recourse. The evolution of herbivores produced stronger and more efficient teeth for pulverizing the toughest of leaves. These herbivores even evolved more advanced digestive systems, fermenting chambers that can render poisonous plants benign. Some animals have also grown taller in order to reach higher into the unprotected areas of trees.

This endless war between plants and plant eaters began on land four hundred million years ago during the Silurian Period, when the first algae inhabited the bare Earth and the herbivorous arthropods evolved to consume them. From that moment on, the war between the two has raged with unabated vigor.

The tuna fish is a technological marvel that never stops swimming.

A true tuna (*Thunnus*) is a fish, sometimes called tunny, of which there are about seven species. From albacore and skipjack to yellowfin and bluefin, these magnificent creatures of the sea are found mostly in temperate and tropical waters. As a food, tuna has become de rigueur in the diets of many Americans. It was even a principle means of nourishment to many of the ancients who populated the Mediterranean Basin. As a fighting game fish, it has few equals.

Curiously, studies indicate that the much loved and much maligned tuna is different from all other species of fish. It is a highly sophisticated creature, which, unlike other fish, is warm-blooded—its body temperature is generally 20 degrees Fahrenheit higher than the surrounding water. Therefore, in order to keep itself warm, it is condemned to a life of continual motion and feeding, or else it will die.

Tunas travel at high speed, foraging the seas for food. It is an energy gamble, since they expend more energy looking for food than any other fish in the sea, save the great white shark. Tunas are deft swimmers and can easily exhaust the efforts of the much respected swimmer, the salmon. As such, tunas find it beneficial to swim with dolphins, whose food-finding capabilities are enhanced by sonar. How do tuna swim continuously?

Research has shown that they are close to hydrodynamic perfection for low drag and high speed. Torpedolike in shape, their fins assume a swept-back position, much like the B-1 bomber at high speed.

Tunas have both red and white muscles, thus they are both sprinters and marathoners. A tuna's circulatory system runs underneath the skin unlike most fish, whose cold blood runs under the spine.

Tunas have richer blood and 20 percent more of it than other fish. To breathe at high speed, they use a type of ramjet technology: holding their mouths open while swimming, thus forcing water to pass through their gills. The downside is that they've lost the muscles necessary to pump their gills as do other fish. Simply put, they could not survive if they stopped swimming, therefore they are forced to swim to live.

Fishermen attest to their awesome power and speed. They are oftentimes clocked at 55 miles per hour, which is remarkable, considering water is eight hundred times denser than air. Consider this: a bullet from a .45 caliber handgun has a muzzle velocity of approximately 1,400 feet per second, yet it can only penetrate water for about six to eight feet. Tunas achieve their speed by turning over about forty-five degrees on their sides, thus assuming the position of an animate hydrofoil. These creatures are simply a sight to behold.

So the next time you pass a can of tuna on the supermarket shelf, think about this high-tech marvel of the sea. It is a super fish that can rocket to a speed of 55 miles per hour in a medium that can stop a bullet in just a few feet, dive quickly to depths that would crush a submarine, and come racing up from the bowels of the deep blue to give a sports fisherman one of the biggest thrills of his life, all the while processing enough water to acquire sufficient oxygen to keep its body temperature near that of a human being.

Bears "do not" hibernate.

In actuality, bears are not true hibernators. They may become very torpid during winter months, but their bodily functions, such as heart rate, breathing, and temperature do not drop to levels that constitute true hibernation. Many scientists refer to this time of prolonged sleep as winter lethargy or incomplete hibernation.

Bears (family *Ursidae*) are most closely related to the dog and raccoon families. The Alaskan brown bear, also called the Kodiak, is the largest living carnivore, weighing up to seventeen hundred pounds. Caution is the prudent approach, for bears can, when aroused, become easily awakened from their deep winter sleep and reach full activity within minutes. By the way, during winter months, bears do take an occasional stroll out of their dens, and if you think you can outrun them, think again. They can achieve speeds in excess of twenty-five miles per hour. Moreover, many of them can climb right up a tree after you, and a good number of them are superb swimmers.

The dove is hardly the bird of peace.

The 1960s ushered in the era of love and peace: one of the most familiar symbols of the peace movement was the dove, but if those who revere the dove (a small pigeon, family *Columbidae*) as a symbol of peace really knew the true characteristics of this bird, they would re-think their choice.

Konrad Z. Lorenz (1903–89), the renowned Austrian pioneer in ani-mal behavior and recipient of the Nobel Prize (1973) for medicine and physiology, sought to find out just how peaceful these beautiful crea-tures really are. As with many of his research projects, Lorenz estab-lished a colony of birds from which he selected his subjects. He placed a male turtledove and a female ringdove in a cage together and left his home (Altenburg) and departed on a trip to Vienna. Upon his return, he was astonished and disturbed to discover the turtledove facedown in the cage, his back devoid of feathers, and bleeding profusely.

Lorenz duplicated the study using wolves and discovered that they did not engage each other in battle. As a classic scientist, who authored the seminal work *On Aggression*, Lorenz kept copious notes on his ob-servations. From his research, he concluded that the wolves knew one of them would most assuredly die; hence, animals that are capable of killing for their food are less apt to turn that power on one another. He also noticed the converse to be true, realizing that those animals that are capable of fleeing their predators exhibit no reluctance to fight to the death.

The next time you think about the dove as the bird of peace, think again.

The giant sequoia is not the oldest living thing.

For generations Sequoia National Park in northern California has been home to the "oldest and largest" living thing on Earth. The giant sequoia called General Sherman, estimated to be between twenty-five hundred and three thousand years old, has always been thought by many to hold that notable distinction.

It may come as a surprise to most, but the General Sherman is not the oldest living thing, even though it is most certainly the largest, weighing nearly three million pounds. A much less impressive tree, found mostly in the White Mountains of eastern California, called the bristlecone pine (*Pinus aristata*), holds the record as the oldest living thing. There are numerous examples of the Great Basin variety of this tree that are over four thousand years old, with one tree, called Methuselah, exceeding four thousand six hundred years of age.

How does the unexciting bristlecone pine (the name derives from the prickles found on its cones) outlive all other trees, including the mighty sequoia? The answer is slow growth and a cool, dry environment, all of which reduce the chance of the tree becoming a victim of insects or diseases. Moreover, the bristlecone pine can exist without many branches or roots. Needles stay on the tree up to thirty years. This prolonged life of its needles enables the tree to withstand many years of drought or severe cold.

Since bristlecone pine trees live so long, they assist scientists in studying past climates by examining their rings. A ring's thickness is a result of temperature and quantity of precipitation.

The bristlecone pine is most surely a botanical wonder.

Moths "do not" eat clothing.

We've all had clothes eaten by moths, haven't we? In truth, moths (*Lepidoptera*, the second largest order of insects) do not eat clothes or anything else during their entire adult lives, short as that may be. It's the larvae of the clothes moth, which hatch into caterpillars that are deposited in clothing, that do the damage. They just love anything made of wool. By the time one sees clothes moths—close relatives of butterflies—in the closet, it's simply much too late.

The myths about dolphins are true.

The dolphin (not to be confused with the dolphin fish, which is used for food and often referred to as *mahi-mahi*) is an aquatic mammal (*Delphinidae*, a small, toothed whale), and a direct relative of the smaller porpoise. Legends as early as ancient Greek times abound, telling of the dolphin's miraculous feats of bravery and intelligence. Plutarch's (c. A.D. 46–120) description of a dolphin that saved Telemachus, son of Odysseus, from drowning and brought him to shore, is but one of countless examples of the dolphin's place in Greek and Roman lore. Even the celebrated Roman official, author, and scientist, Pliny the Elder (A.D. 23/24–79), told of a dolphin-human connection in his *Natural History*, a classic of Latin Literature.

Until the twentieth century, the accounts of the dolphin's miraculous feats of bravery and benevolence were viewed as simply good storytelling, but now scientific research confirms that dolphins do exhibit an obvious affinity toward humans; their kindness and helpfulness have no pale. Even when trapped in the fisherman's net they do not attack their captor and there is no record of dolphins ever having harmed any person. Through the centuries, sailors have welcomed the sight of dolphins as a sign of good sailing.

These magnificent creatures of the ocean, which possess a sagacity that exceeds everything else swimming in the innumerable bodies of water on Earth, have unquestionably lived up to the mix of fact and fantasy that has been linked to them.

Moreover, their high-tech sonar, called *echolocation,* is the envy of anyone who has ever spent a moment underneath the surface of the water. Dolphins can easily navigate through the murkiest of waters. Their ability to learn just about anything, from simple to complex tasks, including the emulation of human speech, is second only to man, and it is not hard to grasp why the early Greeks had speculated that dolphins had once been men.

There are creepy-crawlers on your face.

Believe it or not, your face is a repository for little creepy-crawlers, tiny mites. They have a narrow, cigar-like body, eight short legs, and continually crawl in colonies on your face. They are called *Demodex folliculorum* and *Demodex brevis*. With the aid of a magnifying instrument that will enlarge objects at least thirty times, these mites, though nearly transparent, are sometimes visible.

It seems that these little varmints have been with man since time immemorial. There is no cure, and oddly enough, they may even be beneficial. The *Demodex folliculorum* inhabits hair follicles and deposits its eggs in the sebaceous glands. At night, when all is quiet, it makes it way, along with countless others, across the face, in search of yet another new follicle to call home. The *Demodex brevis* is much the same as its cousin, but chooses to inhabit the glands surrounding the hair follicles.

Although discovered in the nineteenth century, these creepy-crawlers are still much of a mystery. However, it has been speculated that they may contribute to the cleansing of the hair follicles and glands.

The next time you think that something is crawling on your face, you're probably right.

The common cat has two sets of vocal cords.

A domestic cat (genus *Felis*) is born with not one but two sets of vocal cords. The voice box contains one set, the true vocal cords, that make the well-known meow. They are set in motion by means of air passing across them and in turn are regulated by the movement of the arytenoids, the muscles within them, and minute changes in the configuration of the larynx. The other set is sometimes referred to as the false vocal cords. These cords are situated above the true vocal cords and are vibrated on inhaling and exhaling, thus making an automatic, unremitting purring sound.

A word of caution: this purring sound is not always an indication that the cat is content, since cats sometimes purr when hungry or angry.

Man is a fish.

The ordinary fish is unique in the evolutionary process: it is the first animal to have a backbone instead of a shell as a framework for its body; it is the most primeval form of vertebrate life, dating from the Ordovician Period about five hundred million years ago.

The primitive fish form was the wellspring of the vertebrate lineage that eventually led to amphibians, reptiles, mammals, marsupials, apes, and subsequently, man himself. In a sense, man is simply a highly evolved fish.

The apple and the rose are relatives.

It is believed that apples have been a preferred fruit of man for some 2.5 million years. Charcoaled remains of apples dating back to at least 6500 B.C. have been unearthed in Europe and Asia Minor. Whether apples, the king of fruits, grew wild or were cultivated in fields is still a mystery. What isn't a mystery is that they are direct descendants of the family *Rosaceae*, which also includes—you guessed it—the queen of flowers, the rose.

The first known cultivated apples appeared under the rule of King Ramses II of Egypt (1290–1224 B.C.), when orchards were planted along the Nile River Delta. The ancient Greeks followed with a systematic method of cultivation about 300 B.C., producing several varieties. However, the ancient Romans had the greatest success with growing the "golden fruit" and producing thirty-six different varieties, as attested to by Pliny the Elder, in his monumental work, *Natural History*.

As for the apple's connection to the Bible, no mention is made in Genesis. Biblical teachers believe that if the Hebrews had named a particular fruit found among the inhabitants in the Garden of Eden, it probably would have been the pomegranate. Still, Christian folklore heard in India stated that the fruit was the banana, which is actually an herb.

Today, the apple, related to the rose, and the king of fruits, is the most widely grown fruit tree in temperate climates and boasts over seven thousand varieties in the United States alone.

Some living creatures are immortal.

Oh, to live forever! To experience the knowledge of the ages. To never die. Well, that pipe dream is just that, an unrealistic dream, for mankind, anyway. However, some creatures seem to be virtually immortal.

The late Professor L. L. Woodruff of Yale University chronicled the particular history of a select few individuals of the slippery animalcule Paramecium through 11,000 consecutive generations. One cell splits to become two, the two to become four, and so on. It appeared that each cell was immortal, for there was no way of ascertaining just how many years or centuries this exact process of asexual reproduction would continue without any animalcule Paramecium dying of old age. It's astonishing to think that this lowly creature has the secret to eternal life.

However, it must be said that the hydra, a freshwater animal that inhabits lakes and ponds, is in on the secret, too. The cells of the hydra constantly renew themselves, and are never more than a month old. The colonial type polyp known as the coral can also perform this miraculous feat of immortality.

The firefly really does produce light.

The firefly (*Lampyridae*), also called the lightning bug, is a nocturnal luminous insect related to the beetle. About two thousand species inhabit both temperate and tropical areas. A cousin of the firefly is the common glowworm.

Fireflies, or beetles if you will, grow to a length of about one inch and possess light organs composed of fat on both sides of the abdomen. The organs are designed with air tubes and nerves. A nervous reaction takes place that stimulates the air tubes, they in turn emit oxygen, which mixes with a substance in the fat called luciferin, and the end result is an emission of light in the visible spectrum that is used as a mating signal. Each species flashes its own unique light signal.

Some primitive cultures place fireflies in bottles to use as lanterns. They do emit enough flickering illumination to light the way. Certain frogs consume such large quantities of fireflies that they themselves actually glow.

The banana is a curiosity.

Historians and farmers alike find the banana to be a curiosity. Even though it has a treelike appearance and its fruit has been mistaken for a giant fig, the banana is not a fig, it's not even a fruit, it's an herb. Like all herbs, after fruiting, the plant simply dies.

It is believed that the banana made its debut about four millennia ago in the Indus Valley of present-day Pakistan. Its exact origin is thought to be so ancient that even Hindu folklore states that the banana was the forbidden fruit of the Garden of Eden. The banana probably grew wild at first, but it wasn't too long before man civilized the herb to create a banana of increased flavor and that was all but seedless.

The banana didn't find its way out of the Indus Valley until the Arab traders took the delectable herb to Egypt in the seventh century A.D. It finally reached the Americas in 1516, with the help of Christian monks, who planted the herb on the island of Hispaniola. Not until one hundred years after the American Revolution did this delicious herb find its way into the United States.

Some male creatures actually give birth.

This bizarre occurrence happens with two small marine fish, the beautiful and exotic seahorse and its cousin, the pipefish. Both the seahorse and the pipefish are found throughout temperate and tropical waters.

Diminutive as these two fish appear, ranging from two inches to twelve inches, they are capable of receiving the eggs—upwards of two hundred—that are deposited into their pouches by their female counterparts. Once fertilized and safe inside the pouch of either male fish, the eggs incubate anywhere from eight days to several weeks, at which time they are born alive. So, in a very strange way, the seahorse and its cousin the pipefish are the products of a father who is also a mother.

Also, the seahorse has the ability to change its color in an effort to disguise its whereabouts from unwanted interlopers.

Whales are the fastest growing of all animals.

Immortalized in literature; valued as a means of subsistence; prized for its commercial benefits, the whale (order *Cetacea*, which includes dolphins, porpoises, belugas, and narwhals) is the fastest-growing animal in the world. The gestation period for a whale is about fifteen months. During this time, the fetus develops from a microscopic egg to a weight of fifteen tons (thirty thousand pounds) and reaches a length of twenty-three feet before it is born.

After birth, the baby whale continues to grow at an astonishing rate, nourished only by its mother's milk. After weaning it becomes self-sufficient. By the end of the first year of life, a young whale can be as much as sixty-five feet long and weigh up to 65 tons. The adult whale can achieve a weight in excess of 160 tons (blue whale) and grow to a length surpassing one hundred feet. Oddly enough, this tremendous growth rate is accomplished on a diet of small, two-inch crustaceans known as krill.

Corn is a grass.

Surprisingly, corn is the only grain indigenous to the Americas. Actually, it is a tall, annual cereal grass. The American Indians cultivated and crossbred corn long before Columbus's landing in the New World, and their efforts led to the corn we are all familiar with today. It comprised the lion's share of their diets and was known as maize.

Corn is the most versatile of all grains, used not only for food, but to make such things as fuel and plastics. Its presence wasn't known in Europe until Columbus's second trip in 1496.

Some fish are full of antifreeze.

Imagine swimming in polar waters where temperatures are at or below the freezing point much of the time. Normally, fish would freeze to death in such cold temperatures, but nature has seen to it that they survive. How do fish avoid becoming frozen in the frigid waters of Antarctica, while a man would be reduced to a large ice cube?

The simplest way is for fish to remain in deep water, away from the ice that causes immediate freezing. This method is called *supercooling*. However, a much more realistic method is to have something in the body fluids that will not allow them to freeze. In polar fish there exists a white substance made up of glycoproteins or sometimes peptides, substances unique to these fish. Either of these liquids functions very much like the antifreeze in a car radiator. Fish without one of these antifreezes are doomed to die in polar waters.

There is one tree that is without equal.

Piercing the vault of heaven, like a Saturn 5 rocket with its precious cargo, the giant sequoia stands proud. Perched upon a remote, lofty mountain slope, the giant sequoia, classified as *Sequoiadendron giganteum*, is one of nature's magnificent achievements. It sweeps the clouds with majestic grace. The famed Scottish naturalist John Muir called the giant sequoias "the kings of their race."

The origin of the giant sequoia predates the dawn of man by over one hundred million years. Sequoias existed at a time when the largest dinosaurs were dwarfed by the immensity of these mighty redwoods. Ancestors of the sequoia line date back as far as three hundred million years ago.

The name *sequoia* is derived from the Cherokee Indian Chief, Sequoya (c. 1760–1843), who invented a written language for his people and who exhibited moments of superhuman strength and determination. The giant sequoia is a fitting namesake for the exploits of the celebrated Cherokee chief.

It is the largest living thing on Earth, and among the tallest (exceeded in height only by its brother, *Sequoia sempervirens*, the coast redwood) and oldest of trees. Only the California bristlecone pine surpasses the giant sequoia for longevity. But what makes the giant sequoia recherché is its noble presence and unique characteristics, virtually unknown to any other species of tree. It must be said that there are only two significant species of the genus *Sequoia* (sometimes referred to as the redwood). However, a third species, the *Metasequoia* (new sequoia) or dawn redwood, was discovered in central China in 1941. This sequoia grows only to about one hundred feet in height and is deciduous during the winter months, while the two other species are evergreens.

Remnants of sequoias have been unearthed in fossils of the Cretaceous and Tertiary periods, when they lived in the arctic zone. Sometime between one to two million years ago, sheets of ice rolled over much of the Earth, and the last of the sequoias were forced into California and a small portion of southwestern Oregon. Although often spoken of as one in the same, the giant sequoia and the coast redwood, though both redwoods, possess significant differences.

To begin with, their habitats are entirely different. The statuesque coast redwood flourishes in the misty atmosphere of nine coastal counties of California and a portion of Oregon, at elevations less than three thousand feet, while the monstrous Sierra redwood is a denizen of the dry air of six snow-covered Sierra Nevada counties at elevations approaching nine thousand feet. The Sierra redwood, or Big Tree, is generally identified by its more famous sobriquet, giant sequoia.

Unlike the coast redwood, the giant sequoia grows in open stands from a single seed so minute that three thousand seeds weigh barely one ounce. Yet from this single seed sprouts what will one day produce the most Herculean of trees.

In addition, the coast redwood is taller, sometimes reaching heights of over 367 feet, stately, and symmetrical in configuration. The greatest distinction between the two redwoods is the sheer immensity of the giant sequoia. It overwhelms the coast redwood in terms of mass: the General Sherman represents six hundred thousand board feet of straight-grained wood. The giant sequoia is also asymmetrical, with its top forming an uneven, crownlike appearance, as opposed to the more recognized spearlike top of the coast redwood. The second greatest distinction between the two trees is that the giant sequoia lives at least a thousand to fifteen hundred years longer than the two thousand to twenty-five hundred years the coast redwood lives.

The giant sequoia is without equal in the tree kingdom. It is by far the largest and most majestic of all trees. Its diameter sometimes approaches forty feet and the height is often in excess of three hundred feet. First limbs are sometimes found over a hundred feet above the ground and measure up to seven feet in diameter, the size of many full-grown trees of other species.

Many of the most prominent sequoias have been named after former U.S. notables such as Generals Sherman and Grant. The General Sherman Tree is the largest living thing at a height of 272.4 feet, 102 feet in circumference, with the first limb measuring 140 feet in length, and the tree is estimated by some to be about thirty-five hundred years of age. The General Grant Tree—The Nation's Christmas Tree—stands 267 feet tall and exceeds 40 feet across at its base.

The thought of this tree living for thousands of years, the thought that it will one day grow tall enough to kiss the heaven above, the thought that its forefathers were alive before the birth of Christ, leaves one slack-jawed and mystified.

The rarity of the giant sequoia is brought home when one contemplates the deforestation witnessed today. Once numbering in the millions, the mature sequoia population presently numbers approximately twenty thousand. That is indeed a very small number of trees, yet there are hopefully many little giants that will one day become as huge as their forefathers.

The giant sequoia possesses characteristics unique only to its species. It is virtually impervious to fire, disease, and decay. Its taproots rarely extend beyond six feet deep, yet feeder roots can spread over several acres. The bark contains no pitch or resin, the tacky substance that pines and firs produce which results in sudden flash fires. The wood under the bark contains a high concentration of water, which also retards burning. Even the bark's thickness of one to two feet and its consistency protect the tree from heat and cold as well.

Lightning, the cause of many forest fires, usually does not travel down the trunk because of its nonconductive properties. Since the giant sequoia has such an extremely long life, it has time to heal its wounds. It is additionally safeguarded by several natural chemicals, most notably tannin. Tannin creosotes the tree against menacing insects, disease, and the ravages of time.

As one would expect, even the growth pattern of the giant sequoia is unmatched in the world of trees, with many specimens growing at the rate of three feet per year. It's easy to see why the giant sequoias are truly "the kings of their race."

Barnacles make the strongest glue.

Those odd creatures known as barnacles, sessile crustaceans related to shrimp, lobsters, and crabs that live mostly on rocks, hulls of ships, and floating timber, produce the strongest glue in the world. Barnacles permanently attach themselves to these objects by means of a very powerful adhesive. Some fossils of barnacles discovered by paleontologists had attached themselves some 150 million years ago.

The actual composition of this incredible glue is still virtually unknown to scientists.

The camel originated in North America.

To begin with, let's set the record straight: the Middle East is really the Near East. That said, there are two species of camels, the Arabian or one-humped and the Bactrian or two-humped. Oops, what about the dromedary, isn't that a species of camel? No, it is simply a special breed of the one-humped camel used for riding. The uninitiated make the mistake and use the name dromedary in place of Arabian, but this is patently wrong.

Now, as to the camel's origins. Well, how does North America sound? Yes, the camels of *A Thousand and One Arabian Nights* and such evolved on the continent of North America during the Eocene epoch some fifty-three million to thirty-eight million years ago. Many fossils have been discovered, both large and small, with short necks and long necks, with the smallest the size of a rabbit and the largest standing fifteen feet at the shoulder. They ultimately made their way to other continents, with some first migrating to South America while others made their way northwestward to the Baring Strait and into Asia. Together with other behemoths and fierce predators such as mammoths, saber-toothed tigers, mastodons, lions, and several other animals, camels became extinct on the North American continent some eleven million years ago at the end of the most recent Ice Age (Pleistocene epoch).

Just in case you are wondering, camels do not store water in their humps nor in their stomachs, as many a myth would have you believe. But they really can go days or even months without drinking any water.

Mules cannot reproduce.

The mule has long been considered a mainstay during the formative years of colonization in the United States. It has been used for everything from a common farm animal that plowed the fields of the heartland to pulling cannons into battle. Oddly though, the mule, popularized by George Washington, cannot reproduce itself.

The tireless mule is a hybrid animal produced by crossing a male donkey (jack) with a female horse (mare). This combination allows the best genetic qualities of each animal to be transferred to the offspring (the offspring of a male horse and a female donkey is called a hinny). The marriage of these two animals came about when farmers were looking for an animal that was as large as a horse and easy to train, but had the surefootedness and disease resistance of the donkey. Because of this mating, the male mule is always born sterile and the female mule, with rare exceptions, is also born sterile.

From a grain of sand comes the precious pearl.

Generally, when a foreign substance, such as a grain of sand, inadvertently enters the shell of an oyster or another mollusk, a pearl is the result. In response to the irritation, a concretion (pearl) is formed that contains the identical material of the oyster's shell. The most prized pearls come from mollusks whose shells are lined with mother-of-pearl. Pearls are found in various colors, with the black pearl commanding significant sums over the less desired colors.

The cultivated pearl industry has been around since the Chinese of Kiangsu Province began the process in the thirteenth century. Cultivated pearls are produced by placing a particle inside a pearl oyster and waiting sometimes as long as three to five years. The wait may be for naught, for there is no guarantee that what will be produced will be saleable. In the best-case scenario, only about 60 percent of cultivated pearl oysters survive to yield pearls, and of that percentage, less than 3 percent produce gem quality pearls.

Pearls were among the very first natural objects to be prized by ancient civilizations, and the same is true today.

The camel can actually go without water for days.

Although at odds with popular belief, the spine of the camel is not crooked and the hump does serve a most valuable function. The camel is an indispensable beast of burden in desert locales because of its ability to survive under the most adverse conditions. There are two varieties of the camel: the one-humped dromedary, indigenous from India to North Africa, and the two-humped Bactrian, found in Chinese Turkistan and Mongolia.

The secret to the camel's ability to go without water is found in the hump(s). The hump is a dense mass of energy-producing fat that weighs about eighty pounds or more. It is utilized as a reservoir for energy to be called upon on long treks over sweltering desert sands.

When the camel is famished, the hump has a tendency to all but disappear. The fat in the hump is spent while energy is created, and during this process, for every pound of fat burned, it yields roughly a pint of water. Therefore, by excreting a minimal amount of liquid, and by having the ability to recycle its own liquid body wastes, the camel is capable of going for days without water.

Although the camel is indigenous to India, North Africa, and parts of Asia, camels were once used in the Wild West. The United States Army First Camel Corps was established in 1855. At one point, there were thirty-three camels, and there were plans to purchase as many as one thousand more of these beasts of burden. The camel corps was disbanded prior to the Civil War, with many of the camels set free in the deserts of Texas, Arizona, and California.

A chameleon is not the only animal capable of changing its color.

The mysterious true chameleon (*Brookesia* and *Chamaeleo*) is an arboreal lizard found mainly in Madagascar, Africa, southern Asia, India, and Spain, comprising some ninety to one hundred varieties.

It is a well-accepted belief that the chameleon changes its skin color to blend in with its environment. However, it actually changes its color as a behavioral response to such stimuli as light, emotion, motion, and temperature.

The change in color is due to the control of pigment cells in its body called melanocytes. When they remain spherical, a light body tone is produced; when they enlarge and spread out, a darker body tone is produced. A chameleon may appear blue, green, or yellow one moment, then a second later it has changed its appearance to look black or perhaps brown.

This ability to change color is thought to be a characteristic unique to the chameleon, but the octopus, cuttlefish, squid, flounder, and to a limited degree, the seahorse, can perform the same magic, sometimes with better results.

A fly can defy gravity.

The nuisance of all nuisances, the common housefly (*Musca domestica*), can defy gravity. Its presence is all but universal—there are some one hundred thousand species—and its ability to land on ceilings and to walk upside down is a wonder to all who look on in amazement. It was only recently, through the use of an electronic flash mechanism, that it was established just how a housefly does this.

The common housefly, a marvel of nature, has just two wings, but six legs, each equipped with a pair of tiny claws that look like those of a lobster. Beneath the claws is a pair of hairy, glandular pads, called *pulvilli*. The pulvilli secrete a sticky substance that makes them act as suction pads. These pads permit the fly to not only suspend itself upside down but to literally walk with ease, thus seemingly defying gravity.

Some birds migrate twenty-five thousand miles each year.

The diminutive Arctic torn (*Sterna paradi aea*), a seabird only seventeen inches long, holds the dubious record of migrating the greatest distance in one year. Since its summer and winter homes are about eleven thousand miles apart, and its migratory route from northern Labrador to Antarctica is indirect, some terns probably fly a minimum of twenty-five thousand miles in their yearly journey. That's more than once around the world.

This amazing migration permits the Arctic tern to experience more continuous daylight than any other animal: it enjoys endless summer daylight in both the Arctic and the Antarctic.

Blood comes in more than one color.

To be specific, there are numerous colors of blood. Mammals have red blood, lobsters and many other crustaceans have blue blood (the Queen of England most surely denies any consanguinity), certain fish have white blood, and insects have yellow, green, and sometimes red, or even clear blood.

The platypus is an anomaly among mammals.

The platypus (*Ornithorhynchus anatinus*), or duckbill, is unique in the world of mammals. As a native of Australia and Tasmania, the platypus is one of only two egg-laying mammals. The other is the echidna or spiny anteater. They are both egg-laying mammals with milk glands for nursing their young.

The platypus looks very bizarre as well. First discovered in 1797, observers thought it was a hoax, what with its duckbill-shaped snout (used to scoop up food from the bottom of streams), no teeth, no external ears, and webbed feet. The male platypus even has poison glands located in spurs in the rear legs that defend against predators. This unique mammal is also sometimes referred to as the duck-billed platypus.

A spider's web is stronger than iron.

The ubiquitous spider, an eight-legged arthropod of the class *Arachnid*, is represented by over forty thousand varieties. The spider is a primary predator, whose fangs inject poison into its prey. The spider's success as a hunter is due in part to the use of its silk in constructing traps that catch prey. The word *spider* originates from the Old English *spinnan*, "to spin," a reference to its ability to spin webs of silk.

Material for the web is generated from within the abdomen, where three glands spew out the substance through tubes or spinning organs called spinnerets. Once complete, the web is generally suspended vertically in order to snatch airborne insects. The grandest spider web seen to date was twelve feet in diameter and was located in Africa.

If the spider's silk, which is 0.0002 inch fine, is woven into a one-inch-diameter rope, it could withstand the weight of seventy-four tons. Its tensile strength is three times that of a similar rope made of iron.

By the way, the spider is not an insect, but is related to the scorpion, mite, harvestman, and tick. Unlike insects, spiders have no feelers or antennae. Also, spiders have two pairs of jaws and four pairs of legs, whereas insects have three pairs of jaws and three pairs of legs.

Man has more than five senses.

Man and other higher animals utilize sensory perception to react to changes in their environments, both external and internal. Common knowledge prescribes that there are only five senses, but in reality there are many more than five. Besides the prominent senses of taste, hearing, smell, touch, and sight that were noted by Aristotle, there are pain, heat, cold, hunger, Kinesthetic motion (muscle activity), thirst, equilibrium (balance), fatigue, deep stimulation, pressure. . . .

Dinosaurs may have been warm-blooded.

Just check your preconceptions at the door: a new theory, one that breaks with orthodoxy in the world of the dinosaur authorities of science, suggests that dinosaurs (*Dinosauria*), the largest land animals that ever existed (they thrived for some 150 million years), must have been warm-blooded and possibly not even reptiles.

Robert T. Bakker, Ph.D., world-renowned paleontologist, proffers the theory that the higher the metabolic rate of a group of species, the more susceptible it is to abrupt and cataclysmic extinction. He further states that animals such as the alligator or the large turtle are better suited to survival over the millennia because of their extremely phlegmatic metabolism. Thus, to insure that a particular species dies off en mass is to imbue it with a high metabolism: an endless need to consume great quantities of calories, more specifically, protein. Therefore, any major change in the surroundings just might eradicate an entire species.

The Cretaceous Period (144–65 million years ago) witnessed the greatest extinctions in the history of the terrestrial ecosystem, yet some species with low metabolic rates did survive relatively unscathed and are in evidence to this very day: monitor lizards, gill-breathing salamanders, soft-shell turtles, alligators, and crocodiles.

Every dinosaur to the very last did not make it, just possibly because they were warm-blooded, not reptiles as was previously supposed.

Many desert animals do not drink water.

As impossible as it may seem to believe, many desert animals live quite well without drinking water. As an example, the kangaroo rat (genus *Dipodomys*), any of about twenty-five species of hopping rodents indigenous to the deserts of western North America, derives it name from its looks—a combination of rat and midget kangaroo—but in truth, it is neither.

Because of its long hind legs and kangaroolike tail, it can negotiate leaps of over six feet at one time. This ability permits it to save energy, along with being active only after sunset, thus conserving valuable water. It lives most of the day in an underground system of burrows where it stores its food. It obtains needed moisture through the chemical breakdown of the food it consumes, and its highly efficient kidneys have the ability to recycle the water in its body, thus, no water loss. Therefore, the kangaroo rat rarely, if ever, needs to drink water.

The pocket mouse, jerboa, and antelope ground squirrel, as well as other desert animals can, for the most part, survive without drinking water, very much like the kangaroo rat.

Saint Bernard dogs do not carry casks of brandy.

The mighty Saint Bernard dogs do indeed save the lives of travelers lost in snowstorms or buried in avalanches. In fact, in the last three centuries, this breed of dog has saved more than twenty-five hundred lives. The most celebrated of them all was Barry, who, prior to his death in the early 1800s, is credited with having saved forty lives.

Their sharp sense of smell, strength, intelligence, and unerring ability to always find their way have made them indispensable to the monks that inhabit the Hospice of Saint Bernard, founded in the 1000s by Saint Bernard of Menthon in Great Saint Bernard Pass, on the Swiss–Italian border. This hospice in the Alps has been a refuge to travelers for nearly one thousand years.

The breed, whose name derives from the Hospice of Saint Bernard, was probably developed by the monks for rescue work and to assist them in guiding their way through the snow-covered mountains. It is believed that the breed originated from a massive Asian dog that was transported to Europe by the ancient Romans. The dogs ultimately made their way to the hospice during the 1600s. It was a time when foot travel through the Alps was commonplace, and many travelers lost their way or were caught in avalanches. The dogs served to find these endangered souls, and with the help of the monks, they were returned to the hospice, given nourishment, and sent on their way; no one was permitted to stay there for more than one day, unless it was a dire emergency.

Numerous tales surround the exploits of these mighty dogs, the largest breed recognized by the American Kennel Club (up to 170 pounds), but none is more renowned than Saint Bernards rescuing stranded hikers, then warming their insides with a shot of brandy from the casks that hang from their necks. Sorry to say, but the part about the casks of brandy is nothing more than a myth, a myth of epic proportions, that survives to this day.

It seems that the English artist Sir Edwin Landseer (1802–73) is the culprit. He painted a well-known picture of a Saint Bernard with a small cask of brandy suspended from a collar around its neck. However, no records at the hospice make even the remotest mention of the fabled cask. Saint Bernard dogs have never—absolutely never—carried the now legendary casks of brandy. So should you find yourself snowbound in the Swiss Alps, do not worry, a Saint Bernard will most surely find you, but you'll have to bring your own cask of brandy.

The English sparrow is not a sparrow.

Once again, misnomers abound. To begin with, the English sparrow (*Passer domesticus*), more commonly called the house sparrow, is not a sparrow, but more specifically a weaver finch. It is one of the world's most well-known and plentiful small birds (about six inches long). It is a bird that, when raised in captivity—usually in the presence of other singing birds such as songbirds and canaries—can learn to sing quite mellifluously.

As for why it is called the English sparrow, it seems that when these birds were first introduced to the United States around the 1860s, in the hopes of containing the spread of cankerworms that had overtaken shade trees, they were brought over from England. The fact is, these birds were always native to Europe and Asia, and by 1874, they were called by such names as the European or house sparrow, though the English appellation and misnomer seemed to stick.

Bulls "cannot" see the color red.

The matador enters the arena, red cape in hand. He summons the fighting bull, a special breed of cattle, and with bravado and graceful cape work, he outmaneuvers the powerful bovine. The crowd cheers incessantly as he waves the red cape, the muleta, yet again, taunting the bull, calling him to charge. The bull is enraged by the matador's constant waving of the red cape. Or is he?

The fact is, the fighting bull, like all cattle, is essentially color blind. The bull is no more aggravated by the color red than any other color. Moreover, research has shown that bulls and steers are unable to discern red from green, pink, or purple. However, it seems that a bull is attracted to a brightly colored moving object more quickly than a dull-colored one. In essence, bulls are not aggravated by a red cape any more than a purple cape. In fact, it seems that a white cape is a more effective means of causing a bull to charge.

However, red is chosen as the color of the cape because it symbolizes blood, fury, and excitement. But keep in mind, so long as the cape is a bright color and it is in motion, the fighting bull will charge, no matter what the color.

Insects are everywhere.

For some four hundred million years or more insects (class *Insecta*) have propagated and evolved into what is believed to be as many as thirty million distinct species, with only approximately one million having been discovered to date. The continent of North America alone boosts over eighty thousand different species of insects.

Insects are directly responsible for the very existence of plants and animals, and hence, human beings themselves. Insects are found in virtually every type of environment from glaciers to tropical forests, from oceans to mountaintops, and just about everywhere in between.

Insects are the most prevalent of all animals. They represent 85 percent of all animal life and the sum total weight of all the Earth's insects is twelve times greater than the total weight of its human population. On the continent of Africa, termites and ants alone weigh more than the entire population of all species of mammals.

As a group, insects are probably the most bizarre animals on the planet. They smell mostly with their antennae, while some actually taste with their feet, and still others hear by means of sensor hairs located on their bodies or even with ears found on their legs. The range of peculiarities does not end there. Some insects possess five or more eyes, yet others have none. They have no voices to speak of, still they are able to generate sounds that can be detected as far away as one mile. Without lungs, insects breathe through holes found in the sides of their bodies. Many insects perform impressive feats of strength: an ant can lift fifty times its own body weight (if a 175-pound man could do equally well, he would have to lift, with his teeth, 3.6 metric tons), and the flea can broad-jump an astonishing thirteen inches (if a man could do equally well, he would have to jump a distance of seven hundred feet). Insects such as glowworms and fireflies produce light by means of a chemical reaction.

The life spans of insects range from as little as a few hours to many years. Some insects are all but invisible while others are several inches long. They even exhibit human characteristics such as choosing to be social or solitary, farming, building, fighting, caretaking, and hunting. By the way, spiders are not insects.

CHAPTER TEN

THE GRAB BAG

Tulips were once traded on the Amsterdam Stock Exchange.

In the 1600s tulipomania (*tulip*, from the Turkish word meaning "turban") ruled Europe. What is it you ask? Well, it seems that between 1634 and 1637, the lack of a tulip was evidence of bad taste and poor breeding, and as such, tulips were even traded on the Amsterdam Stock Exchange. Brokers speculated in the rise and fall of tulip stocks just as those who buy and sell any present-day stock. Some bulbs brought record prices ranging from $750 to $4,000 each.

The actual cause of tulipomania began after a European gentleman, Augeius G. Busbequis, received a tulip bulb from Suleiman the Magnificent (1494–1566) in Constantinople (Conrad Gesner also lays claim to having initiated the tulip craze in Holland). Most people think that the lovely tulip originated in Holland, but the truth is, it most likely came from central Asia, probably Turkey. Nevertheless, it was not too long before the well-heeled in both Holland and Germany were spending outlandish sums to acquire tulip bulbs directly from Constantinople.

During the ensuing several decades, the Dutch were made delirious with the bulb and they naturally assumed the rest of the world would follow suit. The mania continued to manifest itself in bizarre ways. One individual was known to have paid over twenty-four farm animals, one thousand pounds of cheese, four tons of beer, and other items in order to acquire a very rare bulb known as the Viceroy. Even the stoic British were taken in by the mania that persisted. In 1636, bulbs traded on the Exchange of London. Paris was also smitten by tulipomania as some unscrupulous individuals tried to spark interest in the bulbs. In 1835, a gardener in Chelsea offered bulbs for two hundred pounds each.

As tulip prices rose, everyone from the chimney sweep to the local doctor invested everything in tulips. It was thought the tulip would soon be the panacea for all that ailed the less fortunate. When the bulb burst, thousands of speculators were transformed into homeless beggars and economic chaos continued for years to come.

There is one United States coin that is illegal to own.

The largest and grandest of all United States regular coinage denominations is the double-eagle, whose face value is twenty dollars. It contains nearly one ounce of gold. Minted from 1849 until 1933, the double eagle, also commonly known as the twenty-dollar gold piece, has always been a favorite among numismatists.

The birth of the double eagle came about because of the discovery of gold in California at Sutter's Mill in January 1848. The dramatic increase in the supply of gold caused Congress to pass legislation providing for the minting of both gold dollars and double eagles.

James B. Longacre was the designer of record for the first double eagle, and his design was used until the dramatic design change in 1907. It was the great sculptor Augustus Saint-Gaudens, commissioned by President Teddy Roosevelt, who designed the now famous and admired new double eagle, which is thought to be the most beautiful United States coin ever produced. This magnificent design was issued until 1933, and in that year, the story of the double eagle took a curious turn.

In March 1933, President Franklin D. Roosevelt issued the Gold Surrender Order of 1933 that prohibited private ownership of gold bullion by U.S. citizens, which included gold coins. Although 445,500 double eagles dated 1933 were coined prior to the Surrender Order, none were ever officially released, although two examples were given to the Smithsonian Institution, and twenty-nine more were reserved for the Assay Commission. Yet somehow, an unknown quantity found their way into unauthorized hands.

Some years later, in 1944, a 1933 double eagle was advertised for sale in an auction. The Treasury Department immediately sent officials to the auction house and summarily confiscated the gold piece. The Treasury Department continued its relentless pursuit and seized several more examples of the 1933 twenty-dollar gold piece.

About a decade later, King Farouk of Egypt caused a collection of his coins to be sold publicly. In that collection was an illegal 1933 double eagle. United States authorities entreated the Egyptian government to withdraw the coin, which they did, but the coin was never turned over to United States authorities.

It is estimated that somewhere between five to ten examples of this magnificent and illegal coin exist in private hands today. Some question the United States' position on insisting that the 1933 double eagle be illegal to possess; nevertheless, don't get caught with one.

Some people can send mail, postage-free.

It seems like such a great idea, but who can legally send mail free of charge? A great many people are accorded the privilege of doing so, in most cases, for official business only (former presidents and widows of former presidents are permitted to frank all their domestic mail).

There are two methods by which one can send franked or free mail. The vice-president, along with members of Congress and various other officials, is permitted to make use of the franking privilege (the word *franking* derives from Old French *franc*, meaning free). Only official correspondence, public documents, the *Congressional Record*, and seeds and agricultural reports are carried postage-free.

The sender must put his or her signature, or a reasonable facsimile, on every piece of mail—personal letters are forbidden—in place of a postage stamp. The privilege extends to only mail subject to domestic rates. It must be noted that the privilege is not entirely free, for someone has to pay, and it's the taxpayers. Congress appropriates funds to pay the U.S. Postal Service for the costs of franked mail.

However, the executive and judicial branches of the federal government are granted a different postage-free entitlement. They use what is called the penalty privilege when mailing official matter. Each piece of mail must be sent using penalty envelopes or tags that are imprinted with words that basically say, "Penalty for Private Use, To Avoid Payment of Postage, $300." Each separate entity that avails itself of the penalty privilege reimburses the Postal Service for the price of postage at regular domestic postal rates.

So, if you have any plans to send mail free of charge, it had better be official business and you had better be an official of the U.S. government, a former U.S. president, or the widow of a former U.S. president.

Superstition surrounds the "two-dollar" bill.

Many years ago the two-dollar bill died a less than glorious death. First printed on June 22, 1775, the bill continued as a regular issue for 191 years, but it never achieved nationwide acceptance as anything other than a joke. Even gamblers, whose two-dollar bets one would think would make the use of the two-dollar bill indispensable, turned the other way in droves. When they did use it, they would tear off a corner in hopes that this would negate the hex. As fatuous as this seems, any bills that remain do so as collectibles—keepsakes. Superstition continues to dog the bill.

For some inexplicable reason the two-dollar bill carried a jinx with it and anyone who possessed it. Even before the bills were printed, superstition caused people to be wary of this denomination. Some scholars and numismatists alike have tried to explain the jinx this way. Back in the seventeenth century, during the buccaneer days in the West Indies, one coin that was in use at the time was a large silver piece, valued at about two dollars in present money. At that time it was equivalent to thirteen "reales" in Spanish currency. Because of the bad luck and warped notions associated with the number thirteen, the two-dollar bill was destined to be eschewed by just about everyone. Even bank tellers wanted nothing to do with the bill. It was an orphan.

By 1862, the bill was already disliked, and in 1880, it was used to buy votes in a pre-presidential campaign in Ohio and Indiana. This act caused any man who cashed a two-dollar bill at that time to be labeled a traitor, regardless of whether the bill was obtained to buy a vote or not. The jinx factor just multiplied.

In 1923, the Treasury Department ceased issuing the note, which made everyone happy. Then, two years later, without explanation, the bill was once again printed and the government went on a mission to make it accepted by all. They even organized national speaking tours to excite the populace, but to no avail.

Nevertheless, some of the most wonderful examples of the engravers' art ever seen on paper money are to be found on the two-dollar bill. Numerous dignitaries have adorned the bill, with Thomas Jefferson and his imposing Monticello featured on the bill since 1928. Not even the engraver's art and the celebrated Jefferson could do much to help the bill achieve national acceptance.

Whatever the superstitions of the two-dollar bill might be, and for whatever reasons, remember that there was also a three-dollar bill.

The Oscar is inexpensive.

The value of winning an Oscar (first presented in 1929) is virtually incalculable in terms of public relations for the winner, but its intrinsic value is not very high. Actually, the Oscar, a gold-plated statuette, has a real value of about $900 (2013), even though its resale value is anywhere from $7,000 to $50,000, and possibly more.

The Emmy costs around $900 to produce, with a street value of $500 to $5,000. The Pulitzer Prize, a piece of parchment with the Columbia University insignia emblazoned on a blue cover costs only

$100 to produce but has a resale value estimated at between $100 to $50,000. The winner, in terms of real value, is the People's Choice award. It is fashioned from lead crystal at a cost of about $1,440 per copy. Its resale value is around $2,500.

So the Oscar, named after the uncle of an Academy of Motion Picture Arts and Sciences employee, Margaret Herrick, in 1931, may be inexpensive to produce in real terms, but its public relations value to the winner or its resale value makes it very desirable.

There is no German silver.

Much to the dismay of those who purchase items made of German silver, also called nickel silver, there is no such thing. German silver is not silver from Germany, and it's not even silver. It is simply a combination of copper-based alloys: copper, nickel, and zinc, though sometimes lead and tin are used, but certainly no silver.

The name derives from the silver color that the alloyed metal takes on caused by the nickel and the fact that it was first made in Hildburghausen, Germany.

The first day of the twenty-first century was not January 1, 2000.

January 1, 1900, was not the first day of the twentieth century, either; it was January 1, 1901. The first day of the twenty-first century was January 1, 2001 (the Christian calendar started January 1, of the year A.D. 1; there was no year 0).

Think of it this way: if you begin with January 1, year 1, and end at December 31, year 99, you only have 99 years. In order to complete the century (100 years), one must count one more whole year from January 1, 100, to December 31, 100. So, on December 31, 1999, the twentieth century was only 99 years old, and to make it 100 full years, one must add the year from January 1, 2000 to December 31, 2000.

Thus, the first day of the twenty-first century was January 1, 2001.

Lloyd's of London is not an insurance company.

That's right. Much to the dismay of those who think the famous Lloyd's of London is an insurance company, it's not. It is simply a consortium of more than twenty-five thousand specially chosen Lloyd's underwriters, organized into about four hundred syndicates. Each member acts as a separate entity, underwriting insurance for his own individual account and accepting all risks. The corporation known as Lloyd's of London, which can trace its history back to 1688, does not assume any liability whatsoever. Hence, policyholders are insured with an underwriter at Lloyd's of London, not Lloyd's of London itself, because it writes no policies.

Through the years, underwriters at Lloyd's of London have written insurance for everything from gigantic skyscrapers and ships to beards of celebrities and the capture of the Loch Ness monster. Some of their more famous policyholders include property owners in the San Francisco earthquake and fire of 1906, the *Titanic*'s demise in 1912, and the loss of the *Hindenburg* to fire in 1937.

In addition, Lloyd's of London publishes a daily newspaper giving its members worldwide shipping reports. It is called the *Lloyd's List and Shipping Gazette* and some contend it is the oldest newspaper in London.

So, the next time someone says they are insured by Lloyd's of London, you'll know they're really not.

There is more to U.S. currency than meets the eye.

U.S. currency is known the world over, but what is not known is that it possesses some very interesting aspects unknown to the average citizen. Although the U.S. Treasury Department categorically denies that there are any cryptic anti-counterfeiting tricks in currency artwork, a close examination by some authorities on the subject reveals much to the contrary.

To begin with, on the reverse of the five-dollar bill there's a presumably secret number. A close analysis of the bushes to the left of the Lincoln Memorial shows a shading pattern that seems to spell out a three-digit number: 372. The numerals appear as dark opposing a lighter background. The Treasury Department maintains that the numbers are a mishap of the engraving process.

Of further interest on the five-dollar bill is the Lincoln Memorial itself. With the aid of a magnifying glass one can see that there are the names of twenty-six states engraved across the top portion of the monument. The names also appear on the actual memorial in Washington, D.C.

More specifically, anti-counterfeiting devices on the five-dollar bill include the fineness of the eyes on the portrait, a deliberate narrow line just inside the margin of each 5 on the top left and right corners of the five-dollar bill, and a hair-thin line on the front yet not the back of the five-dollar bill, as well as on the one-dollar, ten-dollar, and twenty-dollar bills. These very fine lines, the cachet of talented engravers, are virtually impossible to duplicate by the less sophisticated photomechanical process and in the photocopy process the lines break up even easier. The type of paper and ink used in producing the currency also serve to foil counterfeiters.

It is estimated that between seven million to ten million dollars' worth of counterfeit currency is made each year in the United States compared to nearly two hundred billion dollars' worth of legal tender circulated during the mid-1980s. The U.S. Secret Service, known today as the protector of the president, was originally created in 1865 to combat the widespread counterfeiting of the first currency issued by the federal government.

The most ubiquitous of all U.S. currency denominations is the one-dollar bill. It is a pictorial representation and advertisement for Freemasonry. The pyramid with the eye above it is a manifest concession to this secret society. The incomplete pyramid illustrates the unfinished Temple of Solomon; the eye is a metaphor for the Grand Architect of the Universe.

It is plainly obvious that Freemasonry was and is an integral part of our currency and history. George Washington, whose likeness appears on the front of the one-dollar bill, was a Freemason as were Presidents Monroe, Jackson, Polk, Buchanan, A. Johnson, Garfield, McKinley (five hundred-dollar bill), Teddy Roosevelt, Taft, Harding, Franklin D. Roosevelt, Truman, and Ford.

So the next time you pull out a five-dollar bill, take a closer look.

You, too, can be buried at Westminster Abbey.

Yes, you, too, can be buried in the celebrated and sacred Westminster Abbey—well, almost.

Though commonly thought to be the resting place of kings, queens, and the like, Westminster Abbey (the present Norman-style structure was consecrated in 1065) has no specific rules or regulations as to who can be interred there. When someone of prominence dies, the deans of Westminster Abbey have the prerogative to invite or not to invite the relatives of the deceased to have the remains of their dearly departed interred in the Abbey. In 1789, one Jack Broughton, an English boxing champion and designer of mufflers, forerunners of modern boxing gloves, was buried in Westminster Abbey.

The Abbey's true name is the Collegiate Church of Saint Peter in Westminster. Oh, yes, calling England's most famous house of worship, and the repository of all that is English, Westminster Abbey is a redundancy, since *minster* or *mynster* (Anglo-Saxon) means a monastery or abbey church.

No matter the color, all eggs are the same.

Poultrymen are constantly trying to make their chickens produce more white-shelled eggs because most households prefer white eggs. Maybe the white shell represents purity and cleanliness. Yet many vegetarians and naturalists hold that brown eggs are healthier than white ones and there are even some societies that favor brown eggs. However, many zoologists state that there is no solid proof that there is a changing relationship between the color of the shell and the nutritional contents of the egg.

Whether the eggshell is colored white, brown, or otherwise, all eggs are essentially equal inside, and the shell color is of no consequence.

Golf courses did not always have eighteen holes.

Scotland, known for its bagpipe, Scotch, and great thinkers, has always held a special place in the hearts of most of us. But to a very devoted and growing number of acolytes, Scotland is also the center of the world to golfers and the Royal and Ancient Golf Club of Saint Andrews is their Holy Grail. But what of the eighteen holes on each standard golf course? Originally, it wasn't that way.

In the beginning, courses were designed with differing numbers of holes, governed by the amount of land available. Some courses had as few as five or six holes, yet Saint Andrews originally had eleven holes, all of which were aligned along the coast: each hole was played out and back, thus making a round twenty-two holes. But the course officials decided that in order to make the course more challenging, they would reduce the number of holes, making many of them longer. On October 4, 1764, the club reduced and modified the number of holes on its original course and the eighteen-hole golf course was born.

U.S. currency paper has unique characteristics.

Although the precise recipe for the manufacture of U.S. currency paper is a well-guarded secret, much is known about the paper. The special bond paper is manufactured by Crane and Company of Dalton, Massachusetts, solely for the U.S. Bureau of Engraving and Printing. The type presently in use has been the same since 1879. The paper is fundamentally made up of 75 percent cotton and 25 percent linen and it is infused with both red and blue fibers.

There are three concealed security features of singular interest. Firstly, the paper is fluorescent when subjected to an ultraviolet light. Secondly, the paper is filled with minute, invisible holes: under extreme magnification fine pinpoints of light pass through the holes. Thirdly, the ink is infused with metallic elements, though not detectable by conventional means—such as the common magnet. Complete success in duplicating the exact paper and ink used has eluded the best of those who have tried. It is a federal offense for unauthorized people to manufacture paper like that used for U.S. currency.

The counterfeiter's job is an exercise in futility when it comes to producing exact copies of U.S. currency, as new anticounterfeiting tricks are continually developed to deter these unprincipled individuals.

There is a palace made of corn.

It's an annual event that began in 1892. Almost every September, the people of historic Mitchell, South Dakota, founded in 1879, give thanks for the state's agricultural bounty. In 1892, the Corn Belt Real Estate Association hatched a plan to lure people to the state. They convinced farmers from adjoining states to make their lives in South Dakota, a state flush with rich soil.

Locals willingly enlisted in the effort to build an exposition hall on Mitchell's Main Street. It was cleverly adorned with native grasses and grains and immense exterior murals were made of countless multicolored ears of corn. Dubbed the Mitchell Corn Palace, the original wooden structure, a unique example of Byzantine architecture, replete with several minarets and towers, was built and decorated in just sixty-four days. It was replaced in 1905, and yet again in 1921, by an immense steel-and-concrete reproduction designed by the architectural firm that gave New York its Radio City Music Hall.

The annual harvest celebration has been headlined by world-famous singers and musicians and takes place during the last full week in September and is known as Corn Palace Week.

Each year before the celebration, artists from the area redecorate the exterior with murals realistically portraying themes ranging from environmental concerns and western history to patriotism, a subject that is very important to these people. As one would expect, the primary medium of the murals is corn, which is embellished with wild oats, rye, and barley.

It is fascinating to note that each winter the pigeons that make the palace their home are instrumental in taking apart the murals that were created for the festival. The internationally known Mitchell Corn Palace has earned the moniker of "the world's most spectacular bird feeder."

Alcohol is served at Disneyland.

The most famous symbol of American family fun, "the happiest place on Earth," Disneyland, actually serves alcoholic beverages on its premises. Alcohol is available at the ultra-exclusive Club 33. It is Disneyland's secret club, so secret that many employees of the park don't even know that it exists and far fewer have ever seen the inside of the club.

Club 33 is located at 33 Rue Royale, second floor, in New Orleans Square, close to the Pirates of the Caribbean attraction and just to the right of the Blue Bayou Restaurant.

Admittance to the club, limited to members and their guests, is through a simple entrance that bears a plaque adorned with the number 33. To actually enter, you must push an intercom button and give your name. Once verified, the door lock is released and you find yourself in an exquisitely decorated foyer with both an elaborate staircase and antique elevator standing at the ready before you. You are then escorted upstairs to a beautifully decorated series of dining rooms accented with dark woods and antiques.

At this point, you can feel the exclusivity of the place. It is said that membership costs about ten thousand dollars and is limited to just one thousand members. Club 33 is open even when the park is closed during the winter months.

All the staff is attired in formal wear with the Club 33 logo emblazoned on their jackets. Everything and everyone is immaculate. Service is exceptional: should you leave your table for a moment, when you return you will find that your napkin has been folded and your water or wine glass filled. The menu is extensive, the food outstanding, and the prices are expensive.

While dining, you are treated to views of the activity outside, which include fireworks or the incredible laser show. Your table is even replete with a matchbook that bears your name. Each dining area is unique and very comfortable. Mrs. Disney's butterfly collection is on display in the Trophy Room.

It is rumored that the club came about because Uncle Walt had planned to live at the park and entertain friends and celebrities. An apartment was built on the third floor of the club as his living quarters. However, Uncle Walt died before the project was completed, and the second floor of the building became Club 33 while the third floor was turned into offices.

There are some peculiarities at Club 33 that are of special interest. Besides its obvious exclusivity, the club is bugged, wired for sound. Miniature microphones are cleverly hidden in overhead chandeliers; a china closet houses a camera; and the Trophy Room includes a speaker in the moose's head—all this just so Uncle Walt could eavesdrop on his guests. Very bizarre.

When you exit Club 33, you take with you a most memorable experience, and the feeling that you were part of Uncle Walt's family, if only for a short time.

Not every boomerang returns to its thrower.

It may seem incongruous to suggest that most boomerangs will not return, but the reality is, they are not meant to do so. The boomerang is a curved throwing stick that has been used mainly by Australia's Aborigines since prehistoric times mostly as an implement of hunting and war. The name *boomerang* derives from an aboriginal name, possibly *wo-mur-rāng* or *wo-mur-ra*, "the throwing stick."

The Aborigines employ two types, the returning boomerang, of which most people are familiar, which is used only in eastern and Western Australia as a child's toy, in sport, and by hunters. It is thrown above birds in flight, which perceive it to be a deadly hawk, then react by flying low into nets strategically positioned by Aborigines.

The other and more popular type, the nonreturning boomerang, is used primarily for hunting and war, and is found mostly in Central Australia and the Northern Territory. It is longer, less curved, flies a straighter course, and is noticeably heavier than the returning type. By the way, this type of boomerang must be retrieved by the thrower.

Evidence suggests that the use of the boomerang is not exclusive to the Aborigines of Australia, for prehistoric boomerangs have been unearthed in regions of Africa, Europe, Asia, and even North America.

London's black-taxi driver is like a doctor.

To apply and receive a driver's license in most cities is fairly quick and painless. The same cannot be said, however, for the exclusive club of taxicab drivers who scurry about London in a peripatetic manner with the utmost precision and determination. They are called the best in the world—the black-taxi drivers.

To become one of London's approximately twenty-thousand licensed black-taxi drivers is an ordeal that includes the mastery of *The Knowledge*. It can take up to five years to finish, but the average time to learn *The Knowledge* is from two to three years. The process extracts a large amount of blood, sweat, and tears from every willing applicant, and one must summon every last bit of intestinal fortitude if he is to survive. So, what is *The Knowledge*, and how difficult could it be to learn?

The Knowledge is an imposing euphemism for a small book describing an area of real estate within a six-mile radius of Charing Cross Station in the center of London, the jewel of the United Kingdom, and one of the world's oldest, most historic, and most populated cities. This section of the city consists of the names of about twenty-five thousand streets that twist and turn for some fifteen-thousand miles and includes buildings, monuments, pubs, hotels, apartment complexes, subway stations, and an endless number of places called "points" by the examining officials of the Public Carriage Office of the Metropolitan Police District.

The aspiring cabbies seeking the "all-London" license must know these twenty-five thousand points cold; that is to say, they must have instant recall of every single point in London. The odds are statistically not very encouraging: wholly two-thirds of all applicants who apply will fail, one or two will sustain serious injuries, and as many more will become divorced while studying *The Knowledge*. The Public Carriage Office makes it known in no uncertain terms that the standards are very precise and will not be compromised under any circumstances. It is because of these standards that the procedure for licensing London cabbies is probably unique.

What is also unique is that these cabbies are independent contractors who own their own cabs, and have no association with the government, other than the strict supervision imposed on them by the Public Carriage Office, an office of government that dates back to the mid-seventeenth century and Oliver Cromwell.

To receive the green-enameled, numbered badge (designating the driver has passed the all-London driver's test) that every black-taxi driver proudly hangs around his neck is nothing short of appearing before the Inquisition. Many cabbies, who took their tests thirty or forty years ago, remember them with the same trepidation, as if it were yesterday.

They say that much of the tension is caused by the examiners themselves, who dress as if they are executioners, testing each applicant on a one-to-one basis. They demand that all potential cabbies dress accordingly and with no jewelry. Each applicant is given a booklet with 468 "runs" in them. The applicant is then asked a "run," say from Saint John's Wood Park to Princess Louise Hospital, or Lowndes Square to Hurlingham Club, or from the Public Carriage Office to the British Museum, by the shortest route. You must recite to the examiner every turn, stop, building, roundabout, and landmark without error, not one. Anything less is frowned upon.

The series of tests lasts several weeks. The examiners justify their methods by saying that it builds character in the cabbies. Its character and knowledge that make London cabbies the best in the world. Nothing less will satisfy the examiners.

Studying *The Knowledge* requires each applicant to forego all other activities in his life. He must be focused on the job at hand, which requires going out on a motorcycle and driving every single "run" several times. It's even wise to explore every side street and alley, because the examiner has at his discretion the liberty to ask "runs" that aren't exactly in the booklet.

There's just no way around learning *The Knowledge;* it's like preparing for a Ph.D. exam. When you pass, you feel like a "doctor of the road." The benefits of becoming a black-taxi driver are independence, an average hourly rate exceeding those of most London workers, and the right to be called one of the best at what you do.

The U.S. government will give you "new" money.

Just imagine: should your cow swallow your wallet or your mattress be destroyed by fire, you can tell the U.S. Department of the Treasury and they will give you new money. Well, its not quite that simple, but should you have currency damaged by some odd circumstance, you can redeem the scraps for new money if you meet certain criteria.

Damaged currency is received and processed by the Office of Currency Standards (OCS) located at the Bureau of Engraving and Printing (founded in, 1862, it is the largest printer of security documents in the world) in the nation's capital. A detailed description of how the currency was damaged must accompany every submission to the OCS. If the currency was completely destroyed, then a letter explaining in precise detail just how the currency was destroyed must accompany proof of rightful ownership.

Once the claim has been processed, the actual payment is made by government check, but it is redeemable for brand-new money. So, should any of your paper money end up in the clothes dryer, placed in the stove for safekeeping, or mutilated by a playful child, there is salvation.

Big Ben is "not" a clock.

London: the city that spans the ages. London: the town of a thousand pubs. London: the Houses of Parliament and Buckingham Palace. London: the clock they call Big Ben.

But wait a minute. Big Ben is not the clock and not the Parliament tower, but rather the bell that sounds the hour. The bell, cast in 1858, weighs in at 13.5 short tons (twenty-seven thousand pounds) and is nine feet in diameter and 7.5 feet high. A four-hundred pound hammer strikes the bell, sounding the note of "E."

Big Ben, which is located in the clock tower of the Houses of Parliament, was named for one Sir Benjamin Hall, who was the designated commissioner of works when it was installed.

The bell first sounded the hour in 1859. In later years the clock attached to Big Ben, which is world-famous for its accuracy (within one second), came to be identified with the name Big Ben as well, although this is wholly incorrect.

The Olympic torch relay did not begin during the ancient Olympic Games.

Contrary to public belief, the much publicized Olympic torch relay does not date back to the ancient Olympic Games first played in 776 B.C. Oddly enough, it is a rather modern practice which first occurred during the controversial Olympic Games of the XIth Olympiad at Berlin.

To dispel but a few of the myths surrounding the games of 1936— the first modern games were held in 1896 in Athens, Greece—they were not held by the Nazi's as most believe, and they were not awarded to Germany. In fact, the games are always awarded to a city and not a nation. So Berlin held the games and not the Nazi's. By the way, Berlin was awarded the games before the Nazi's came to power.

As for Adolf Hitler, he was simply a patron of the games, who had no overt authority. On one particular occasion he ventured beyond the pale in an effort to politicize the games. He was immediately admonished for having done so, and he apologized to Baillet Latour, President of the International Olympic Committee. Lastly, as is widely rumored, Hitler did not refuse to shake the hand of the great athlete, Black American Jesse Owens, because he had no opportunity to do so.

So the Olympic torch relay that carries the Olympic flame from Olympia, Greece, to the site of each successive Olympic Games is full of pomp and circumstance, as the flame symbolizes the light of spirit, knowledge, life, and a messenger of peace. Yet what appears to be an ancient tradition is but only decades old.

NOTES

This is the point in the book where I sense that the end of my research and writing is near. I have spent myriad sleepless days and nights trying my level best to get it right; to present the facts in an informative and entertaining style.

A book of this nature requires a list of sources that would make even an experienced librarian shudder. But the truth is, during my research I encountered, on numerous occasions, inconsistencies and contradictions, even between what are considered to be some of the most reliable reference sources available anywhere. When confronted with these endless occurrences, I was left with no choice but to cast my net out to yet other sources in an effort to reconcile the problems. Moreover, I have attempted to leave no stone unturned in my search for the uncommon, the surprising, the confounding, the curious, and the mysterious. I have also sought, when appropriate, to give the reader a better sense of the time frame during which an event transpired or a personage was involved in an event, by giving the dates of occurrences and the dates of births and deaths as well.

Also, every effort was made to present the precise chronology of each event, the exact dates, the correct spellings of people and places, and most importantly, "the truth." Moreover, there were particular instances when there was more than one plausible answer. In those cases, I chose to present the reader with such, in an effort to be impartial.

ACKNOWLEDGMENTS

A special acknowledgment to my parents, Darinka and Mike Perko, for always allowing me to find my own way.

To Natalija Nogulich, for her unwavering support.

To Hrayr Shahinian, MD, a good friend.

To Charles Holland, Esq., for his wise counsel.

To Francesco Grisanzio, Stephen M. Stahl, MD, Sandy Long, the Authors Guild, Franklin M. Chu, MD, and Erasmus, thank-you.

Kudos to the staff of the Beverly Hills Public Library, my home away from home, for its tireless assistance.

And to those who knowingly and unknowingly inspired me to write this book, I humbly thank-you.

Lastly, to my wife and children, whose patience and understanding carried me through it all: we can go to the lake now!

ABOUT THE AUTHOR

Marko Perko is a graduate of the University of Southern California. He has always had an insatiable thirst for knowledge of all types, and as such, he is highly regarded as a modern-day Renaissance man, historian, polymath, and polemicist. He is the author of the critically acclaimed and wildly popular book entitled *Did You Know That. . .?* In addition, he is the writer of the international best-selling knowledge-based board game *Twenty Questions*. He is the co-author of *Khamsin*: A Thriller. He is also the founder of the highly praised Marko Perko *online* (www. MarkoPerko.com) Website, the creator of the Cultural Enrichment Programs™, and is active in software development—www.Krypti.com.

Perko has also written for and edited numerous publications, and has worked as a columnist, speechwriter, composer, lecturer, and playwright. He is a member of The Authors Guild; The American Society of Composers, Authors and Publishers; Broadcast Music, Inc.; and the British Library.

Presently, he is at work on his next book, lecturing, and developing a television series based upon his book *Did You Know That. . .?*

Marko Perko lives in California with his wife Heather. They have two children: Marko Perko III and "Skye Mackay" Perko.

See: www.MarkoPerko.com

SELECTED BIBLIOGRAPHY

Abrams, Irwin. The Nobel Peace Prize and the Laureates: An Illustrated Biographical History, 1901–1987. Boston: G. K. Hall & Co., 1988.

Abramson, Rudy. "Will It Fly? Test Set for Wright Rival." *Los Angeles Times*, September 1984.

Ackermann, A. S. E. *Popular Fallacies: A Book of Common Errors.* Detroit: Gale Research Co., 1970.

Alcock, John. "South Mountain, a Park for All Seasons." *Arizona Highways*, July 1989.

Alden, J. R. *George Washington: A Biography.* Baton Rouge: Louisiana State Press, 1984.

Almanac of Famous People. 4th Ed. 3 Vols. Detroit: Gale Research Inc., 1989.

American Book of Days. 3rd Ed. New York: The H. W. Wilson Co., 1978.

"American Notes." *Time Magazine*, June 1989.

Anderson, D. D. *Abraham Lincoln.* New York: Twayne Publishers, Inc., 1970.

Antarctic Science. Cambridge: Cambridge University Press, 1987.

Appelbaum, D. K. *Thanksgiving: An American Holiday, An American History*. Facts On File, Inc., 1984.

Applewhite, E. J. *Washington Itself*. New York: Alfred A. Knopf, Inc., 1981.

Augarde, Tony. *The Oxford Dictionary of Modern Quotations*. Oxford: Oxford University Press, 1991.

Auld, W. M. *Christmas Traditions*. New York: Macmillan Company, 1931.

Bakker, R. T. *The Dinosaur Heresies*. New York: William Morrow and Co., Inc., 1986.

Barber, Charles. *Early Modern English*. London: Andre Deutsch Limited, 1976.

Barnhart Dictionary of Etymology. Bronx: The H. W. Wilson Company, 1988.

Bartlett, John. *Familiar Quotations*. 14th & 15th Eds. Boston: Little, Brown and Co., 1968, 1980.

Bass, T. A. *Camping With the Prince: And Other Tales of Science in Africa*. Boston: Houghton Mifflin Co., 1990.

Benet's Reader's Encyclopedia. 3rd Ed. New York: Harper & Row, Publishers, Inc., 1987.

Benet's Reader's Encyclopedia of American Literature. New York: HarperCollins Publishers, 1991.

Berliner, B., Corey, M., and Ochoa, G. *The Book of Answers*. New York: Prentice Hall Press, 1990.

Berman, Avis. "Art Destroyed, Sixteen Shocking Case Histories." *Connoisseur*, July 1989.

Biographical Directory of the United States Congress 1774–1989. Bicentennial Ed. Washington, D.C.: United States Government Printing Office, 1989.

Black, H. C. *Black's Law Dictionary*. 6th Ed. St. Paul, Minn.: West Publishing Co., 1990.

Boller, Paul F., Jr. *Quotesmanship*. Dallas: Southern Methodist University, 1967.

Boller, P. F., Jr., and George, J. *They Never Said It*. New York: Oxford University Press, 1989.

Bombaugh, C. C., *Facts and Fancies for the Curious*. Philadelphia: J. B. Lippincott, 1905.

Boucher, François, *20,000 Years of Fashion: The History of Costume and Personal Adornment.* Expanded Ed. New York: Harry N. Abrams, Inc., Publishers, 1987.

Bowers, Q. David. *United States Gold Coins: An Illustrated History.* Los Angeles/Wolfeboro: Bowers and Ruddy Galleries, Inc., 1982.

Braude, J. M. *Speaker's and Toastmaster's Handbook of Anecdotes By and About Famous Personalities.* Englewood Cliffs, N. J.: Prentice-Hall, Inc., 1971.

Brennan, R. P. *Levitating Trains & Kamikaze Genes.* New York: John Wiley & Sons, Inc., 1990.

Brewer's Dictionary of Phrase and Fable. Centenary Ed., Revised. New York: Harper & Row, Publishers, 1981.

Britannica Encyclopedia of American Art. Chicago: Encyclopedia Britannica Educational Corporation, 1973.

Brooks, Elston. "Here's Z Reel Story on 'Razzamatazz,'" *Fort Worth Star-Telegram*, September 1986.

Brown, A. E. *Monarchs of the Forest: The Story of the Redwoods.* New York: Dodd, Mead, and Co., 1984.

Brown, Les. *Us Brown's Encyclopedia of Television.* 3rd Ed. Detroit: Gale Research, Inc., 1992.

Brown, M. W., Hunter, S., Jacobus, J., Rosenblum, N., and Sokol, D. M. *American Art: Painting—Sculpture—Architecture—Decorative Arts—Photography.* New York: Harry N. Abrams, Inc., 1979.

Brown T. W. *Sharks: The Silent Savages.* Boston: Little, Brown and Co., 1973.

Broyard, Anatole. "The English Novel Unsheathes Its Claws." *New York Times Book Review*, February 1989.

Bryson, Bill. *The Mother Tongue: English & How It Got That Way.* New York: William Morrow & Co., 1990.

Burchfield, Robert. *The English Language.* Oxford: Oxford University Press, 1985.

———. *Unlocking the English Language.* New York: Hill and Wang, 1991.

Burnam, Tom. *More Misinformation.* New York: Lippincott & Crowell, Publishers, 1980.

———. *The Dictionary of Misinformation.* New York: T. Y. Crowell, 1975.

Calkins, K. L. "As Someone Famous Once Said.. . ." *The Wall Street Journal*, January 1988.

Callahan, P. S. *Insects and How They Function*. New York: Holiday House, 1971.

Cannon, J., and Griffiths, R. *The Oxford Illustrated History of the British Monarchy*. Oxford: Oxford University Press, 1988.

Carpenter, Allan. *The Encyclopedia of the Central West*. New York: Facts On File, Inc., 1990.

Carper, Steve. *No Milk Today: How to Live With Lactose Intolerance*. New York: A Fireside Book, 1986.

Christopher Columbus Encyclopedia. 2 Vols. New York: Simon & Schuster, 1992.

Cirlot, J. E. *A Dictionary of Symbols*. London: Routledge & Kegan Paul, 1971.

Claghorn, C. E. *Biographical Dictionary of American Music*. West Nyack, N. Y.: Parker Publishing Company, Inc., 1973.

Clairborne, Robert. *Loose Cannons and Red Herrings: A Book of Lost Metaphors*. New York: W. W. Norton & Co., 1988.

———. *Our Marvelous Native Tongue: The Life and Times of the English Language*. New York: Times Books, 1983.

Clark, Eugenie. "Gentle Monsters of the Deep: Whale Sharks." *National Geographic*, December 1992.

Coyle, L. P. *The World Encyclopedia of Food*. New York: Facts On File, Inc., 1982.

Current Biography Yearbook. 1940–1990 Ed. New York: The H. W. Wilson Company, 1971.

Davis, Burke. *Our Incredible Civil War*. New York: Ballantine Books, 1960.

Davis, K. C. *Don't Know Much About Geography*. New York: William Morrow and Co., Inc., 1992.

———. *Don't Know Much About History*. New York: Crown Publishers, Inc., 1990.

Decisions of the United States Supreme Court (1965–66 Term). Rochester: The Lawyers Co-operative Publishing Company, 1966.

Dictionary of American Biography. 10 Vols. & Supplements. New York: Charles Scribner's Sons, 1932–1990.

Dictionary of National Biography. 22 Vols. London: Oxford University Press, 1968.

Dictionary of Scientific Biography. 18 Vols. New York: Charles Scribner's Sons, 1970–1990.

Dictionary of Superstitions. Oxford: Oxford University Press, 1989.

Dictionary of the Middle Ages. 13 Vols. New York: Charles Scribner's Sons, 1989.

Dillon, Francis. *The Pilgrims: Their Journeys & Their World.* Garden City: Doubleday & Co., Inc., 1975.

Dunkling, Leslie. *A Dictionary of Days.* New York: Facts On File, Inc., 1988.

Edey, M. A., and Johanson, D. C. *Blueprints: Solving the Mystery of Evolution.* Boston: Little, Brown and Company, 1989.

Emery, Noemie. *Washington: A Biography.* New York: G. P. Putnam's Sons, 1976.

Encyclopedia Americana. International Edition. 30 Vols. Danbury, Conn.: Grolier, Inc., 1991.

Encyclopedia of Food. New York: The Baker & Taylor Company, 1923.

Encyclopedia of the Animal World. 11 Vols. Sydney: Bay Books, 1980.

Facts On File Yearbook. New York: Facts On File, Inc., 1941 to date.

Feldman, A., and Ford, P. *Scientists & Inventors.* New York: Facts On File, Inc., 1979.

Feldman, David. *Why Do Clocks Run Clockwise? and other Imponderables.* New York: Harper & Row, Publishers, 1987.

Ferling, J. E. *The First of Men: A Life of George Washington.* Knoxville: The University of Tennessee Press, 1988.

Fernández-Armesto, Felipe. *Columbus.* Oxford: Oxford University Press, 1991.

"First in flight: Wrights or Wrong?" *Design News,* July 1988.

Fitzgibbon, Theodora. *The Food of the Western World.* New York: Quadrangle/The New York Times Book Co., 1976.

Flatow, Ira. *They All Laughed . . . From Light bulbs to Lasers: The Fascinating Stories Behind the Great Inventions That Have Changed Our Lives.* New York: HarperCollins Publishers, Inc., 1992.

Fleming, Charles. "C'est Possible: but Is a Hop, Skip and Jump Really the Right Stuff?" *The Wall Street Journal,* October 1990.

Folklore of American Holidays. 1st Ed. Detroit: Gale Research Co., 1987.

Funk & Wagnalls Standard Dictionary of Folklore, Mythology, and Legend. 2 Vols. New York: Funk & Wagnalls Company, 1949.

Funk, C. E. *A Hog On Ice & Other Curious Expressions.* New York: Harper Colophon Books, 1948.

Giscard d'Estaing, Valérie-Anne. *The World Almanac Book of Inventions.* New York: World Almanac Publications, 1985.

Glenny, Michael. "The Amber Room." *Arts & Antiques*, March 1989.

Goldwyn, Martin M. *How a Fly Walks Upside Down . . . and Other Curious Facts.* Secaucus: Citadel Press, 1979.

Gould, S. J. *Wonderful Life: The Burgess Shale and the Nature of History.* New York: W. W. Norton & Company, 1989.

Grambs, David. *Words About Words.* New York: McGraw-Hill Book Company, 1984.

Great Lives From History: British and Commonwealth Series. 5 Vols. Pasadena: Salem Press, 1987.

Grzimek's Animal Life Encyclopedia. 13 Vols. New York: Van Nostrand Reinhold Company, 1984.

Guide to American Law: Everyone's Legal Encyclopedia. 12 Vols. St. Paul, Minn.: West Publishing Company, 1984.

Hale, J. R. *Age of Exploration.* New York: Time, Inc., 1971.

Hanser, Richard. "Of Deathless Remarks." *American Heritage*, June 1970.

Hay, Peter. *Movie Anecdotes.* New York: Oxford University Press, 1990.

Hellemans, A., and Bunch, B. *The Timetables of Science.* New York: Simon and Schuster, 1988.

Hendrickson, Robert. *American Literary Anecdotes.* New York: Facts On File, Inc., 1990.

———. *The Dictionary of Eponyms: Names That Became Words.* New York: Stein & Day, 1972.

Herman, J. B. "The Spell of Words: Orthographic Oddities." *SCAN/INFO*, October 1992.

Hibbert, Christopher. *Rome: The Biography of a City.* New York: W. W. Norton & Co., 1985.

Hillinger, Charles. "Charles Hillinger's America, Louisiana's Famed

Causeway is a Bridge Over Troubled Waters." *Los Angeles Times*, February 1990.

Höhn, Reinhardt. *Curiosities of the Plant Kingdom*. New York: Universe Books, 1980.

Holy-Days and Holidays. Detroit: Gale Research Co., 1968.

"How Much is That Grammy in the Window." *Spy Magazine*, April 1989.

Hubbell, Sue. "Earthquake Fever." *The New Yorker*, February 1991.

Hughes, Robert. *The Fatal Shore: The Epic of Australia's Founding*. New York: Alfred A. Knopf, 1986.

Humphreys, David. *Life of General Washington: with George Washington's Remarks*. Athens: The University of Georgia Press, 1991.

Hunger, Rosa. *The Magic of Amber*. Radnor: Chilton Book Company, 1979.

Illustrated Encyclopedia of Mankind. 22 Vols. New York: Marshall Cavendish, 1990.

Illustrated Encyclopedia of the Animal Kingdom. 20 Vols. New York: The Danbury Press, 1971.

Inventors and Discoverers: Changing Our World. Washington, D.C.: National Geographic Society, 1988.

Jobes, Gertrude. *Dictionary of Mythology, Folklore, and Symbols*. 3 Parts. New York: Scarecrow Press, Inc., 1961.

Jones, Bill. "The Surrender Order of 1933." *The Numismatist*, March 1990.

Jordan, William. "The Magnificent Machine of the Sea." *Los Angeles Times Magazine*, July 1986.

Kane, I. N. *Famous First Facts: A Record of First Happenings, Discoveries, and Inventions in American History*. 4th Ed. New York: H. W. Wilson, 1981.

——– *Facts About the Presidents: From George Washington to George Bush*. 5th Ed. New York: The H. W. Wilson Company, 1989.

Kasson, J. F. *Rudeness & Civility: Manners in Nineteenth-Century Urban America*. New York: Hill and Wang, 1990.

Kennedy, Michael. *The Oxford Dictionary of Music*. Oxford: Oxford University Press, 1985.

Kenner, Hugh. "The Phantom Chestnut." *Arts & Antiques*, October 1989.

Kiester, Edwin, Jr. "A Curiosity Turned into a Silver Bullet." *Smithsonian*, November 1990.

Kimes, Beverly. *The Star and The Laurel: The Centennial History of Daimler, Mercedes and Benz 1886–1986*. Montvale New Jersey: Mercedes-Benz of North America, 1986.

Krythe, M. R. *All About American Holidays*. New York: Harper & Brothers, 1962.

Lambert, Bruce. "Executive Who Helped Develop Seat Belts." *New York Times*, September 1992.

Langguth, A. J. *Patriots: The Men Who Started the American Revolution*. New York: Simon & Schuster, 1988.

League of Women Voters of the United States. *Who Should Elect the President?* Washington, D.C.: League of Women Voters of the U.S., 1969.

Leish, Kenneth. *The White House*. New York: Newsweek, 1972.

Lewin, E., and Lewin, A. E. *The Thesaurus of Slang*. New York: Facts On File, Inc., 1988.

Limburg, P. R. *Stories Behind Words*. Bronx: The H. W. Wilson Company, 1986.

Little, Brown Book of Anecdotes. Boston: Little; Brown and Company, Inc., 1985.

Liungman, Carl G. *Dictionary of Symbols*. Santa Barbara: ABC-CLIO, Inc., 1991.

Lorenz, Konrad. *Here Am I—Where Are You?: The Behavior of the Greylag Goose*. New York: Harcourt Brace Jovanovich, Publishers, 1988.

———. *On Aggression*. New York: Harcourt Brace Jovanovich, Publishers, 1966.

Mabberley, D. J. *The Plant Book: A Portable Dictionary of the Higher Plants*. Cambridge: Cambridge University Press, 1989.

Mackay, Charles. *Extraordinary Popular Delusions and the Madness of the Crowd*. New York: Farrar, Straus, and Giroux, 1932.

Manchester, William. *A World Lit Only By Fire: The Medieval Mind and the Renaissance*. Boston: Little, Brown and Co., 1992.

Mann, C. C., and Plummer, M. L. *The Aspirin Wars: Money, Medi-

cine, and 100 Years of Rampant Competition. New York: Alfred A. Knopf, 1991.

Mariani, J. F. *The Dictionary of American Food & Drink.* New Haven: Ticknor & Fields, 1983.

Marks, P. M. *And Die in the West: The Story of the O.K. Corral Gunfight.* New York: William Morrow and Co., Inc., 1989.

Marshall Cavendish Illustrated Encyclopedia of Plants and Earth Science. 10 Vols. New York: Marshall Cavendish, 1988.

Marshall Cavendish International Wildlife Encyclopedia. 24 Vols. New York: Marshall Cavendish, 1989.

Martin, Judith. *Miss Manners' Guide to Excruciatingly Correct Behavior.* New York: Atheneum, 1982.

Mason, George. "Phenomena, Comments and Notes." *Smithsonian,* April 1991.

McCrum, R., Cran, W., and MacNeil, R. *The Story of English.* New York: Elisabeth Sifton Books-Viking, 1986.

McCullough, David. *Brave Companions: Portraits in History.* New York: Prentice Hall Press, 1992.

McGraw-Hill Encyclopedia of Science & Technology. 7th Ed. 20 Vols. New York: McGraw-Hill Book Company, 1992.

McGraw-Hill Encyclopedia of World Biography. 16 Vols. New York: McGraw-Hill Book Company, 1973.

McPherson, J. M. *Abraham Lincoln and the Second Revolution.* New York: Oxford University Press, 1991.

———. *Battle Cry of Freedom: The Civil War.* New York: Oxford University Press, 1988.

Mead, Chris. *Bird Migration.* New York: Facts On File, Inc., 1983.

Metropolitan Police: Public Carriage Office List of Questions. London: The Receiver for the Metropolitan Police District, 1991.

Montagu, A., and Darling, E. *The Ignorance of Certainty.* New York: Harper & Row, Publishers, 1970.

———. *The Prevalence of Nonsense.* New York: Harper & Row, Publishers, 1967.

Montalbano, W. D. "Beauty of Florence's Art Distresses Some Tourists." *Los Angeles Times,* Art, November 1987.

Montgomery, Sy. "Vampire Bats." *Los Angeles Times*, August 1991.

Morris, William, and Morris, Mary. *Morris Dictionary of Word and Phrase Origins*. 2nd Ed. New York: Harper & Row, Publishers, Inc., 1988.

Morwood, William. *Traveler in a Vanished Land: The Life and Times of David Douglas, Botanical Explorer*. New York: Clarkson N. Potter, 1973.

Myers, R. J. *Celebrations: The Complete Book of American Holidays*. Garden City: Doubleday & Co., Inc., 1972.

Nash, J. M. "Wake Up, East and Midwest: The Next Big One May Not Hit California After All." *Time*, October 1990.

National Cyclopaedia of American Biography: Being the History of the United States. 63 Vols. New York: James T. White & Co., 1898 to date.

New Arthurian Encyclopedia. New York: Garland Publishing, Inc., 1991.

New Catholic Encyclopedia. 18 Vols. New York: McGraw-Hill Book Company, 1967.

New Encyclopedia Britannica. 15th Ed. 32 Vols. Chicago: Encyclopedia Britannica, Inc., 1989, 1992.

New Illustrated Science and Invention Encyclopedia. 27 Vols. Westport, Conn. H. S. Stuttman, Inc., 1987.

New Oxford Companion to Music. 2 Vols. Oxford: Oxford University Press, 1984.

Oxford English Dictionary. 2nd Ed. 20 Vols. Oxford: Clarendon Press, 1989.

Panati, Charles. *The Browser's Book of Beginnings: Origins of Everything Under, and Including, the Sun*. Boston: Houghton Mifflin Co., 1984.

Partridge, Eric. *A Dictionary of Slang and Unconventional English*. 8th Ed. New York: Macmillan Publishing Co., 1984.

Pasquier, Roger F. *Watching Birds: An Introduction to Ornithology*. Boston: Houghton Mifflin Co., 1977.

"Pluto Not a Planet, Astronomers Rule." Available from: <http://news.nationalgeographic.com/news/2006/08/060824-pluto-planet.html/>.

Podolsky, D. M. *Skin: The Human Fabric*. New York: Torstar Books, Inc., 1984.

Pomfret, J. E., and Shumway, F. M. *Founding the American Colonies: 1583–1660*. New York: Harper & Row, Publishers, 1970.

"Pope Says Galileo Was Right About Earth." *New York Times*, November 1992.

Poundstone, William. *Big Secrets*. New York: Quill, 1983.

———. *Bigger Secrets*. Boston: Houghton Mifflin Co., 1986.

Powers, C. T. "A Ph.D. for Would-Be Cabbies." *Los Angeles Times*, October 1992.

Prange, G. W. *At Dawn We Slept: The Untold Story of Pearl Harbor*. New York: McGraw-Hill Book Company, 1981.

Prevention's Giant Book of Health Facts: The Ultimate Reference for Personal Health. Emmaus, Pa.: Rodale Press, 1991.

Prud'Homme, A., Stanchina, K., and Dampier, C. "A Treasure in Amber." *People Weekly*, Discovery, October 1992.

Rice, P. C. *Amber: The Golden Gem of the Ages*. New York: Van Nostrand Reinhold Co., 1980.

Rice, Susan. *Mother's Day*. New York: Dodd, Mead and Co., 1915.

Richardson, Dow. "They Didn't Say It." *New York Times Magazine*, January 1945.

Rombauer, I. S., and Becker, M. R. *Joy of Cooking*. New York: The Bobbs-Merrill Co., Inc., 1975.

Samuels, Peggy and Harold. *The Illustrated Biographical Encyclopedia of Artists of the American West*. Garden City: Doubleday & Company, Inc., 1976.

Seale, William. *The President's House: A History*. 2 Vols. Washington, D.C.: White House Historical Association, 1986.

Shenkman, Richard. *I Love Paul Revere, Whether He Rode or Not*. New York: HarperPerennial, 1991.

———. *Legend, Lies & Cherished Myths of American History*. New York: William Morrow and Co., Inc., 1988.

Shugart, C., and Engle, T. *The Official Price Guide to Watches*. 10th Ed. New York: House of Collectibles, 1990.

Simpson, Eileen. "Culture Shock: Victims Go Right Up Museum Walls." *Travel Holiday*, November 1990.

Sinclair, Andrew. *The Sword and the Grail: Of the Grail and the Templars and a True Discovery of America.* New York: Crown Publishers, Inc., 1992.

Skinner, S., and Martens, R. A. *The Milk Sugar Dilemma: Living With Lactose Intolerance.* East Lansing, Mich.: Medi-Ed Press, 1985.

Staff, Frank. *The Valentine and Its Origins.* New York: Frederick Praeger, Inc., 1969.

Stimpson, George. *Information Roundup.* New York: Harper & Brothers Publishers, 1948.

Stimpson, G. W. *Why Do Some Shoes Squeak? and 568 Other Popular Questions Answered.* New York: Bell Publishing Co., 1984.

Tannahill, Reay. *Food in History.* New York: Crown Publishers, Inc., 1988.

Taviani, P. E. *Columbus: The Great Adventure—His Life, His Time, His Voyages.* New York: Orion Books, 1991.

Tebbel, John. *George Washington's America.* New York: E. P. Dutton and Company, Inc., 1954.

This is the West. New York: Rand McNally & Company, 1957.

Thoreau, H. D. *Waiden and Other Writings of Henry David Thoreau.* New York: The Modern Library, 1950.

Times Atlas of the Oceans. New York: Van Nostrand Reinhold Co., Inc., 1983.

Times Atlas of the World. 7th Comprehensive Ed. New York: Times Books, 1985.

Tingay, Lance. *Tennis: A Pictorial History.* New York: G. P. Putman's Sons, 1973.

Tisdale, Sally. *Stepping Westward: The Long Search for Home in the Pacific Northwest.* New York: Henry Holt and Company, 1991.

Tuleja, Tad. *Curious Customs: The Stories Behind 296 Popular American Rituals.* New York: Harmony Books, 1987.

———. *Fabulous Fallacies.* New York: Harmony Books, 1982.

Unexplained II: Mysteries of Mind, Space, and Time. 7 Vols. New York: Marshall Cavendish, 1985.

Unsworth, Walt. *Everest: A Mountaineering History.* Boston: Houghton Mifflin Co., 1981.

"Wright is Wrong?" Available from: <http://www.cbsnews.com/8301-504803_162-57599046-10391709/update-wright-is-wrong/>.

Usher, R. G. *The Pilgrims and Their History*. Williamstown, Mass.: Comer House Publishers, 1977.

Van Doren, Charles. *A History of Knowledge: Past, Present, and Future*. New York: Birch Lane Press, 1991.

Villarreal, Rudy. "Redemption of Mutilated U.S. Currency." *The Numismatist*, March 1990.

"Vital Statistics." *U.S. News & World Report*, March 1990.

Walker, W. F., Jr. *A Study of the Cat: With References to Human Beings*. Philadelphia: Saunders College Publishing, 1982.

Wallace, I., Wallechinsky, D., and Wallace, A. *Significa*. New York: E. P. Dutton, Inc., 1983.

Wallechinsky, D., and Wallace, I. *The People's Almanac*. Garden City: Doubleday & Company, Inc., 1975.

Walters, Jim. "The Ex-Farm Boy Who Found Pluto." *Los Angeles Times*, January 1987.

Ward, Philip. *A Dictionary of Common Fallacies*. 2 Vols. Buffalo, N. Y.: Prometheus Books, 1989.

Weaver, H. E. *Redwood Country: A Guide Through California's Magnificent Redwood Forests*. San Francisco: Chronicle Books, 1983.

Weekley, Ernest. *An Etymological Dictionary of Modern English*. New York: E. P. Dutton, 1921.

"Welcome to the Corn Palace." *Country Living*. October 1992.

White House: An Historic Guide. Washington, D.C.: White House Historical Association, 1982.

Who's Who In America. Chicago: The A. N. Marquis Company, 1899 to date.

Williamson, David. *Kings and Queens of Britain*. Devon: Webb & Bower, (Publishers) Limited, 1986.

Wilmerding, Lucius, Jr. *The Electoral College*. New Brunswick, N. J.: Rutgers University Press, 1958.

Wolf, T. H. "How the Lowly 'Love Apple' Rose in the World." *Smithsonian*, August 1990.

Wolff, Perry. *A Tour of the White House With Mrs. John F. Kennedy*. Garden City: Doubleday & Co., Inc., 1962.

World Book Encyclopedia. 22 Vols. Chicago: World Book, Inc., 1992.

Word Mysteries & Histories: From Quiche to Humble Pie. Boston: Houghton Mifflin Co., 1986.

Woutat, Donald. "Tulipomania Revisited, 350 Years Later, There's Talk of Full-Bloom Folly." *Los Angeles Times*, October 1988.

Yeoman, R. S. *A Guide Book of United States Coins.* 46th Ed. 1993. Racine, Wis.: Western Publishing Company, Inc., 1992.

Zweig, Stefan. *Conqueror of the Seas: The Story of Magellan.* New York: The Viking Press, Inc., 1938.

CPSIA information can be obtained
at www.ICGtesting.com
Printed in the USA
BVHW031304270321
603578BV00007B/39